BOSTON

BEACON FOR THE NEW HORIZON

BY JACK HYNES & GREGORY KLEE

CORPORATE PROFILES BY ANN HANDLEY

ART DIRECTION BY BRIAN GROPPE

TOWERY PUBLISHING, INC.

BOS

BEACON FOR THE

▼ ALEX S. MACLEAN / LANDSLIDES

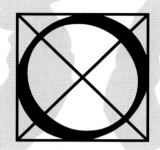

▼ RICHARD PASLEY

▼ RICHARD PASLEY

TON

NEW HORIZON

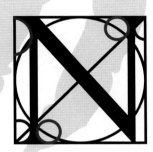

*S*TILL GOING STRONG AND still doing business from the same old stand, the Union Oyster House has been a Boston restaurant since 1826. The building itself dates back to 1715 when, as a general store, it was known as the Sign of the Cornfield.

BOSTON WAS FOUNDED IN 1630, 10 years after the Pilgrims landed at Plymouth. Though the view of the harbor is considerably different from that which greeted the area's earliest settlers, Boston today still holds the promise for a brighter tomorrow.

PAGES 4 & 5, PHOTO BY LOU JONES

LIBRARY OF CONGRESS CATALOGING-IN-PUBLICATION DATA

Hynes, Jack, 1929-
    Boston : beacon for the new horizon / by Jack Hynes : corporate profiles by Ann Handley ; art direction by Brian Groppe.
        p. cm. — (Urban tapestry series)
    Includes index.
    ISBN 1-881096-13-0 : $39.50
    1. Boston (Mass.)—Pictorial works. 2. Boston (Mass)—Description and travel. I. Handley, Ann, 1963- . II. Title. III. Series.
    F73.37.H96 1994   94-33479
    974.4'61—dc20   CIP

TOWERY PUBLISHING, INC., 1835 UNION AVENUE, MEMPHIS, TN 38104

PUBLISHER: J. Robert Towery
EXECUTIVE PUBLISHER: Jenny McDowell
VICE PRESIDENT OF NATIONAL SALES: Steve Hung
PROJECT DIRECTORS: Dawn Olson, Mary Whelan, David Fallon
TECHNICAL DIRECTOR: William H. Towery

EXECUTIVE EDITOR: David Dawson
SENIOR EDITORS: Michael James, Ken Woodmansee
ARTICLES EDITOR: Stinson Liles
EDITORIAL CONTRIBUTORS: Sarah Lawson, Alan Earls
COPY EDITOR: Carlisle Hacker

ASSISTANT ART DIRECTOR: Anne Castrodale
ASSISTANT PROFILE DESIGNERS: Terri Jones, Lawanda McClellan

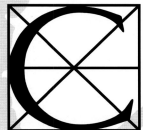

C O N T E N T S

VISITORS TO BOSTON FROM THE west are first greeted by the dramatic downtown skyline as they reach the terminus of the Massachusetts Turnpike. Dominating the scene are the Prudential and John Hancock towers—modern-day sentinels of the new Boston.
PAGES 8 & 9, PHOTO BY RICHARD PASLEY

BY JACK HYNES

And here's to dear old Boston,

Home of the bean and the cod,

Where the Lowells speak only to the Cabots,

And the Cabots speak only to God.

—JOHN COLLINS BOSSIDY, 1910

BOSTON IS OFTEN PERCEIVED BY SOME AS THE GRANDE

dame of American cities, or, perhaps, America's quaint little old lady. But those of us born

and reared here—as well as those who later discover the city's charms—are quick to correct

that perception of primness.

For Boston has finally shed its antiquarian reputation and,

From its earliest days Boston has always been character-ized by the hustle and bustle of a city on the move. The heavily traveled Southeast Expressway (opposite) will soon be replaced by a multibillion-dollar central artery into the heart of the city and beyond.

without loss of its special grace, has emerged as a city pulsing with new energies, eager to

compete with others in the global marketplace. Indeed, Boston has "arrived" at this stage

in its history, albeit somewhat reluctantly, and has deftly managed to avoid the glitz and

gloss to remain a livable city with a heart.

It was not easily come by, this curious blend of the old and

Boston's heritage is truly reflected in its relationship with the harbor. Historic Faneuil Hall (opposite) is a proud, elegant reminder of Colonial Boston—a city landmark for over 250 years.

new. Boston was founded in 1630 on a bed of granite at the edge of the sea. And even

today the city is at one with the ocean. It's fitting, then, that visitors arriving by air first

view Boston from over the harbor. The wharves and docks of Colonial days have given rise

to 20th-century office towers and hotels angled to capture the spectacle of the bustling

harbor below. And when the east wind comes up, as it so often does at evening, the interior

of the city is enveloped in a misty shroud of fog, its salty tang unmistakably delicious.

That same mysterious fog greeted the early residents of

Boston. They were a proud and rebellious lot, determined to carve out their part of the

New World unfettered by foreign hands. And they soon began sowing the seeds of

revolution that their great-grandchildren would fight and die for more than a century

later on Lexington Green and Bunker Hill.

But to really discover Boston, put on your walking shoes, for

there are more points of historic interest within the core city and within easy walking

distance than in any other city in America.

HE CITY PROPER IS A

fascinating polyglot of neighborhoods, each with its own

particular historic and ethnic charm. Spend the better

part of a day following Boston's Freedom Trail, a

two-and-a-half-mile walk back in time into the nation's earliest days. You will stroll

through Boston Common, first used by the new settlers as a grazing meadow for their

cows and sheep, and later as a drill field for the Colonial militia as they prepared for the

War of Independence.

Opposite the Common at the crown of Beacon Hill stands

the State House, its golden dome flashing in the sun, its graceful symmetry a monument to

Step back in time on the crooked, cobbled lanes of Acorn Street in Beacon Hill (opposite), a reminder of a gentler age. The gas street lamps and the grace of a Charles Bulfinch-designed entryway on Mt. Vernon Street are typical of many of the homes in this part of town.

the incomparable Charles Bulfinch, the genius architect who designed it. Bulfinch left his indelible mark on many of Boston's present-day buildings. The old and gracious homes on Beacon Hill display the subtle elegance of the Bulfinch hand—Greek Revival and the Federal style with graceful entryways, iron foot scrapers, rich courses of red brick, and recessed Palladian window arches.

From the architectural treasure trove that is Beacon Hill, you might wander nearby

At the Granary Burying Ground—established in 1660—a simple, timeworn stone marks the grave of Revolutionary War hero Paul Revere. Atop the crest of Beacon Hill stands the Massachusetts State House, where laws of the Commonwealth have been legislated for generations. A statue of Union General Joseph Hooker stands guard (opposite).

to an even earlier Boston. Stop by the Old Granary Burying Ground—laid out in 1660—where many of Boston's first citizens are interred, including three signers of the Declaration of Independence and the victims of the Boston Massacre in 1770. Make your way to Kings Chapel—the first Anglican church in the New World and later the first Unitarian church n America— where Sunday services are still held. Many of its furnishings were provided by British royalty: its vestments and red seat cushions were a gift from Queen Anne the pulpit was given by King James II, and its silver communion plate was a gift from King George III. Alongside Kings Chapel is a small graveyard where many of Boston's early settlers are buried. ✒︎☞

A SHORT DISTANCE AWAY FROM KINGS CHAPEL STANDS

the Old South Meeting House. Built in 1639 as a church, it was later replaced as a town

hall of sorts, where rebel leaders Samuel Adams and John Hancock delivered their fiery

speeches of secession. It was also at the Old South Meeting

House that a mob of fellow revolutionaries met on the

evening of September 16, 1773, and, disguised as Indians,

made their way to the harbor and seized chests of the tea

from British ships docked at Griffen's Wharf. This act of

defiance has come to be known as the Boston Tea Party,

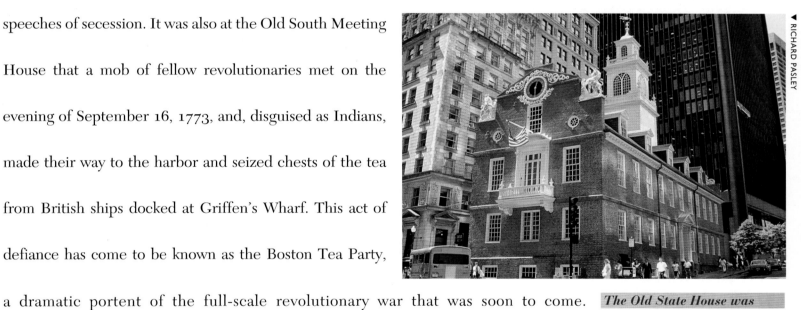

a dramatic portent of the full-scale revolutionary war that was soon to come.

Continue your stroll just down the street to the Old State

House, which was erected in 1713 as the official seat of government for both the state

and the city. From the building's ornate balcony, the Declaration of Independence was

read to the gathered citizenry shortly after its signing in Philadelphia in July 1776. ☞

The Old State House was erected in 1713 as the original seat of British government in the colony. Nearby is a replica of the Beaver, from whose decks a band of Colonial rebels dressed as Indians dumped Her Majesty's tea into the harbor (opposite).

AND IT WAS HERE IN FRONT OF THE OLD STATE HOUSE on a blustery March evening in 1770 that an angry mob of young Colonials, emboldened by a few too many pints at a nearby tavern, came upon a lone British sentry standing guard on State Street. The mob taunted the redcoat and threw snowballs until a contingent of British troops was dispatched from a nearby barracks. Then the confrontation escalated. The crowd of Colonists, already seething at the British occupation of their city, refused the officer's order to disperse, and in the din and furor that followed, shots were fired into the crowd. When the smoke had cleared, five men lay dead on the cobbled street. One of the victims was Crispus Attucks, a young black man now enshrined in history as one of the first martyrs in the War for Independence. Observances at the site of what has come to be known as the Boston Massacre are held every year on its anniversary. 🖝

In 1990 thousands of Bostonians turned out to greet Nelson Mandela, a present-day hero in the fight for equality. Every April an authentic reenactment of the Battle of Lexington (opposite) recalls heroes of the past as participants commemorate the "shot heard 'round the world."

ARTHER ALONG AND YOU COME TO ANOTHER HISTORIC

shrine that today does double duty as a retail and fast-food emporium that would leave

an early settler awestruck. Faneuil Hall was built in 1742 by philanthropist Peter Faneuil

as a marketplace and meeting hall for the citizenry of early Boston. With its adjacent

Quincy Market building, the six-acre square is today a tourist's delight with its bazaar

of shops, restaurants, and street performers. The marketplace has also served as a guide

for other cities looking to reclaim and refurbish abandoned urban areas. ✒️👉

The pillars of Quincy Market welcome the multitudes of tourists who swarm through the shops inside, while the Old Custom House tower keeps a watchful eye (opposite). Faneuil Hall, built in 1742, serves as the elegant centerpiece for the Quincy Market complex.

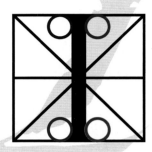

IF THE LURE OF PIZZA, FRIED CLAMS, AND YOGURT CONES

is not exactly what you had in mind for a light lunch, turn yourself a few blocks away

from Quincy Market and head into Boston's North End. For Bostonians, the North End means Italian. With its jumble of narrow, twisting streets, the neighborhood is one of Boston's oldest, and home to some of the city's finest restau-

From fresh breads to baked beans to pizza, Boston serves up anything you could possibly want to eat. But most would pass up the beans for a large North End pizza.

rants. No yogurt cones here, thank you; this is for serious diners who don't count calories.

But the North End was not always Boston's Little Italy.

When the potato famine devastated Ireland in 1842, thousands left the Emerald Isle to make a new life in America. Many Irish immigrants landed here in Boston, and since the

North End was but a short walk from the docks, they found ready access to living accommodations and jobs. The Irish stayed and prospered in Boston, especially in politics.

The true Bostonian's major interests, diversions, and obsessions are sports and politics, and not necessarily in that order. The North End neighborhood, with its teeming population of newly arrived Irish, served as a powerful springboard to elected office. One of Boston's mayors after the turn of the century was the colorful John F. Fitzgerald. They called him "Honey Fitz" and he served his Boston well. But he is better known today as the father of Rose Fitzgerald Kennedy, mother of President John F. Kennedy and Senators Robert and Edward Kennedy. Rose Fitzgerald was born in Boston's North End on Garden Street in 1892. ☞

In 1917 John F. Kennedy was born in this house on Beale Street in the town of Brookline just south of the city. Boston's North End is a place where old traditions still abound, including friendly conversation over espresso (opposite).

HEN NOT DEBATING POLITICAL ISSUES, BOSTONIANS prove themselves to be avid followers of the area's sports franchises. The Red Sox. The Celtics. The Bruins. All have brought moments of great glory—and, at times, devastating heartbreak—to the

There's nothing quite like the sight of a seventh-inning stretch at hallowed Fenway Park, the home of the Red Sox. The old Boston Garden (opposite), for years the home of the Celtics and Bruins, has become a part of the city's history. Today a new Garden has been constructed on the same spot.

generations of sports lovers who live in Boston. Even the places where the action occurs—Fenway and the Boston Garden—have become almost hallowed in these parts, as if they remain forever populated by the ghosts of the legendary athletes who for decades have

knocked home runs, nailed last-second jump shots, or put slap shots in the back of

the net. 👉

▲ JAMES LEMASS

▲ DAVID COMB

BUT WE'RE STRAYING A BIT FROM OUR WALKING TOUR.

From the North End neighborhood of Honey Fitz it is a bit of a hike over to Charlestown, another enclave of history. But assuming you are well fortified with fried calamari, linguine with white clam sauce, and a couple of Chiantis and an espresso, you may need the exercise.

Keep your eye on the Bunker Hill monument towering over the neighborhood that hugs the edge of the harbor. The monument, which is made of granite quarried from Boston's neighboring town of Quincy, was raised to commemorate those 441 patriots who died at the Battle of Bunker Hill on the morning of June 6, 1775, attempting to repulse three charges by British troops. The gallant patriots lost the battle, but the British paid a terrible price with over 1,000 troops lying dead at the close of that hot summer day. King George was so incensed when he learned of the debacle that he relieved General Thomas Gage of his command and summoned him back to England.

Nowhere else in the country is the old so perfectly blended with the new as in Boston. The Bunker Hill Monument (opposite) towers over the Charlestown neighborhood, commemorating the fierce battle on a hot summer day in June of 1775.

A peculiar and little-known footnote to the battle: actually, it was not fought on Bunker Hill, but on the adjoining Breeds Hill. Why the historical mix-up, no one is certain. Regardless, the 221-foot monument stands as another reminder of Boston's preeminent role in the shaping of America.

Also located at Charlestown, and certainly worth a visit, is the oldest commissioned warship in the world, the USS *Constitution*—"Old Ironsides"—built at McKay's Shipyard in 1798. She distinguished herself in the War of 1812 when British shells found her hull impregnable. The *Constitution* is permanently berthed in Charlestown with a full complement of U.S. Navy officers and crew dressed in period uniforms. The ship is visited daily during the year by busloads of schoolchildren and tourists who are given a fascinating tour by the well-versed crew.

In the summer of 1992, thousands of people flocked to the harbor to view the arrival of full-masted tall ships from dozens of foreign countries. Dressed in naval uniforms of 1797 (opposite), the crew of the USS Constitution *welcomes visitors to the ship known as "Old Ironsides."*

ROM THE WATERFRONT, YOU MIGHT RETRACE YOUR

Boston has long been a major center of international business. Every morning, commuters pour from subway stations into the city's downtown financial district. Boston's tallest landmark, the glass-sheathed John Hancock Tower (opposite), rises over the Old Trinity Church in Copley Square.

steps through the financial district, where you'll experience architecture that ranges from

contemporary, glass-sheathed towers to squat, granite-block reminders of yesteryear.

You might want to take a slight detour through Boston's

Chinatown for a sampling of midafternoon dim sum at one of the area's restaurants.

Boston's Chinatown is the fourth-largest Asian neighborhood in the country. And, in

recent years, the area has seen an influx of Vietnamese who add to the city's culture and

intrigue, and lend additional shading to the charming complexities of Boston.

The arrival of Vietnamese and Cambodian refugees in the *Asian art, both contemporary and ancient, is on display throughout Boston's Chinatown. The pagoda-roofed entry to Chinatown (opposite) is the gateway to the fourth-largest Asian neighborhood in the country.*

late 1970s has served as a recent reminder of Boston's continuing attraction as a promising

haven for those forced from their homelands by war or famine. The city has always been

a melting pot for the disenfranchised. Here, amid the memories of those similarly

oppressed who came before, there is a promise of freedom and opportunity that remains

the very bedrock of Boston. ☞

T IS NOW BUT A SHORT STROLL OVER TO BOSTON'S Public Garden. Separated from its neighbor, Boston Common, by Charles Street, the Public Garden is a flower-bedded oasis in the center of the city. At one time a saltwater marsh, it was reclaimed by the city leaders in 1859 and converted into one of the most beautiful public parks in America. Its main entrance is graced with a bronze statue of George Washington astride his horse as general of the Continental Army. The winding pathways are lined with flowers and shrubs, and tall, graceful trees from various parts of the world provide shade and respite for young and old. 🖝

The graceful pedestrian bridge spanning the Public Garden lagoon is best experienced from one of the park's famous swan boats. A young fan of "Make Way for Ducklings" (opposite) gets acquainted with a member of the bronze brood on display in the Public Garden.

And for the forever young, what is more pleasant on a fine spring day than a cruise on the Public Garden swan boats? They silently cruise their man-made lake as they have since 1876 when Robert Paget designed and built the foot-pedal boats, inspired by the swans from the opera *Lohengrin*. The swan boats continue to be operated by later generations of the Paget family, proving once again that nothing in Boston is of very short duration.

Boston is proud of her public parks and takes special pride in knowing that Frederick Law Olmsted used Boston as his focal point in designing a series of parks surrounding the city which are referred to as the "Emerald Necklace." Extending for over seven miles, it is the longest public parkland in urban America. 👉

The Public Garden swan boats await the beginning of yet another day of cruising the lagoon. Since 1876 the boats have been a summer-time family tradition, as well as a favorite motif for artists.

BUT WHAT ABOUT TODAY'S BOSTON? WE HAVE SEEN

it as a "walking city" replete with history and traditions. However, present-day Boston is

especially unique in that it is such a livable city.

It is a city of neighborhoods, each with its own character

and style. They form a close ring around the core city, or downtown as the natives call it.

The satellite neighborhoods are really small towns within themselves, and a great many

of their families have lived in the same neighborhood—perhaps even the same house—

for three or four generations. Several take their name from old English towns—

Brighton, Dorchester, Roxbury, Hyde Park. All are within a short subway or bus ride of

downtown.

Early morning brightens the rooftops of one of Boston's residential communities. Many families can boast of having roots in a neighborhood that trace back five generations.

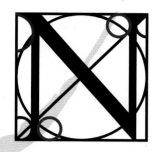

OW LET US TAKE UP THE MATTER OF THE FAMOUS *Edward Kennedy, senior U.S. senator from Massachusetts, is one of Boston's favorite sons (above). The Christian Science Church headquarters in Boston's Back Bay (opposite) features the stunningly beautiful Maparium Room.*

Boston accent, although native Bostonians would deny there is any such thing. But there

are certain peculiarities of speech that bear the mark of Boston. For instance, "mark of

Boston" would be heard as "mahk of Bawstin." The best-known example is, of course,

"I pahked my cah in the Hahvud yahd." With a little practice, you could be speaking like

a native in no time. Of course your friends may not understand you, unless they are

from Boston.

Even Boston's most illustrious son, President John F.

Kennedy, retained his Boston accent while serving in Washington. He managed to confuse

the White House press corps on many an occasion by inserting *r*'s such as he did when

he referred to his problems with Cuba, which came out "Cuber." ☞

BUT IT IS NOT JUST THE ACCENT THAT SETS BOSTONIANS

apart. The natives have a beguilingly parochial view of the rest of America. Firm in the

conviction that "we were here first," Bostonians look upon people from afar—that need

only be 100 miles away—as late arrivals. As one Beacon

Hill dowager once put it in response to why, with all her

wealth, she never traveled: "But my deah, why would I

travel when I'm already heah?"

Boston's reluctance to

change had its serious downside in the years immediately

The ubiquitous parking
meter is the nemesis of all
Boston drivers. But if the
parking meters don't get you,
maybe one of Boston's men
in blue will.

following World War II. While other American cities moved energetically forward to

meet new challenges, Boston lagged behind, trapped in its own provincialism. It became

an urban backwater, a tattered and tired old relic.

The rebirth of Boston first came about with the election of a new mayor in 1949. I am understandably proud to say that it was my father, John B. Hynes, who forged a coalition of frustrated businessmen, recently returned veterans, and rank-and-file city workers, all concerned and dismayed at the politics-as-usual attitude of the old guard and its longtime boss and mayor, the legendary James Michael Curley.

For nearly a century, the Boston Marathon has attracted the world's premier runners. Cosmos Ndeti of Kenya won the event in 1993 and 1994. The Fourth of July celebration on the city's Esplanade (opposite) is the site for the Boston Pops' annual concert.

Under Hynes, the city embarked on a major program of urban renewal, first bringing the Prudential Center to an abandoned railroad yard in the Back Bay, then staking out a new government center with a contemporary-styled city hall, and later forming plans for a sweeping renovation of the waterfront.

When Hynes retired from office 10 years later, old Dame Boston had received a new lease on life. And when he turned over the keys of the office to his successor, Boston had turned around. The city had found itself again, and there was a new spring in the steps of the people. The city was on the move again, and it has never looked back.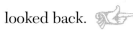

ODAY, BOSTON LOOKS FORWARD EAGERLY TO THE challenges of the next century. It has been over 350 years since John Winthrop and his hardy band of settlers first made camp on Beacon Hill. Winthrop was the first to give Boston its mission and heritage when he wrote, "For we must consider that we shall be a city upon a hill. The light of all the people are upon us and we shall be made a story and a byword through the world."

That mission prevails. And the city's proud heritage, burnished by time, stands ready now to accept the new triumphs intertwined with the old traditions. Indeed, Boston is a very special place.

From Newbury Street, with its lifelike murals, to the contemporary gleam of the John Hancock Tower (opposite), the Back Bay area of the city provides a rich mixture of architectural styles.

So here's to dear old Boston,

Home of the brave and the true,

Where her past speaks softly to its present,

And her future is in the cup of God's hand.

THE GOLDEN DOME OF THE
State House and the clock tower
of the Old Custom House give
testimony to Boston's past, while
the contemporary skyscrapers of
today are graceful reminders of
the city's promising future.
PAGES 52-53, PHOTO BY DAVID COMB

THE BRIGHTLY LIT CITGO SIGN
shining over Kenmore Square is a
favorite landmark and a welcome
sight for weary runners nearing
the end of the famed Boston
Marathon.

*T*HE SOUTHEAST EXPRESSWAY, one of the city's major people movers, nears its terminus in the heart of Boston's towering financial district.

𝒥UST 50 YEARS AGO, THE recently refurbished Old Custom House clock tower was the tallest structure in the city. Today, that distinction belongs to the John Hancock Tower.

$\mathcal{M}$ANY OF BOSTON'S OLDER office buildings display a fascinating myriad of architectural details not found in modern-day glass and steel high-rises.

$\mathcal{T}$HROUGHOUT THE CITY, THE
old and the new are in constant
contrast. The flashing weather
beacon atop the John Hancock
Mutual Life Insurance Building is
framed by the mirrored panes of
the John Hancock Tower.

*D*USK ENVELOPS THE DOME of the First Church of Christ Scientist Mother Church. The religious sect has been headquartered in Boston since 1893.

𝒯HE BOSTON HARBOR HOTEL, one of the city's finest luxury hotels, was once the Federal Reserve Bank Building. Much of the original architectural detail, including the domed ceiling, has been preserved from its earlier days.

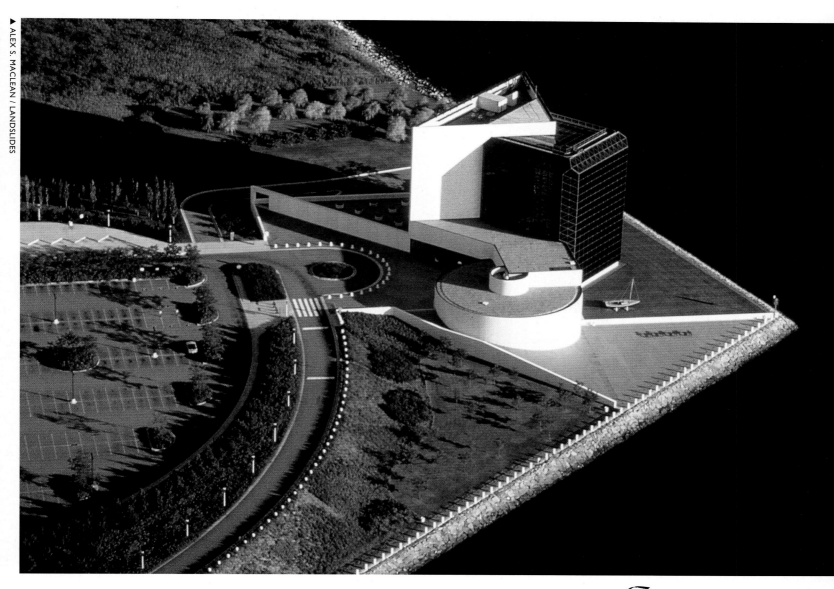

𝒯HE JOHN F. KENNEDY LIBRARY and Museum honors the life and legacy of the popular 35th president through 25 exhibits, three theaters, and 20 video presentations.

The John F. Kennedy Library and Museum honors the life and legacy of the popular 35th president through 25 exhibits, three theaters, and 20 video presentations.

$\mathcal{T}$HE I.M. PEI-DESIGNED John Hancock Tower, which rises 60 stories above Copley Square, is the most dominant symbol of the new Boston. There's no better view of the city than from the observatory on the top floor.

$\mathcal{S}$OME OF THE CITY'S MORE out-of-the-ordinary sights are found high in the sky, like the gold-leafed grasshopper weather vane that stands atop historic Faneuil Hall. Paul Drummey of Period Hardware, a modern-day craftsman in the tradition of Paul Revere, replicates authentic weather vanes and lamps from Boston's Colonial period.

Copper gaslights, reminiscent of the city's earlier days, today stand sentinel on many of the streets in the Back Bay and Beacon Hill neighborhoods.

CHRISTMAS SEASON IN BOSTON means the return of *The Nutcracker*, a colorful pageant that year after year delights young and old alike.

All seasons favor antique lovers. Browsing through the cluster of shops at the base of Beacon Hill on Charles Street can turn up some unusual treasures from the past (OPPOSITE).

A BRONZE LIKENESS OF Benjamin Franklin stands watch in front of the old City Hall. Franklin's parents are buried nearby at the Granary Burying Ground.

The broad fountain in the plaza at Copley Square is a favorite spot for taking strolls on a hot summer's day. Trinity Church and Hancock Tower provide a typical Boston backdrop (OPPOSITE TOP).

Two early arrivals for the Fourth of July Boston Pops concert on the Esplanade stake out a spot alongside the bust of Maestro Arthur Fiedler, originator of the Pops and its conductor for over 30 years (OPPOSITE BOTTOM).

BEACON FOR THE NEW HORIZON

𝓑OSTON IS TRULY A CITY OF movers and shakers. Richard Styron (TOP LEFT) is the former president and CEO of the Federal Reserve Bank of Boston. Robert Parker (TOP RIGHT) is the creator of the fictional Spenser character, a Boston private eye whose escapades have been chronicled in 25 books and a popular TV series. Suffolk County District Attorney Ralph Martin (BOTTOM LEFT) is the first African-American attorney ever elected to the office.

William Weld (BOTTOM RIGHT), the governor of the Commonwealth of Massachusetts, is a former U.S. attorney whose ancestors arrived on the *Mayflower*.

𝒦ATHLEEN DENNEHY (TOP LEFT) is superintendent of the State Prison for Women-MCI Farmingham. Margaret Marshall (TOP RIGHT) is the former head of the prestigious Boston Bar Association.

Jack Connors (BOTTOM LEFT) is a founding partner of Hill, Holliday, one of the country's largest ad agencies. John Doyle (BOTTOM RIGHT) heads up his own award-winning advertising agency.

$\mathcal{S}$AMPLING THE CIGARS IS ONE advantage to having your own old-time tobacco shop, like the Leavitt-Peirce shop in Harvard Square.

Longtime Boston Celtics' Coach and General Manager Arnold "Red" Auerbach, one of Boston's living legends—and most well-known cigar aficionados—is memorialized in bronze at Quincy Market.

Any time of day, the restaurants of Quincy Market are among the city's most popular. From inter-national delicacies to fast food, this facility is not for the weight-conscious (OPPOSITE).

SOUTH
MARKET
BUILDING

2

OFFICES
FLOORS 3·4·5

TA
LEAT

HARVARD & CO

SOU
MA
BUI

SOU
MARK
BUIL

FOLKI

SHOP
FLOORS 1 & 2

SOUTH
MARKET
BUILDING

4

OFFICES
FLOORS 3·4·5

boston pe

AT

M

SHOP
FLOO

SC

SO
MA
BU

a

*I*N THE 1980S, THE HEART
of the old downtown retail district
was converted to a pedestrians-
only shopping mall called Downtown Crossing. The mall is
anchored by Filene's Basement, a
bargain hunters' paradise.

*T*HE SPIRE OF THE OLD SOUTH Meeting House (LEFT) remains a focal point in downtown Boston. It was here at the Old South that a group of patriots, determined to defy the Crown, planned the Boston Tea Party in December of 1773.

"Nellie" and her hansom cab (ABOVE) provide the perfect means for viewing the Old South and the wealth of other historical treasures in the city's downtown area.

*T*HE FOUNTAIN AND PLAZA AT the Mother Church of the First Church of Christ Scientist (TOP) provide a cool respite for summertime city dwellers.

These Boston firefighters battling a stubborn blaze in Kenmore Square (BOTTOM) could undoubtedly use a little cooling off after a hard day's work.

The Back Bay's Prudential Tower, or the "Pru" as it is commonly known, served as the spark that ignited Boston's rebirth in the 1950s. As the work above goes on, there is time for a midday chat on the plaza of the Federal Reserve Bank Building.

MEN
WORKING
ABOVE

THE BOSTON HARBOR TUNNEL is part of the gigantic new Central Artery. The project is the largest public works undertaking in the history of the country, and the cost will reach into the billions. The structure will be named the Ted Williams Tunnel in honor of one of Boston's favorite sports legends.

*T*ODAY, BOSTON IS FORGING new parameters in the global marketplace. The city's experienced scientific workforce has adapted quickly to the increasing demand for new ideas, products, and horizons.

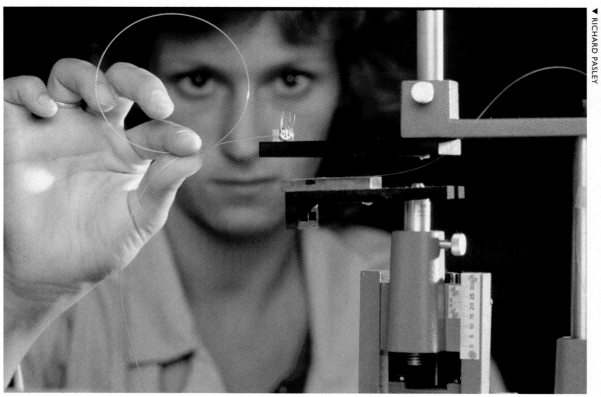

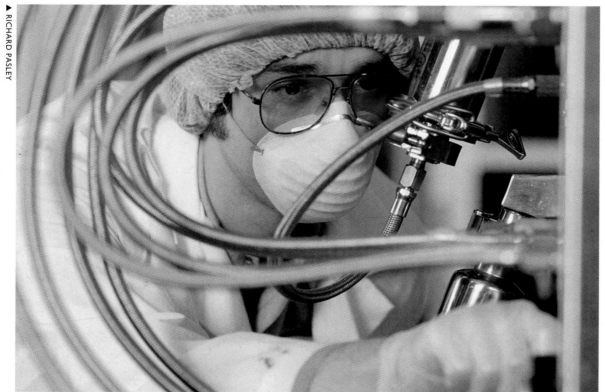

$\mathcal{T}$HE IMPETUS FOR BOSTON'S progressive vision stems from the classrooms and laboratories of the world-class academic institutions located in the city.

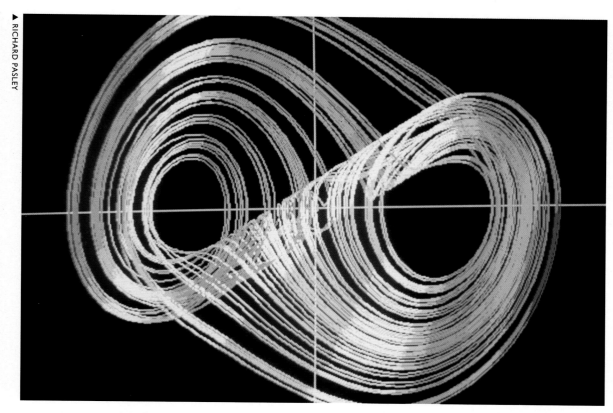

RICHARD PASLEY

ℱROM NIGHT COURSES AT Northeastern University to the advanced media laboratories at the Massachusetts Institute of Technology to parents and students learning about computers together at an inner-city school, Boston is focused on being one of the world's major cities in the 21st century.

SARAH PUTNAM

BOSTON'S VISION FOR THE future is clearly focused, thanks to the city's resolute sense of purpose. The area has been the birthplace and ignition point for numerous research and development companies, and many, like Polaroid and Monsanto, have become giants on the world's economic stage.

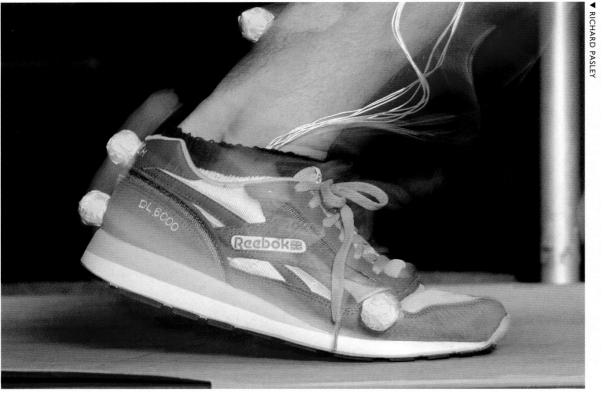

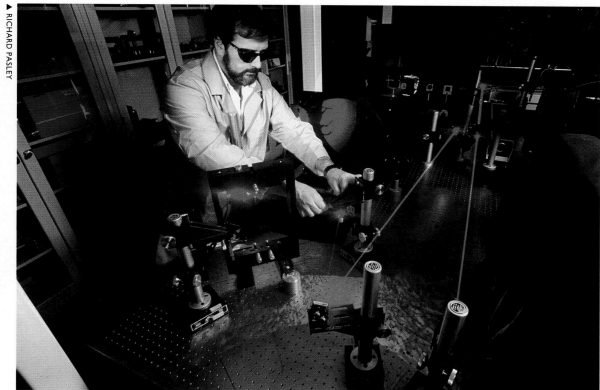

*T*HE NEW WESTIN HOTEL, one of several major hotels built in Boston in recent years, provides its guests with easy access to the sparkling shops of Copley Place and the Prudential Mall.

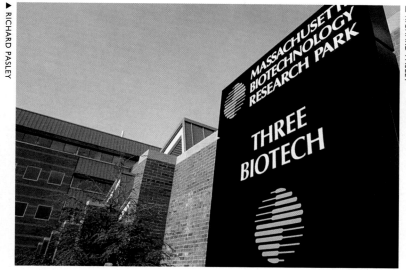

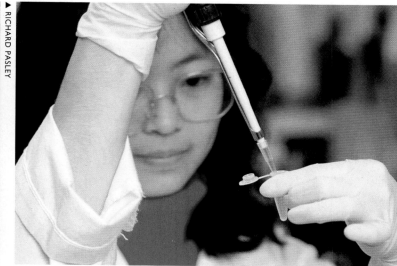

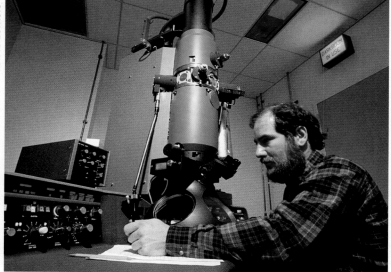

*T*ECHNOLOGY ABOUNDS IN the Boston area. In addition to the city's medical schools—Harvard, Tufts, and Boston University— the Biotechnology Research Park at the University of Massachusetts Medical School in Worcester and the Whitehead Institute in Cambridge are also creating new, high-tech frontiers.

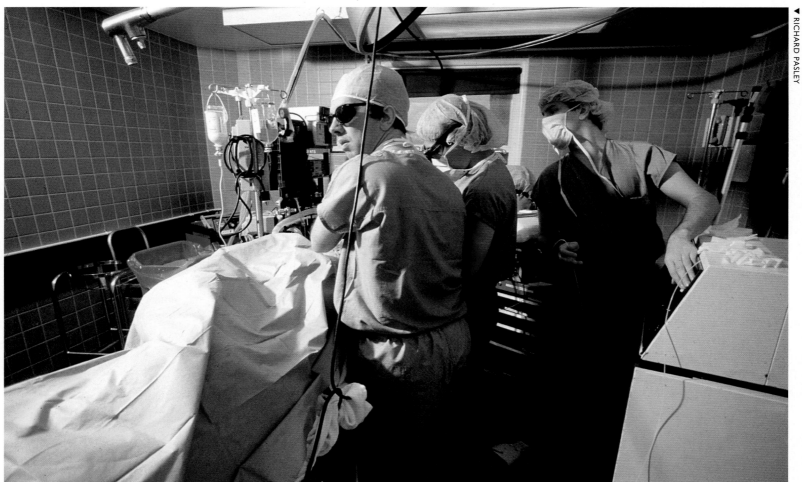

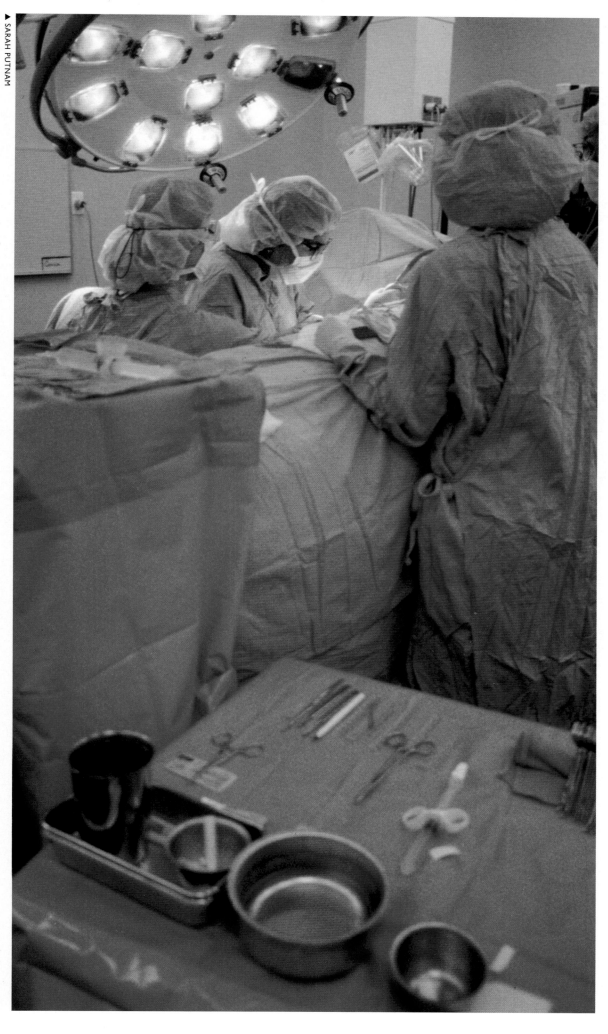

*D*RAMATIC NEW TECH-niques in laser and fiber-optic surgery are being employed and taught in the operating rooms of Boston's major hospitals, which are indisputably among the finest in the world.

$\mathscr{N}$EW ADVANCES IN INDUS-
trial technologies are taking place
in Boston as well—from harness-
ing nuclear power to making pasta
the "new" old-fashioned way
(OPPOSITE).

BOSTON IS HOME TO A kaleidoscope of fine restaurants representing a rainbow of ethnic backgrounds, whether it be a coffee bar, Donuts a la Mike, or the innovative children's pastry-making class at the venerable Ritz Carlton.

RICHARD MITCHELL

*O*THER POPULAR SPOTS ARE the Commonwealth Brewery in the city or the Blue Room in Cambridge (BOTTOM RIGHT). In the North End, Frank Susi poses proudly outside the Abruzzese Meat Market on Salem Street (BOTTOM LEFT).

WEBB CHAPPELL

WEBB CHAPPELL

$\mathscr{T}$HE BRICK WALL OF CAFE
DuBarry on fashionable Newbury
Street is adorned with an alfresco
painting of famous Bostonians.
Nearby is Boston's popular Bull
and Finch Pub, commonly known
as Cheers. Every year, thousands
of visitors line up to check out the
neighborhood bar that was the
inspiration for the highly successful television comedy series.

𝒯HE CITY HONORED THE cast of "Cheers" by renaming a nearby alley "Kirstie." Even though the show has ceased production, the Bull and Finch Pub remains Boston's best-known and most popular bar.

$\mathcal{O}$F COURSE, THERE ARE A wealth of other odd tourist attractions to see, including the giant milk bottle standing in the entrance of the Children's Museum on the waterfront. If it's musical entertainment you're looking for, you don't have to look far—musicians are scattered throughout the city on street corners and in local taverns.

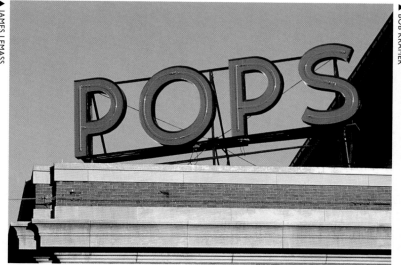

$\mathcal{M}$ANY RESIDENTS OF Boston are proud of their green-thumb contributions to the charm of city living. This winner of an inner-city garden contest is seated alongside his prizewinners.

*D*URING SPRINGTIME, Boston's most colorful floral display occurs when the tulips bloom along the lagoon walkways in the Public Garden.

THE CHILDREN OF BOSTON are as diverse as the city's neighborhoods. Whether waiting to board a school bus or contributing to Franklin Park's sidewalk art, Boston is truly a city for the young and young at heart.

BOSTON:

$\mathcal{P}$RESCHOOLERS SHARE IN the fun at the Mount Pleasant Tot Lot in Roxbury.

*A*t Newbury Comics in the Back Bay, Mike Dreese keeps the shelves stocked with the latest editions. Newbury Street is home to over 200 quaint shops and restaurants nestled in the brick bay fronts of the area's 19th-century townhouses.

please
leave all parcels
at front desk

𝒯HE OLD BRATTLE BOOK
Shop downtown is a book lover's
paradise, where browsing is an art
form. From new editions to first
editions, the Brattle is always
chock full with books.

*I*T IS SAID THAT THE BOSTON area is one large college campus. Harvard University (TOP) first opened its doors in the fall of 1636, and has since become one of the most prestigious universities in the world. Boston University (BOTTOM LEFT), on the edge of the Back Bay, and hallowed Wellesley College (BOTTOM RIGHT) are also well known for academic excellence.

▲ JAMES LEMASS

▲ BOB KRAMER

▲ MARK SEGAL / PANORAMIC IMAGES, CHICAGO, 1994

*I*NDEED, FROM THE RAM-
parts of Harvard Law School
(BOTTOM LEFT) to the towers of
the heights at Boston College
(BOTTOM RIGHT), higher education remains an indelible part of
life in the city.

▲ LOU JONES

▲ JAMES LEMASS

𝒩EEDLESS TO SAY, THERE are a lot of diversions in the city to keep students busy, like an impromptu jazz concert on the Quad at Northeastern University (LEFT). The newsstand in the center of Harvard Square is as much of an institution as its university neighbor across the street (TOP). Street singers lend a European flavor to the unique sights and sounds of the Harvard campus (BOTTOM).

A VARIETY OF MUSIC CAN be heard throughout the year in Boston. Ray Charles performs at the Hatch Shell on the Charles River Esplanade (TOP). The Heretics go late into the night at The Paradise, one of the city's popular rock clubs (BOTTOM). When the New England Patriots aren't using their stadium in Foxboro, it often draws capacity crowds for rock concerts by groups like the Rolling Stones (RIGHT).

𝒯HE PORT OF BOSTON HAS always been a great liberty call for seamen, such as these Russian sailors sampling the scene at Quincy Market.

*T*HE CITY'S NIGHTLIFE GOES up tempo on weekends when clubs, restaurants, and theaters cater to a multitude of students, locals, and tourists.

$\mathcal{D}$URING THE CHRISTMAS season, the old Park Street Church provides a Colonial backdrop for festive Boston Common. It was in this church that "America," composed by Bostonian Samuel Francis Smith, was first sung in 1832.

*I*N THE BACK BAY, A GIANT, illuminated spruce tree is the backdrop for holiday caroling outside the Prudential Center. Rest assured, there's plenty of Christmas shopping going on inside at the center's collection of world-famous designer stores.

NICHOLAS CARROLL

DAVID COMB

*C*REATIVE WINDOW DRESS-ing can cause even a longtime Bostonian to do a double take along the row of shops in Boston's Back Bay shopping district (ABOVE).

The Old Custom House tower overlooks another night of activity at Quincy Market (OPPOSITE).

The assemblage of shops, bars, and eateries within the old brick and granite market building has been a focal point of tourism in Boston since its opening more than 20 years ago.

HAT COULD BE FINER
than a summer evening on the
banks of the Charles River—
listening to the Boston Pops at
the Hatch Shell (OPPOSITE TOP)
or a concert by talented musicians
at the New England Conservatory
of Music (OPPOSITE BOTTOM).

Gala soirees at the refurbished
Boston Opera House add even
more glitter to the city's arts scene
(LEFT).

*J*ASPER WHITE, BOSTON CHEF extraordinaire, contemplates perhaps another change in the fabulous menu at his five-star restaurant, Jaspers, near the waterfront (OPPOSITE).

There's contemplation of a different sort at the Museum of Fine Arts. The museum exhibits collections ranging from old European masters to fascinating artifacts from Egypt (TOP LEFT).

Several of the area colleges boast of their own museums such as the Tufts University Art Center (BOTTOM LEFT).

*O*NCE THE HOME OF BAKED beans, Boston's dining options today are as varied as any city in the world.

*F*ROM OUTDOOR CAFES ON Newbury Street to the popular New Orleans Jazz Brunch at the Hampshire Hotel, the fine dining experience is a way of life in Boston.

*F*OR A TASTY TRIP BACK IN time, sit yourself down at one of the city's old-fashioned diners. Not much has changed in these establishments over the past 50 years, except the prices.

$\mathscr{W}$ITH SOME IMPRESSIVE
"iron" as a backdrop, Linda
Pimental strikes a pose on one
of Boston's area beaches.

A LESS-STRENUOUS AP-proach is taken by healer and author Joan Barysenko, while her golden retriever ponders a romp on the beach.

$\mathcal{O}$N SATURDAY MORNINGS, smart shoppers head for the open fruit and produce stalls along dock square, where prices are often negotiable and ripe for bargain hunters. Over in nearby China-town, native delicacies and staples are offered at a variety of traditional markets (OPPOSITE).

BOSTON'S ASIAN COMMUnity has always been a major part of the color and charm of the city (OPPOSITE). Here, the old ways endure and ancient cultures prevail.

Residents peruse a display of bonsai at the August Moon Festival, one of several such observances celebrated in Chinatown.

A HOT-AIR BALLOON IS readied for takeoff as Boston's First Night celebration gets under way. Held for the past 18 years, First Night officially begins at 1 p.m. on December 31 and ends with spectacular fireworks over the harbor that ring in the new year.

*F*IRST NIGHT DRAWS throngs of costumed revelers into the city with a colorful premidnight march from the Back Bay to the waterfront. It has become, in recent years, a spectacular event for the whole family. New Orleans may have its Mardi Gras, but Boston has First Night.

BOSTON'S FISH PIER IS THE busiest on the East Coast. Dozens of trawlers unload their catch daily from the deep waters off George's Bank (RIGHT).

The renowned New England lobster is found a bit closer to shore. Trapped in baskets, their powerful claws are taped; then they are shipped to market. Not as popular, but farther down on the price-per-pound scale, are other gifts from the sea, like these terrapins (OPPOSITE BOTTOM).

BOSTON:

BEACON FOR THE NEW HORIZON

*C*ARGO-LADEN SHIPS BOUND for Boston are aided in their quest for dock space by tugboat operators experienced in the delicate task of nudging mammoth freighters into their berths.

℞onald "Mighty Mouse" Blow is a tugboat skipper who knows the water and the way (RIGHT). While up on the Charles River, which flows into the harbor, recreational boating *is* the way.

*I*N BOSTON, YOU ARE NEVER far from the water, and many residents take full advantage. Some prefer the swift tranquility of rowing on the Charles with the city as a backdrop.

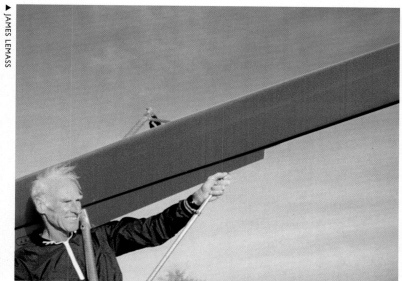

*B*UT FOR THOSE WHO ENJOY saltwater spray, a number of yacht clubs rim the harbor to satisfy the lure of the open sea.

*F*OR THE CITY'S YOUNGSTERS, the most popular water spots in town include nearby lakes and the many municipal swimming pools spread throughout Boston.

RICHARD PASLEY

BOSTON ALSO OFFERS plenty of places for aquatic observers. The New England Aquarium has living exhibits from seals and sea lions to sharks and stingrays.

The Museum of Science has its own version of Jurassic Park (TOP).

JAMES LEMASS

BOB KRAMER

O N SUMMER EVENINGS, "Swing, batter!" is a cry often heard at the city's many sandlots. For some inner-city youths, the neighborhood playground is a home away from home for softball, shooting hoops, or just hanging out.

CHOOSING UP SIDES FOR A game of basketball on asphalt could be the starting point for a future Celtics star. Shooting hoops is serious stuff in Boston neighborhoods, even if the basket happens to be a milk crate.

*F*ROM PEOPLE-WATCHING TO playground basketball, Boston's streets provide a true glimpse into the heart and soul of the city.

BOSTON SPORTS FANS ARE imperivous to heat, cold, rain, or a disastrous win-loss record. The New England Patriots are a case in point. Their fans are die-hard loyal, remaining forever hopeful that the team will one day win the Super Bowl.

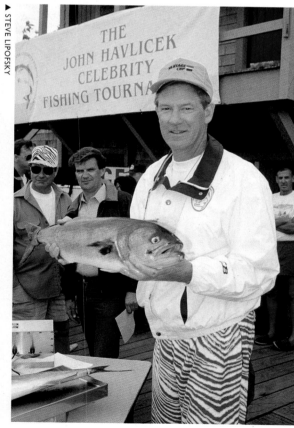

*B*UT FOR CELTICS FANS, winning championships is nothing
new. Bostonians have thronged
City Hall Plaza numerous times in
the past to pay homage to their
victorious heroes, and they expect
to be there again in the future.

The jersey numbers of former
Celtics greats John Havlicek and
Larry Bird (BOTTOM LEFT AND
RIGHT) hang high from the rafters
of Boston Garden, along with
those of other stars from the past.

FENWAY PARK, THE HALLOWED home of the Red Sox, is as legendary as the baseball greats who have played there over the years. One of those stars, Carl Yastrzemski—seen here with former New York Yankee Joe DiMaggio—is still a larger-than-life figure in Boston.

Though there are plenty of stars on the field, it's the folks in the front office who ensure that a day at Fenway is enjoyable for Red Sox fans, young and old alike.

*F*ORMER BOSTON BRUINS
superstar Bobby Orr is said by
many to be the greatest player to
ever lace up the skates. Orr and
his family still live in the Boston
area, and he remains active in a
variety of local causes.

$\mathcal{T}$HERE IS NOT A MORE RABID fan in the country than a Bruins fan. For these loyal and leather-lunged folks, nothing beats season tickets for "Da Broons."

$\mathcal{F}$OR THE ARDENT FOLLOWERS of the sport of kings, there's nothing like a winning trifecta at Suffolk Downs. Located close to Logan Airport in east Boston, Suffolk Downs is only a short subway ride from downtown. And races are held nearly year-round.

𝐾NOWN THE WORLD OVER, the Boston Marathon is the city's premier sporting event. Runners from all 50 states and dozens of foreign countries come in April to compete in the 26.2-mile race from Hopkinton to Boston.

The first Boston Marathon saw but six runners at the starting line. Nowadays, there are as many as 10,000. The race's primary sponsor has been the John Hancock Company, whose corporate head-quarters overlooks the finish line.

*I*f the Boston Marathon is
the city's premier sporting event,
then certainly the premier parade
is the St. Patrick's Day Parade in
south Boston.

𝒯HOUSANDS LINE THE ST. Patrick's Day Parade route on what is often a cold and blustery March day—a day for little people and leprechauns.

*T*HE GENTLE CHANGE OF seasons in the city is heralded by blooming trees on stately Commonwealth Avenue, and by residents basking in the sunshine splashing their front steps.

*T*HOUGH SNOW-COVERED
Boston has its own scenic charm,
the ivy-covered fronts of Back
Bay buildings (BOTTOM) give
lush, green testimony to a long-
awaited spring in the city.

BEACON FOR THE NEW HORIZON

*E*VEN IN SPRING, AN OCCA-
sional ice storm can send the city's
residents back into winter mode.

*A*T THE FIRST NIGHT celebration, elaborate ice sculptures
on Boston Common elicit gasps of
astonishment from all who pass by.

THE STATUE OF GEORGE
Washington looks out over the
Commonwealth Avenue Mall
from the entrance to the Public
Gardens. The city fathers named
Boston's longest street after him,
and it remains so today.
PAGES 162-163, PHOTO BY JAMES LEMASS

$\mathcal{T}$HE GRANITE DOME OF THE
Massachusetts Institute of Technology looms over the Cambridge
skyline at dusk. MIT was founded
in Boston in 1861. The world's
first computer was developed at
the school in 1928.

*T*HE EARLY MORNING SUN illuminates the mansard rooftops of the South End. This section of the city is the result of a major landfill project in the 1860s.

*I*N THE EARLY 1600S, WHEN Boston was a mere village, many of the area's earliest settlers built homes on the narrow streets of the North End.

*T*HE NORTH END BECAME home for thousands of Irish immigrants in the latter part of the 19th century. Today, the North End is Boston's Little Italy, a colorful, close-knit neighborhood of families who have lived there for generations.

COPUCCI

OMESTIC GROCERIES...

COME SUMMERTIME, THE
North End is the scene for several
street festivals. Residents along
Hanover Street have a perfect
view from their windowsills, and
many display their offerings to
their saint of choice (OPPOSITE).

$\mathcal{M}$ARCHERS SOLEMNLY TREK
their way along the parade route
during the Feast of St. Anthony—
obviously one of the more popular
saints. Festivals can last for two or
three days, and they are accompa-
nied by much feasting and dancing.

*R*OXBURY YOUNGSTERS GET
set to rehearse for their annual
Black Nativity Pageant, a musical
version of Langston Hughes' poem
depicting the birth of Christ.

*W*ITH THE ADVENT OF SPRING, parishioners at Mission Church in Roxbury prepare for Palm Sunday.

174

ELMA LEWIS, FOUNDER AND matriarch of the Black Nativity Pageant, also heads her own School of Fine Arts in Roxbury (OPPOSITE, BOTTOM). The Cathedral of the Holy Cross in the South End (OPPOSITE, TOP) is the site of the ordination of priests, and serves as home church for the cardinal of the Archdiocese of Boston.

As it has for over 250 years, Park Street Church stands watch over Boston Common at sunset (LEFT).

ON THE FOLLOWING PAGES, Trinity Church, in the Back Bay, was designed by Henry Richardson. The Gothic structure has been hailed by many architects as the finest church ever built in America (LEFT).

Just a few blocks from Trinity Church, another grand architectural presence is the First Church of Christ Scientist, the Mother Church for Christian Scientists the world over (RIGHT).

PAGES 176-177, PHOTOS BY JAMES LEMASS

served as an outdoor pulpit for a variety of groups—the Quakers set up a meeting house in the Common in 1656 (OPPOSITE, TOP).

In the North End, a Franciscan priest pauses for prayer and reflection in a peaceful church garden (OPPOSITE, BOTTOM).

New priests of the Roman Catholic Church are ordained at Holy Cross Cathedral in the South End (LEFT). The Boston Archdiocese is one of the largest in the United States.

THE BEAUTIFUL NEW ORANGE
Line Mass Transit Station in
Forest Hills is a turnaround point
for commuters traveling in and out
of the city (TOP). The Green Line
is the people mover from the
suburbs west of the city
(BOTTOM RIGHT).

*S*OUTH STATION, REFUR-bished at the turn of the century, was once one of the busiest rail terminals in the world. Amtrak trains also serve the Boston commuter, many of whom use the time to catch up on work using a laptop computer.

MANY MORNING COMMUTERS
still travel by car, passing through
the tollgates on the Mystic-Tobin
Bridge headed for downtown
(RIGHT).

A jungle of signs faces the
northbound commuter on the
return home, but this daily night-
mare will soon become history
with the completion of the massive
new Central Artery project
(OPPOSITE, TOP).

Coming and going, the traffic
on the turnpike extension under
the Back Bay sees little letup day
or night (OPPOSITE, BOTTOM).

𝒯HE NORTHERN AVENUE Bridge on the waterfront is a rusting relic that is slated for demolition (TOP).

A dapper South End resident poses beneath another relic being dismantled, the old elevated subway line on Washington Street (BOTTOM).

*F*OR WORKERS ON THE WATER-
front, a hand or two of pinochle
pass the time until their ship
comes in.

$\mathcal{E}$VEN THE MOST COMMONLY
traveled thoroughfares, such as the
Tobin Bridge, seem foreign when
viewed from new points of view
(ABOVE AND OPPOSITE).

*O*UTSIDE THE CITY, A WARM
sun sets on the suburb of Malden,
a small city unto itself.
PAGES 188-189, PHOTO BY RICHARD PASLEY

MOST OF THE RESIDENTS OF the suburbs commute to Boston for work and return home in the evening to their communities. The city is close enough to allow them to enjoy the many cultural, entertainment, and sports events that Boston offers.

Most of Boston's suburban communities have their own special character and charm. Many, such as Reading, Lexington, and Quincy, have their own Colonial history as well.

Lexington is home to Erikson's Ice Cream Store, a reminder of the small-town charm that can be found in the suburbs of Boston (OPPOSITE, TOP).

The civic fountain is a popular spot in the suburb of Quincy. Presidents John Adams and John Quincy Adams were both born and raised in the small town (OPPOSITE, BOTTOM).

▼ NICHOLAS CARROLL

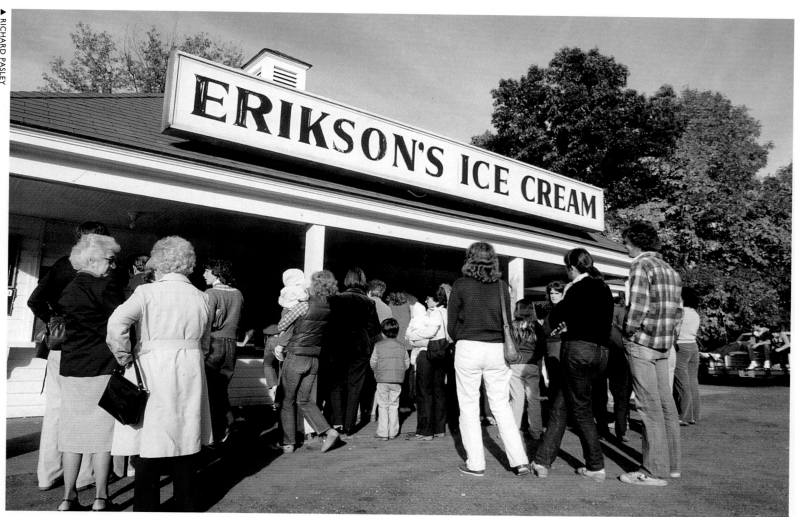

*K*IDS EVERYWHERE ARE MAG-
netized to the "mall," and New
England youngsters are no
different. The Arsenal Mall in
Watertown suits this group just
fine (OPPOSITE).

Boston's suburban towns continue to grow as the demand for
new housing picks up. These new
colonial homes are going up in
Sudbury, 30 miles west of the city
(TOP LEFT). Also going up are new
malls and shopping centers, such
as this one in Framingham (TOP
RIGHT). Folks in Billerica enjoy
a beautiful, bucolic setting
(BOTTOM).

The Old North Bridge in Concord echoed the march of Colonials on that historic day on April 19, 1775.

CONCORD IS HOME TO WALDEN Pond, the spot where Henry David Thoreau withdrew from the world and wrote the classic *Walden*.

Southeastern Massachusetts and Cape Cod are the world's largest producers of cranberries. Cranberry bogs like this one in Carver are a common sight throughout the area (BOTTOM).

*T*HIS OLD FISH SHANTY ATOP A granite pier in Rockport is a popular motif for local artists. A motif of a different sort can be found on the Boston waterfront (BOTTOM).

THE BOSTON HARBOR ISLANDS
have become popular recreational
areas as these canoeists and grape
pickers on Grape Island have
discovered. The group of small
islands in the outer harbor was
largely ignored until recently.

*T*HERE ARE ABOUT 30 ISLANDS that make up the Harbor Islands archipelago. Currently, there are plans to transform the islands into a park to be administered by the National Park Service.

$\mathcal{F}$ROM ENJOYING A DAY AT THE
beach to flying kites at Franklin
Park, the Boston area is an ideal
place to enjoy the simple pleasures
unheard of in most cities its size.

*B*OSTON'S BEACHES ARE NOT the only places to enjoy water activities. The Charles River, which runs through the heart of town, is one of the city's most endearing landmarks.

*T*HIS COULD BE MISTAKEN FOR a pastoral autumn scene in the New England countryside, but it's really a view of a pond and park tucked within the Fenway community. The park is part of the Emerald Necklace designed by Frederick Law Olmsted in 1884.

$\mathcal{T}$HE PARADE OF TALL SHIPS IN Boston Harbor is a perfect opportunity to view windjammers under full sail with a full complement of passengers.

𝒯HE **FULL-RIGGED REPLICA OF** the *Mayflower* also takes part in the Tall Ships event. The *Mayflower* is permanently berthed in Plymouth Harbor near the living reproduction of Plimoth Plantation (**LEFT**).

Scurrying up the main mast to unfurl a tall ship's sails is not a task for the faint of heart (**TOP RIGHT**).

*T*HE *Man of the Sea* STATUE looking out over the harbor in Gloucester (LEFT) is dedicated to the men who have died trying to tame the open seas, while the *Minuteman* statue in Lexington (RIGHT) honors those who fought heroically in the war for independence.

𝒫LIMOTH PLANTATION depicts the lives of the Native Americans and Pilgrims who first settled the area. J. Alleyn Bradford, whose antecedent was Governor William Bradford, is joined by Paula Maher, a descendant of the Indian tribe that befriended the Pilgrims (OPPOSITE).

The re-creation of the original Pilgrim settlement is authentic to the smallest detail. Those portraying the early settlers are schooled in the dress and speech of the period, and the buildings and other structures have also been researched for authenticity.

𝓑OSTON LIGHT, AMERICA'S
first lighthouse, has been a shining
beacon in the outer harbor since
1716.

A PANORAMIC VISTA OF TODAY'S
Boston is proof that the city is
destined to persevere for centuries
to come.
PAGES 214-215,
PHOTO BY ALEX S. MACLEAN / LANDSLIDES

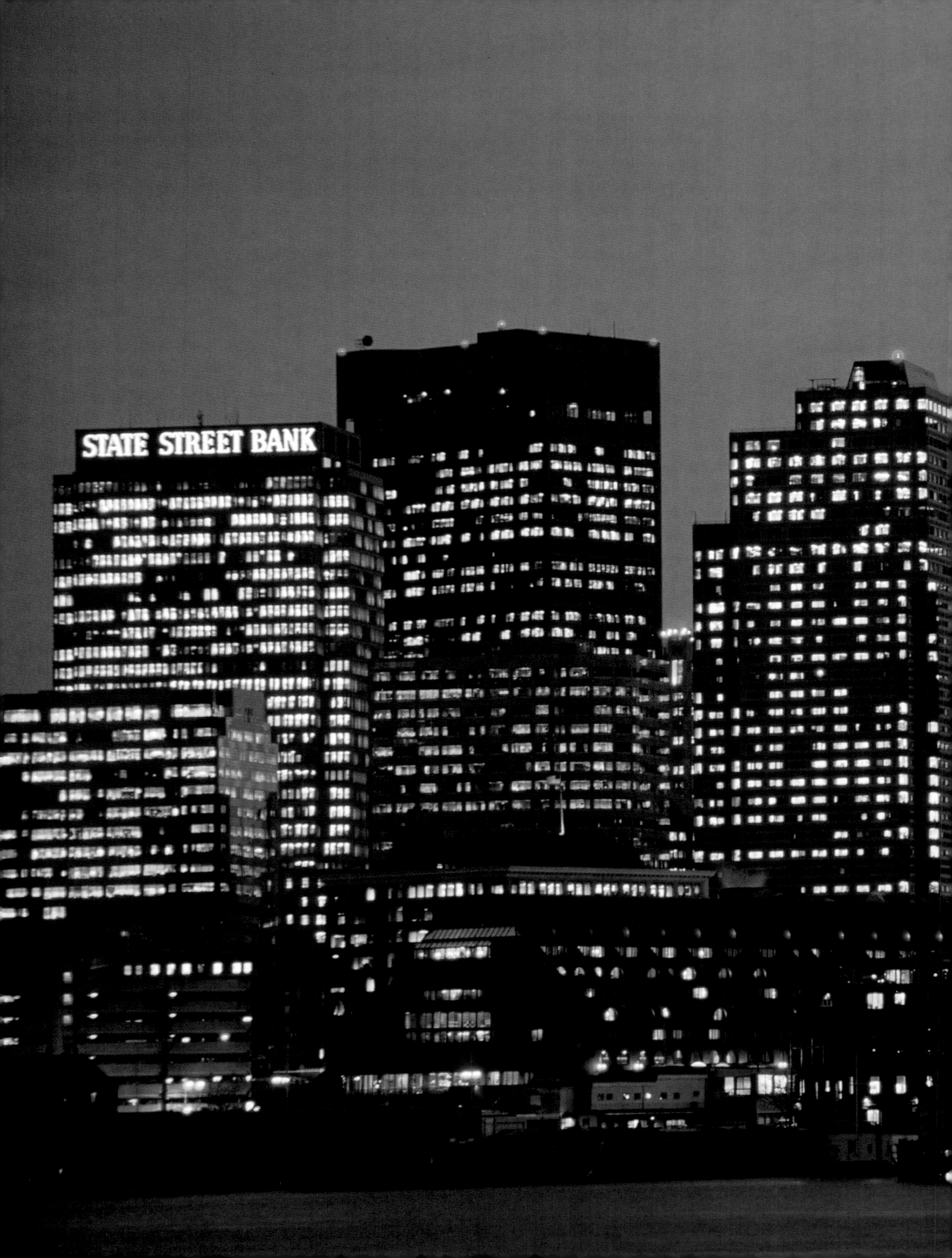
STATE STREET BANK

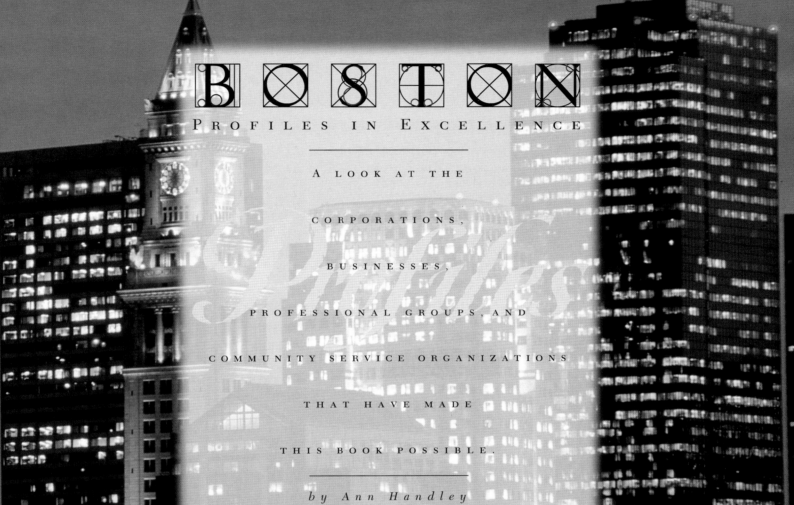

BOSTON
PROFILES IN EXCELLENCE

A LOOK AT THE

CORPORATIONS,

BUSINESSES,

PROFESSIONAL GROUPS, AND

COMMUNITY SERVICE ORGANIZATIONS

THAT HAVE MADE

THIS BOOK POSSIBLE.

by Ann Handley

▼ JAMES LEMASS

BOSTON

PROFILES IN EXCELLENCE

1792	State Street Bank and Trust Company
1800	Greater Boston Chamber of Commerce
1811	Massachusetts General Hospital
1836	Shawmut National Corporation
1850	Arkwright
1863	South Boston Savings Bank
1868	St. Elizabeth's Medical Center
1871	Mount Auburn Hospital
1872	The Boston Globe
1873	Sedgwick James of New England, Inc.
1875	Meredith & Grew, Incorporated
1889	Stone & Webster Engineering Corporation
1893	New England Baptist Hospital
1894	New England College of Optometry
1894	Perini Corporation
1895	Hill & Barlow
1896	Deaconess Hospital
1899	Peabody & Arnold
1900	Whittier Partners Group, L.P.
1901	The Gillette Company
1901	OSRAM SYLVANIA INC.
1914	The Stop & Shop Companies, Inc.

▼ JAMES LEMASS

ONE OF THE MOST FINANCIALLY SOUND BANKS IN THE

United States, State Street Bank and Trust Company has more than 10,000 employees worldwide. While its primary businesses include securities processing, recordkeeping, investment management, and related services, it is a full-service bank with a broad base of customers around the

world. Focusing its commercial lending activities on middle-market companies in New England, State Street also provides commercial banking services to a variety of specialized industries on a nation-wide basis.

A TRUSTED SERVICER OF FINANCIAL ASSETS

Since 1924, when State Street was appointed custodian of the first U.S. mutual fund, the company's securities processing business has evolved into a highly sophisticated array of information technology-based services. Institutional investors—including mutual funds, pension funds, insurance companies, and nonprofit organizations—turn to State Street to help them

As a global financial asset servicer and manager, State Street supports its customers' investment strategies—wherever they are located, wherever they invest.

Through treasury centers in Boston, London, Luxembourg, Munich, Hong Kong, Tokyo, and Sydney, the bank offers capital markets services 24 hours a day worldwide.

execute and monitor their investment strategies. For example, when a mutual fund decides to buy a stock or bond, State Street takes possession of the security and performs the necessary accounting functions related to the purchase, including collecting dividends or interest. Today, State Street is the largest U.S. mutual fund servicer. Building on this expertise, the company has also become the nation's largest master trust custodian and is responsible for more than $1.6 trillion of assets in total.

Managing $139 billion in assets, State Street is also one of the leading U.S. investment managers. While a large portion of these assets is managed on behalf of in-

stitutions, the company is also a leading trustee and money manager for individuals in New England.

Other services that State Street offers include cash management, foreign exchange, investment banking, and corporate trust.

State Street's unique focus in the financial services industry has proved to be a profitable one. In 1993, revenue grew 18 percent, surpassing $1 billion for the first time in the company's long and distinguished history. Likewise, financial assets under management increased 28 percent, and earnings per share were up 13 percent.

GROWING WITH BOSTON SINCE 1792

State Street is actually an alliance of a number of Boston banking institutions. When its oldest ancestor, Union Bank, was established on June 25, 1792, it brought the number of chartered financial institutions in the city to three. Union Bank's charter was signed by John Hancock, Massachusetts' first governor.

At the time, Union Bank's founders placed advertisements in local newspapers seeking a "convenient building situated either on Cornhill (now Washington Street) or State Street." Rooms were eventually rented at the corner of State and Exchange streets. The location was ideal for the new enterprise: close to the State House and across the street from Israel Hatch's Coffee House, where the stagecoach departed and people gathered to discuss current events.

State Street's namesake predecessor was established in

1891 and was located, of course, on State Street. With the State House at one end and Long Wharf at the other, the thoroughfare became the center of Massachusetts politics and commerce. The city's first merchant, John Coggan, set up shop at the corner of State and Washington, effectively launching retail trade in Boston. The first public reading of the Declaration of Independence in Massachusetts took place on State Street.

The current State Street Bank and Trust Company was formed in 1961 after a series of mergers united 13 financial institutions. In 1978 the State Street Plan was written, and the organization initiated an unusual business strategy: During a period when balance sheet size was thought to be the measure of a successful bank, State Street focused on creating sustainable growth in earnings per share. The Plan's contents remain the company's guiding principles today.

COMMITTED TO MEETING HIGH EXPECTATIONS

"State Street's goal is to be a quality institution for our customers, our employees, our stockholders, and the society in which we live," the State Street Plan begins. To that end, the company began in 1986 to survey its customers regularly, using the results to improve the quality of its service. In 1987 the company established an education and training facility designed to ensure that each employee has

the skills necessary to provide the highest quality service to customers.

Long ago, State Street established itself as a philanthropic presence in the Boston community. That commitment continues to this day. In 1993, for example, State Street donated over $3.2 million to charitable organizations. Through a campaign organized by the company, State Street employees contributed more than $1 million to the United Way of Massachusetts Bay in 1993—the largest United Way contribution made by employees of Massachusetts institutions.

THE LONG VIEW

Today, State Street creates solutions for servicing and managing financial assets that benefit investors around the world. Supporting their increasingly complex, global investment strategies, State Street helps its customers succeed in meeting their objectives.

Balancing its commitment to the local community with its desire to deliver world-class service to customers around the globe, State Street continues to hold a leadership position in

Boston as one of the largest employers in eastern Massachusetts. At the same time, the company takes a longer view of its role.

"Our services facilitate the movement of funds into higher-performing assets," says Chairman and Chief Executive Officer Marshall N. Carter. "We believe we are helping to build a global investment system through which savings can move across the world to the most fruitful investments—allowing individuals everywhere to participate in the world's economic progress."

▶ JOHN SWAN

In the late 18th century, State Street was the center of Massachusetts politics and commerce (above left).

While its business activities are worldwide, State Street Bank has traditionally provided leadership and financial support to the Boston community (above right).

The bank provided financing for Stony Brook Gardens, a cooperative, affordable housing development in Boston (below).

MEMBERS OF THE GREATER BOSTON CHAMBER OF COMmerce's oldest ancestor were very different from their counterparts today. Early members were grain and produce farmers who formed what they called the Grain Exchange, established around 1800. As the organization grew, it came to represent 1,000 members from a wider range of indus-

tries. In 1885 the exchange merged with another area merchants' group to form the principal trading body of the rapidly growing city. Meetings were held at the Quincy Market Rotunda until 1892, when the landmark Grain Exchange Building, with its curved facade and crownlike roofline, was completed.

On June 15, 1909, the Massachusetts legislature founded a new entity—known as the Boston Chamber of Commerce—by combining the existing trade organization and the Boston Merchants Association. In 1952 the Chamber added "Greater" to its name to reflect its growing membership base.

MEETING THE NEEDS OF MODERN BUSINESS

At the time of the Chamber's founding, members felt that the emerging complexities of the 20th century demanded a unified voice that would represent business interests and promote the just and equitable principles of trade. Those tenets remain true today, especially as the scope of issues affecting business and the local economy continues to grow.

Throughout the 20th century, the Greater Boston Chamber's role has broadened to encompass such concerns as governmental regulation of business, environmental protection, state and municipal fiscal policy, development of new energy sources, expanded transportation services, educational resources, development and renewal issues, inner-city needs,

and health care reform, among other important areas.

Responding to the increasingly complex issues facing today's businesses, the Chamber formulated a plan in 1992 that would help focus its efforts on a set number of initiatives and utilize its resources more effectively. The result was a 12-point list of public policy priorities that includes such goals as lessening the cost of doing business in the Commonwealth of Massachusetts and supporting the construction of a new convention center to stimulate increased tourism in Greater Boston.

The Chamber's focused approach has resulted in a number of unqualified successes. For example, the organization recently fought successfully for a rollback of unemployment insurance rates, saving Massachusetts businesses an estimated $180 million in 1994. The Chamber also helped bring about the inclusion of $21 million in water and sewer rate relief for Massachusetts Water Resources Authority ratepayers in the state's 1994 budget.

The Greater Boston Chamber is changing in other ways as well. "We have become much more of a business than we used to be," says Chamber President William Coughlin. The organization's membership, too, is evolving. While still including many of the area's oldest and largest businesses, the Chamber's membership roster has grown to include increasing numbers of new and emerging technological companies.

AGGRESSIVELY SHAPING THE LOCAL BUSINESS ENVIRONMENT

The Greater Boston Chamber of Commerce is hard at work on a number of programs designed to make the area more hospitable to business. One such effort is aimed at increasing access to capital for area businesses that need seed money at start-up and additional cash for expansions. Initiatives include supporting a state fund for loans to small businesses and advising member businesses on loan sources.

Other Chamber priorities include supporting educational reform, developing apprenticeships for area high school students, promoting international trade opportunities for Boston businesses, and working to enhance the city's image as a business center for the 21st century.

As part of its general goal of reducing the cost of doing business in the Boston area, the Chamber is working to moderate or eliminate increases in the cost of labor, taxes, government regulations, and insurance expenses. The Chamber is also an active player in the debate over health care reform. "We want to make sure that the state constructs its

program in a way that is fiscally responsible, and will not put Massachusetts at a competitive disadvantage with its neighboring states," Coughlin states.

The Chamber will continue to advocate for the construction of a new Boston convention center, sometimes referred to as the megaplex. "The convention business is exploding," says Coughlin. "We are losing millions of dollars of convention business because our facilities are too small and outdated."

Paying close attention to Boston's $7 billion, 10-year Central Artery/Tunnel Project to ensure that it is conducted in a manner least disruptive to local businesses is another Chamber priority, Coughlin says. The Chamber, through its affiliation with the Artery Business Committee, wants to make sure that the "Big Dig," as the project is frequently called, won't place undue hardship during construction on companies located in the downtown area.

Additionally, the Chamber is continuing to push for the development of the Crosstown region of the city—the underutilized area of Boston that runs from the Longwood Medical area

through the Southwest Corridor, to the Newmarket section. The Chamber believes Crosstown should be the site of considerable new investment because it offers available land, proximity to medical and educational institutions, access to transportation, and substantial public-sector investments in infrastructure.

The list goes on, and it's easy to see that the Greater Boston Chamber of Commerce is aggressive on many fronts in efforts to strengthen the region's economy.

A diverse membership base enables the Chamber to assemble a wealth of business and professional talent—from the area's largest employers to emerging businesses and budding entrepreneurs in all segments of the economy (top).

The Greater Boston business community is served by a Chamber that is a forceful advocate for state and city public policies that support economic growth (above).

Opposite page: Chairman of the Board Fletcher Wiley (left) and President William Coughlin are key members of the Chamber's current leadership team.

223

Massachusetts General Hospital

HE CITY OF BOSTON IS WIDELY REGARDED AS A MEDICAL mecca, and the venerable Massachusetts General Hospital (MGH) stands at the forefront of patient care, professional education, and medical research. ■ A recent *U.S. News & World Report* survey of the nation's hospitals rated the MGH the top hospital in New England, and fourth overall

in the country, with top 10 rankings in 11 different specialties, including orthopedics, geriatrics, and cardiology. Additionally, Massachusetts General Hospital remains the oldest and largest teaching hospital of Harvard Medical School, offering future leaders in medicine an opportunity to study with today's most renowned medical experts.

Equally significant, the MGH conducts the largest hospital-based research program in the United States, with an annual research budget of more than $170 million. The institution's long-standing focus on medical research has led to a number of notable discoveries, including the first demonstration of "painless" surgery using anesthesia in 1846, the first successful replantation of a severed human limb, development of artificial skin for burn treatment, and the discovery of the genes for Lou Gehrig's and Huntington's diseases.

SERVING THE COMMUNITY'S MEDICAL NEEDS

The MGH has remained committed to serving the routine and complex medical needs of the community throughout its history. When the MGH was founded in 1811 by a small group of Boston physicians as the first general hospital in New England and only the third in the country, the sick relied primarily on home remedies and contacted doctors as a last resort. Even then, physicians provided little additional help, as techniques and medications were limited.

A report by the 19th-century state legislative committee

that recommended approval of the hospital's charter articulated the spirit of the Massachusetts General Hospital mission, which continues to hold true today: "The hospital is intended to be a receptacle for patients from all parts of the Commonwealth, afflicted with diseases

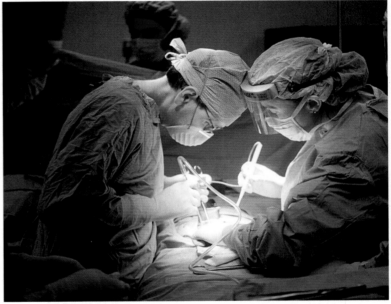

of a particular nature, requiring the most skillful treatment, and presenting cases for instruction in the study and practice of surgery and physicianship. Persons of every age and sex, whether permanent residents of the town, or occasional residents therein, those in indigent circumstances, these are among that . . . portion of the community for whom it is intended."

Now, more than 180 years later, Massachusetts General Hospital annually records more than 35,000 admissions and nearly 750,000 visits to its outpatient programs and Emergency Services, serving people from Boston neighborhoods, across the state,

throughout the country, and around the world. They come to the MGH knowing that regardless of their ability to pay, they will receive the finest medical care available. True to its original mission, the MGH continues to serve Boston's poor.

In 1988, the MGH became the city's first private hospital to open a clinic specifically to serve the medical needs of Boston's homeless population. Care providers also make regular "house calls" to the city's homeless shelters to assist the many individuals who do not or cannot visit the clinic. Massachusetts General Hospital has likewise been dedicated to meeting the growing need for health care in Boston-area neighborhoods, linking patients to the full range of services offered by the MGH. The hospital operates three neighborhood health centers, which serve approximately 200,000 local res-

With a 180-year history of internationally recognized accomplishments, the MGH stands at the forefront of patient care, professional education, and medical research.

idents each year, delivering geriatric care for homebound patients and working with community leaders to address problems of drug abuse, violence, and infectious disease.

In March 1994 the Massachusetts General Hospital further committed to expanding the range and efficiency of its delivery of care. The MGH formally affiliated with Brigham and Women's Hospital, another leading Harvard teaching hospital in Boston, to form Partners Health-Care System, Inc. Together, these academic medical leaders are creating a high-quality, efficient health care delivery system in partnership with community-based primary care providers.

Since its founding, the Massachusetts General Hospital has remained dedicated to providing excellent and compassionate patient care, educating the next generation of medical leaders, and finding cures for disease. With a 180-year history of internationally recognized accomplishments, it is not surprising that the MGH is widely regarded as one of the world's foremost medical institutions. Equally important, however, the hospital has always extended its care to any and all people in need. Massachusetts General Hospital continues to fulfill the mission inspired and articulated by its founders Drs. James Jackson and Charles C. Warren: "When in distress, every man becomes our neighbor."

Massachusetts General Hospital annually records more than 35,000 admissions and nearly 750,000 visits to its outpatient programs and Emergency Services, serving people from Boston neighborhoods, across the state, throughout the country, and around the world.

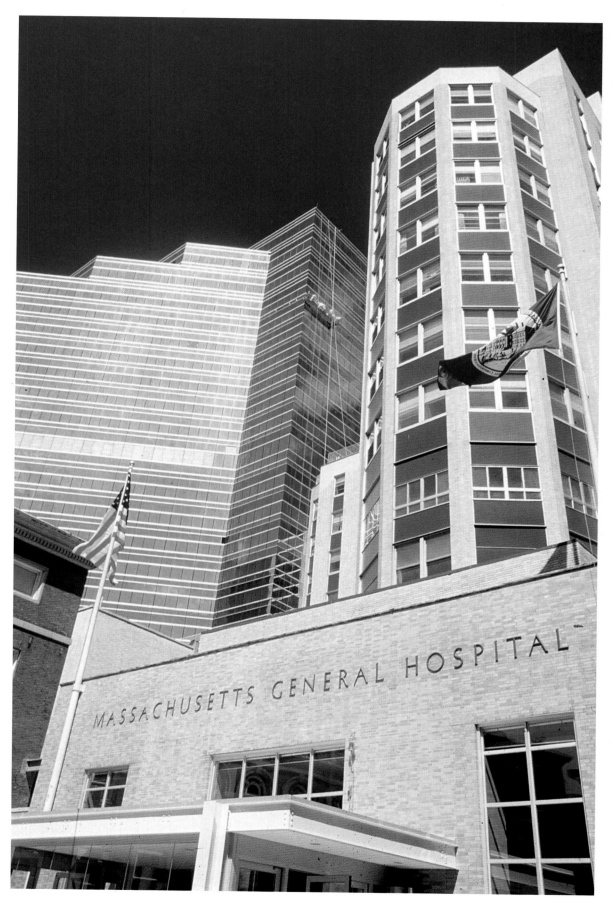

HAWMUT BANK IS ONE OF THE OLDEST INSTITUTIONS IN Boston, dating back to 1836. Originally called Warren Bank to honor a hero in the Battle of Bunker Hill, the name was changed to Shawmut—the American Indian word for the Boston peninsula. An appropriate name, because the bank has spent a century and a half playing an integral role in the growth and development of Boston and its surrounding communities.

FUELING SUCCESS IN BOSTON-AREA COMMUNITIES

From its earliest days, Shawmut has proved its strength and commitment to serving the financial needs of Bostonians. The bank weathered the financial panics of the 1830s and 1870s (when many other financial institutions failed) and earned its federal charter during the turbulence of the Civil War.

Shawmut's strength and commitment to providing its customers with the latest financial services led to its entry into the "modern" age in 1914—the year that Shawmut joined the new Federal Reserve Bank system. A few years later, the bank offered its first loans for purchasing automobiles. Expanded branch banking and wider services followed, including mortgages in 1926.

After World War II, the expanding economy led Shawmut to move into consumer loans for other kinds of purchases. In addition to benefiting the area's consumers, Shawmut's loans helped build the nation's infrastructure. The bank helped to finance the nation's railroads, gas and electric utilities, and even telecommunications giant American Telephone and Telegraph (AT&T).

Shawmut continued its pattern of growth and in 1975 opened One Federal Street, a striking new headquarters building in downtown Boston. Following a difficult period for the banking industry as a whole during the late 1980s, Shawmut emerged as a strong player. Reserves were up, nonperforming assets were reduced to a low level, and expansion was the watchword.

Today's Shawmut National Corporation is a super-regional bank holding company with $31 billion in assets and over 300 branches and 500 ATMs. It ranks as the 27th-largest bank in the nation and is a leading provider of financial services to small and medium-sized companies. Shawmut is also a major supplier of financial services to corporate customers, correspondent banks, and government units throughout New England as well as in select national markets.

In keeping with its longtime stature as a business, the bank is also a leader in the community. Shawmut has supported a number of local projects, including consumer education seminars, special loan funds created in conjunction with state

Established in Boston in 1836, the bank takes the name Shawmut from the American Indian word for the Boston peninsula.

THE NATIONAL
Shawmut Bank
OF BOSTON

1836 — 1936

ONE HUNDREDTH ANNIVERSARY

MEMBER FEDERAL DEPOSIT INSURANCE CORPORATION

and federal programs, and ATMs adapted to meet the needs of non-English-speaking and visually impaired customers. Additionally, Shawmut is involved in fund-raising efforts for the Jane Doe Walk for Women's Safety.

Shawmut has also initiated outreach efforts to low-

today's banking world. Banks must master the demands and opportunities of rapidly advancing technology and address the shifting competition within the larger financial services industry.

With its outstanding New England banking franchise and a diverse mix of consumer, small-

instrumental in the development of Shawmut Center, New England's premier sports and entertainment complex. Scheduled for completion in 1995, Shawmut Center is the new home of the Boston Bruins and the Boston Celtics, and will host a variety of other special events. These proj-

and moderate-income neighborhoods, providing more flexible underwriting requirements. In addition, the bank has Urban Business Banking units within its Small Business Banking Group.

THE STRENGTH TO BUILD A SOLID FUTURE
Although the basic requirements for success in banking in the 1990s are the same as they have been for centuries, there are many additional complexities in

business, and corporate customers, Shawmut believes it is well positioned for the future.

Now that Shawmut has achieved a strong presence in the region, the organization is ensuring prosperity for the future by building on that presence. To that end, the bank is becoming even more involved in the community. Shawmut, for example, sponsored the Volvo International Tennis Tournament in New Haven, Connecticut, and has been

ects, in addition to enhancing the quality of life for the entire region, have increased the bank's name recognition.

Of all the public perceptions of the bank, though, Shawmut National Corporation is most proud of its reputation as a trusted business partner. That hard-earned reputation has been the foundation of the bank's success and is the cornerstone of its plans for the future.

Shawmut Bank has been instrumental in the development of Shawmut Center, New England's premier sports and entertainment complex. Scheduled for completion in 1995, the facility is the new home of the Boston Bruins and the Boston Celtics, and will host a variety of other special events.

RKWRIGHT IS A SUPPLIER OF RISK MANAGEMENT SERvices for large commercial, industrial, and institutional companies worldwide. Its primary services center on risk assessment, loss control, property underwriting, and brokerage capabilities, which are delivered to customers headquartered in North America or Europe. The organization's

Situated along Route 128, "Massachusetts' Technology Highway," Arkwright is headquartered in Hobbs Brook Office Park in Waltham. Managed by Middlesex Mutual Building Trust, an Arkwright Mutual Insurance Company subsidiary, the award-winning office park boasts eight buildings on 87 acres, 45 tenants, and 1.1 million square feet of office space.

solid reputation is built on its proven abilities to help customers identify, evaluate, control, and finance risk; Arkwright's loss prevention expertise and superior engineering solutions are considered essential components in the business plans of some of the world's most successful corporations. Headquartered in Waltham, Massachusetts, Arkwright has

and paper manufacturing, utilities, technology, health care, and financial and education organizations.

With more than $750 billion in protected property values, Arkwright Mutual Insurance Company, Arkwright's direct underwriting arm, insures roughly 17 percent of the largest corporations in the United States. Brokered business is placed through

writing and property conservation skills to create an effective risk management program. The company is most noted for its emphasis on loss prevention engineering services, which are delivered through its staff engineers and the 1,200 engineers of its jointly owned subsidiary, Factory Mutual Engineering and Research. Additionally, Hobbs Group has a staff of claims specialists and certified safety professionals, and provides property and casualty loss control engineering and claims services through its international network.

Another key component of Arkwright's international success in the field of risk management is the jointly owned Factory Mutual Test Center, a computerized, 60,000-square-foot facility where products, packaging, or equipment can be tested to determine flammability and explosion potential. The results of such tests demonstrate the need for risk management and provide invaluable data to customers implementing a loss prevention program.

Arkwright also owes much of its success to its ability to find creative solutions to help customers minimize their exposures. As such, the organization is continually on the lookout for newer and better ways to manage risk. In recent months, Arkwright Mutual Insurance Company has formed several subsidiaries that improve the way the Arkwright organization can evaluate risk. One company, Arkwright Technical Services, Inc., offers computerized tomography, a nondestructive form of equipment examination

offices in the United States, Canada, and Europe.

Founded nearly 150 years ago, the Arkwright organization employs more than 1,000 people, with an additional 3,000-plus employees within Arkwright Mutual Insurance Company's jointly owned operations. Arkwright's services are targeted toward a diverse customer base that comprises a variety of segments, including pharmaceuticals, real estate, steel manufacturing, pulp

Hobbs Group, Inc., an Arkwright Mutual Insurance Company subsidiary, which meets a wide range of commercial insurance needs, including casualty, workers' compensation, construction wrap-ups, and specialty insurance coverages.

THE ARKWRIGHT ADVANTAGE

Arkwright Mutual Insurance Company goes beyond the bounds of simply insuring property by providing customers with under-

William J. Poutsiaka is Arkwright's president and chief executive officer. His vision for the company is to be recognized as a global, technically focused, engineering-driven risk management organization with significant underwriting capacity.

that is more timely and less costly than traditional methods. Another company, Arkwright Risk Services, Inc., offers innovative financial solutions for those customers who have difficult-to-insure risks, such as earthquake or pollution.

A HISTORY ROOTED IN LOSS CONTROL

While its strategy for managing risk reflects the needs of today's rapidly changing business world, Arkwright's philosophy is actually more than a century-and-a-half old.

In the midst of the depression of 1835, a local mill owner named Zachariah Allen undertook a concerted effort to control losses at his facility, with the intent that his insurance premium might be lowered to reflect a better risk. During this time, however, insurance companies relied on the "good risks" to help finance the "bad risks"; that is, facilities with good loss experience offset those with more frequent and severe losses. As a result, Allen's request for reduced premium was denied.

Frustrated, Allen met with other mill owners who had philosophies similar to his own, eventually forming a mutual fire insurance company dedicated to insuring only "good risk" properties. These companies believed in the value of loss control and prac-

ticed property conservation techniques within their facilities. Allen believed losses at these better-protected factories would be fewer and less severe, meaning less premium would be needed to finance potential losses. Furthermore, any remaining premium at year-end would be returned to each policyholder in the form of dividends.

Operating under the name Manufacturer's Mutual Fire Insurance Company, Allen's company focused on writing business in the Rhode Island area. Fifteen years later, Allen wrote to James Read, a Boston merchant with an ownership interest in several cotton mills, urging him to organize a mutual insurance company in Boston. Together with a number of other textile manufacturers, Read formed Boston Manufacturers Mutual Fire Insurance Company on March 15, 1850, marking the official founding date of Arkwright Mutual Insurance Company.

Ten years later, a second industrial mutual company in the Boston area sprang up; named after Sir Richard Arkwright, a leader in the British textile industry, Arkwright Mutual was incorporated. Over the years, several local insurance companies began merging with Boston Manufacturers. Arkwright Mutual did the

same in 1967, forming what was then known as Arkwright-Boston. In the following decades, after merging with Mutual Boiler

Insurance Company and Philadelphia Manufacturers Mutual Insurance Company, Arkwright-Boston officially changed its name in 1987 to Arkwright Mutual Insurance Company.

Today, the Arkwright organization is still dedicated to Allen's original belief that the most effective method of helping businesses prevent or control losses is by taking proactive steps to reduce the risk that a loss will occur.

Arkwright supports the use of better analytic tools to aid in the pricing of risk. Toward this end, the company is leading the way in the development of advanced computer-modeling techniques to enhance its ability to underwrite and manage its customers' risk exposures.

HEN SOUTH BOSTON SAVINGS BANK WAS ESTABLISHED IN 1863, South Boston's population was only 30,000 and the country was torn by the struggles of the Civil War. Over 100 manufacturers existed in South Boston and flourished throughout the greater part of the 1800s. ■ A small group of enterprising, public-spirited men established the bank,

seeing a promise of more growth in South Boston and the need for a financial institution to support its residents. The tradition continues today.

The bank has flourished over the years—growing from one office and initial deposits of $550 (made by the bank's original six members) to seven offices and assets of over $2 billion. One important feature of the bank that has not changed is its dedication to providing a safe haven for South Boston and area residents to save their money, secure mortgages, and seek financial advice.

Established in South Boston in 1863, the bank remains a safe haven for area residents to save their money, secure mortgages, and seek financial advice.

viously were employed at South Boston Savings. It is the kind of bank where the CEO answers his own telephone and probably knows the person calling. Some families have been doing business with the bank since its inception. In fact, the first savings account, opened in 1863, is still active today!

South Boston Savings' relationship with the community has helped carry it through some tumultuous economic times. During the Great Depression, for example, many bank customers uncertain about the economy demanded immediate withdrawal of

their money. The story goes that a South Boston Savings employee went to the vault, took out all the money, and laid it on a table behind the tellers. He told depositors they could have their money, but he urged them, for the good of the community, to leave their accounts intact. The people listened, and

South Boston Savings survived one of its worst crises.

The bank has done more than continue over the years—it has prospered. South Boston Savings became publicly traded in 1983, and since then its assets have more than tripled from $600 million to a current total of $2 billion, making it one of the largest savings banks in New England.

SERVICE AND CONVENIENCE

South Boston Savings offers a complete line of banking services, including savings accounts, mortgages, NOW accounts, money market accounts, individual retirement accounts (IRAs), Keogh plans, student loans, and automatic teller machines (ATMs).

The bank provides customers the convenience of banking at various offices located in South Boston, Dorchester, Needham, North Quincy, Quincy, West Roxbury, and Weymouth, as well as a mortgage origination office in South Boston. In addition, banking services are available to customers at home or away with the convenience of ATMs located worldwide, or through Bank-by-Mail and Infophone.

South Boston Savings has thrived in a time when many small, independent savings banks are vanishing. For more than 130 years, the bank has stayed true to its original mission: serving the needs of the community.

LOYALTY TO THE COMMUNITY

South Boston Savings' commitment to its roots has created tremendous loyalty in the community. Many of the bank's employees reside in South Boston, and many have followed in the footsteps of their parents and grandparents who pre-

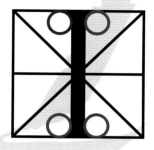

Meredith & Grew, Incorporated

I N 1875 MEREDITH & GREW WAS FOUNDED AS ONE OF THE first commercial real estate firms in Boston on the Yankee principles of integrity, vision, and hard work. More than a century later, the firm continues to be one of the foremost and influential commercial real estate forces in the city, with a distinguished history and many long-lasting relationships.

GROWING AND DEVELOPING BOSTON

Meredith & Grew first opened its doors to a city that was vastly different than that of today. The landfills that would create much of Boston's waterfront were not yet complete, and the landmark Custom House was the sole tower on the city's skyline. Today, Boston is a global center of commercial and intellectual activity with leading business, educational, and health institutions, and the skyline boasts a magnificent mix of historical and modern buildings.

Much like the city of Boston itself, Meredith & Grew has undergone great growth and development throughout its 120-year history. Once primarily a brokerage firm, the company has evolved into a full-service commercial real estate company with specialties including advisory services; appraisal and consulting; brokerage services on regional, national, and international levels; market research; property and asset management; and real estate finance.

Meredith & Grew believes that change is the only constant. If a company is to thrive amid the competition and economic volatility that characterizes today's business environment, it must anticipate and capitalize on the opportunities brought by change, not simply react to them.

Armed with this business philosophy and an unwavering commitment to its founding principles, Meredith & Grew has successfully and skillfully endured the many economic challenges that have come to pass since 1875. The

company is proud of its reputation as a strong and trusted force in an unpredictable and perpetually changing industry.

Since its beginning, Meredith & Grew has remained committed to providing services of the highest standard to a wide range of business entities including corporations, partnerships, institutions, developers, trusts, and individuals. Throughout its history, the company has maintained many long-term client relationships and has skillfully guided its clients through the peaks and valleys of the real estate cycle, as well as through economic booms, recessions, and depressions. Regardless of the economic trend, Meredith & Grew's focus remains on the changing needs of its clients.

With many years of professional experience behind it, the firm continues to take on new, exciting challenges on behalf of clients, however far-reaching the requirements of the job. Through its affiliation with ONCOR International, Meredith & Grew is able to meet client needs beyond Boston—in 180 other market areas

Since its founding in 1875, Meredith & Grew has been an influential force in the growth and development of Boston.

throughout the United States, Canada, Europe, and the Far East.

As Boston approaches the 21st century and a new era, Meredith & Grew is proud to be involved in the continued development of the city and wishes to thank its clients for their enduring trust and confidence.

T. ELIZABETH'S MEDICAL CENTER OF BOSTON IS ONE OF the major tertiary care teaching and research centers in a city of world-class medical institutions. It was founded as a hospital for poor women in Boston's South End in 1868. Some 30 years later—in 1899—it was still in the South End that St. Elizabeth's began its long relationship with Tufts

University School of Medicine.

"St. E's," as the hospital is affectionately known, moved to the Brighton section of Boston in 1915 where it has continued to grow and expand services. Today, this 454-bed, full-service medical facility has earned a national reputation in several specialty areas: cardiology, neurology, oncology, and women's health. It also houses one of Boston's first neonatal intensive care nurseries.

Over the years, St. Elizabeth's has remained true to its founding mission—to provide highly personalized, state-of-the-art medical care. From patients having a routine checkup in one of St. E's outpatient centers to

critically ill newborns on life support in the neonatal intensive care unit, everyone can expect individualized treatment.

CARDIOLOGY CENTER

The Cardiology Center has long been a St. Elizabeth's specialty. Staffed by a team of experienced cardiologists and cardiothoracic surgeons, the Cardiology Center offers state-of-the-art diagnostic tests: echocardiography, stress tests, catheterization, heart monitors, and electrophysiology. The center also has the sophisticated tools for assessing blood flow to the heart. It offers patients the latest in drug therapy, noninvasive procedures such as angioplasty,

and open-heart surgery.

In addition, its Cardiovascular Research Center is a leader in the field of clinical research. Recently, the National Institutes of Health gave approval to a St. E's team of researchers to perform the first human gene clinical trials in cardiovascular gene therapy, which are believed to be the first worldwide. In addition, St. Elizabeth's has served as a

A 30-bed neonatal intensive care nursery provides round-the-clock, individualized care for critically ill and extremely premature newborns (below right).

Located in the Brighton section of Boston, St. Elizabeth's is today a 454-bed, full-service medical facility with a national reputation in several specialty areas (below).

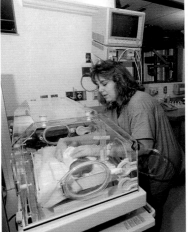

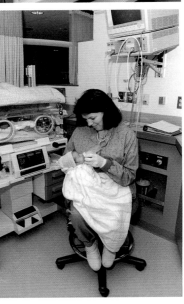

national center for investigational trials for atherectomy catheters to shave plaque from artery walls, endovascular stents to keep arteries open, laser angioplasty, antiarrhythmia drugs, pacemakers, and implantable defibrillators.

NEUROLOGY CENTER

The Neurology Center is another St. Elizabeth's specialty. It is a nationally recognized leader in the treatment of complex nerve diseases such as Guillain-Barré syndrome, myasthenia gravis, multiple sclerosis, tremor and movement disorders, Lou Gehrig's disease, Alzheimer's disease, strokes, and brain tumors.

The Neurology Center has one of the few neural intensive care units in New England to serve patients with neuromuscular respiratory failure and acute cerebrovascular disease. In addition, it has patient care units for neuro-oncology, behavioral neurology, autonomic disorders, dystonia, and Parkinson's disease.

In addition, the Neurology Center has been awarded a number of substantial National Institutes of Health grants to study respiratory control, autonomic function, Alzheimer's disease, peripheral neuropathy, muscle diseases, and others. All of these projects are clinically oriented, directly benefiting St. Elizabeth's patients.

CANCER CENTER

The Cancer Center at St. Elizabeth's is staffed by a broad-based group of oncologists and surgeons covering a variety of specialties. This integrated network of doctors offers comprehensive treatment for the full range of malignant tumors. These multidisciplinary medical teams evaluate and treat patients with breast, prostate, colorectal, and lung cancer. Since the Cancer Center participates in numerous clinical trials testing cutting-edge therapies, patients have the opportunity to receive

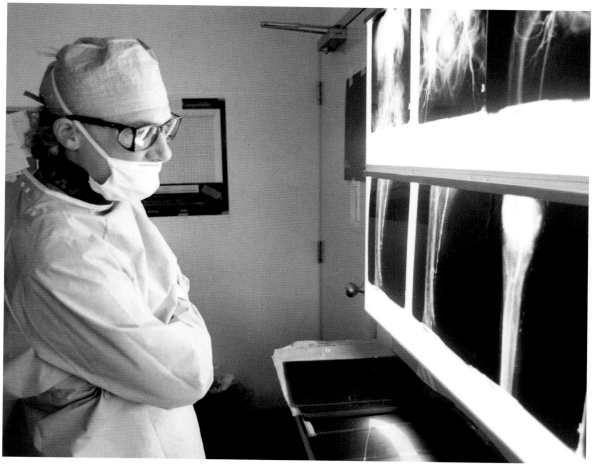

innovative treatments not available at other cancer centers.

The Cancer Center is part of the Hematology/Oncology Department. The hematology program offers transfusion services and treatment of blood disorders such as anemia and hemophilia, as well as blood diseases like leukemia.

WOMEN'S HEALTH CENTER

The Women's Health Center, located in the new, state-of-the-art St. Margaret's Center for Women and Infants, offers full-service obstetrical and gynecological care on both an inpatient and outpatient basis to women of all ages. The inpatient obstetrical program provides services for both normal and high-risk pregnancies. A 30-bed neonatal intensive care nursery, staffed by perinatologists, nurses, and respiration therapists, provides round-the-clock, indi-

vidualized care for critically ill and extremely premature newborns. In addition, St. Elizabeth's has an experienced gynecological team to provide treatment for extremely complicated medical and surgical problems.

The comprehensive outpatient program offers a variety of services for women of all ages, all within the St. Margaret's Center facility: obstetrics, gynecology, midwifery, maternal/fetal medicine, primary care, endocrinology, cardiology, psychiatry, and surgery. The Center for Breast Care and the MidLife Center both utilize a multidisciplinary approach to treatment.

Diagnostic services offered by the Women's Health Center include mammography, ultrasound, bone densitometry (to diagnose osteoporosis), cardiac stress, and lipid testing. A variety of counseling services are also available.

A first in cardiovascular research: St. E's cardiovascular team, headed up by Jeffrey Isner, M.D., chief of cardiovascular research, recently won approval from the National Institutes of Health to begin cardiovascular gene therapy on humans.

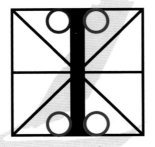

I N 1872, WHEN EBEN JORDAN AND FIVE OTHER LOCAL businessmen decided to launch *The Boston Globe*, the city was already home to 10 newspapers competing for readers and advertisers. Convinced Bostonians would respond to "a superior commercial and business journal of outspoken independence," the group pooled $150,000 and on March 4

produced the first *Globe*—all eight pages of it.

The public, however, wasn't excited by the new publication. Circulation remained low, and the Great Boston Fire on November 9, 1872, which gutted 65 acres of the city's downtown property, prompted most of the newspaper's original investors to abandon the project due to financial hardship. As the sole remaining backer, Jordan turned to General Charles H. Taylor. A former Civil War soldier, stringer for the *New York Tribune*, and secretary to the governor of Massa-

adding material for women and children, and introduced a baseball column to attract young people. Five years after taking over, Taylor had turned it into the most innovative paper in the city, with a circulation of 50,000.

Taylor, who transformed the *Globe* into a strong and respected voice, headed the *Globe* until his death in 1921. Since then, management has continued in the hands of the Taylor family. William O. Taylor stepped into his father's shoes in 1921 and guided the paper until 1955, when he was succeeded by his son, William Davis

and cellular communications. By the early 1990s, the company had returned to its newspaper roots, divesting itself of most of the other properties at significant profit to shareholders.

The biggest change in ownership came in 1993, when Affiliated merged with The New York Times Company in the largest newspaper merger and acquisition in U.S. history. The move was prompted by the impending dissolution of two century-old trusts that controlled 68 percent of Affiliated's voting power. The trusts, scheduled to

Since the 1870s, the Taylor family has provided strong leadership for **The Boston Globe.** *From left: General Charles Taylor, builder of the* Globe *and publisher from 1873 to 1921; William O. Taylor, son of Charles and publisher from 1921 to 1955; William Davis Taylor, son of William O. and publisher from 1955 to 1978; and William O. Taylor II, son of William Davis and chairman of the board and publisher from 1978 to the present.*

chusetts, Taylor signed on as temporary business manager in August of 1873. He never left.

Today, the publication is the region's dominant daily newspaper.

A HISTORY OF INTEGRITY
Under Taylor's stewardship, the *Globe* was one of the first newspapers in the country to embrace impartial coverage of political issues. Taylor also expanded the paper's "family" coverage by

Taylor. In 1978 General Taylor's great-grandson, William O. Taylor II, took over the office of publisher, which he occupies today.

In 1973 *The Boston Globe* became part of a publicly traded company as a subsidiary of the newly formed Affiliated Publications, a holding company owned primarily by members of the Taylor and Jordan families. In subsequent years, Affiliated expanded its reach with investments in television, radio, magazines,

cease in 1996, were held on behalf of about 140 descendants of Jordan and Taylor, many of whom were not part of the newspaper business. Publisher William O. Taylor was concerned that control of the newspaper would be lost, with potentially adverse effects on the newspaper's integrity.

The 1993 merger was seen as the best way to preserve the character and mission of the *Globe*. The agreement included provisions for the *Globe* to main-

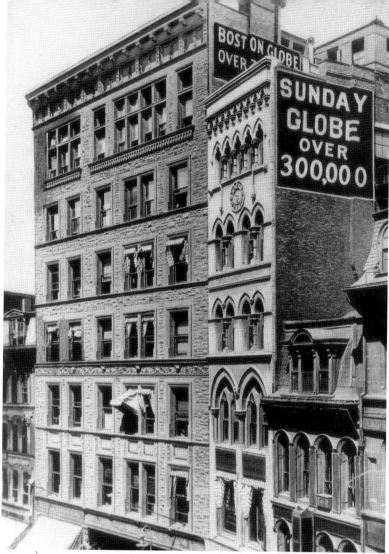

tain editorial control of the paper and remain a Massachusetts-based corporation, as well as to retain other business activities.

MEETING THE CHANGING NEEDS OF BOSTON-AREA READERS

Over the years, the *Globe* has been an innovative and sometimes controversial newspaper. The paper burst onto the national scene, for example, during the Vietnam War years, publishing the Pentagon Papers and becoming one of the first newspapers to call for an end to U.S. involvement in Southeast Asia. Its coverage of the desegregation of Boston Public Schools in the early '70s—which at one point led to shots being fired through the *Globe*'s windows—resulted in a Pulitzer Prize for public service in 1975.

The *Globe*'s innovative development continued over the years, even during difficult financial times. In 1987, during a recession, the paper inaugurated "New Hampshire Weekly," the first of six regional Sunday sections. These "zoned editions" cover local stories and serve specific geographic areas.

Also during the recession, a time that put a squeeze on advertising revenues throughout the newspaper industry, the *Globe* established music and movie sections, redesigned its magazine, beefed up the book pages, and added sections for younger readers.

The Boston Globe has a current daily circulation of more than 500,000 and a Sunday circulation of 814,000. The newspaper has collected 12 Pulitzer Prizes for journalistic excellence, including a 1980 award for investigative reporting on waste and mismanagement within the city's public transportation system and a 1984 series on black employees in the workplace, in addition to the one for coverage of school desegregation in 1975.

As the *Globe* has grown, it has also become a philanthropic force in the area. The Boston Globe Foundation, for example, funnels $2 million annually into local nonprofit agencies, funding projects as diverse as arts education, help for abused children, and literacy. In 1986 the foundation gave $1 million to the Boston Public Library for branch reading programs and the renovation of its main building. The *Globe* also grants numerous college scholarships to local students.

But the newspaper's best-known philanthropic effort is Globe Santa. Since 1956 this seasonal program has raised money to buy Christmas gifts for needy children. Globe Santa has received more than $1 million annually from readers in recent years, allowing it to reach 66,000 children every year.

Change is a regular event at the *Globe*, and the newspaper will continue to adapt to community and reader needs. As it has for more than a century, *The Boston Globe* will maintain its New England perspective, and will remain deeply involved in the community that shaped it.

The Globe's main headquarters today is in the Dorchester section of Boston (above right). The paper also has a printing plant in Billerica and a packaging and assembly plant for Sunday inserts in Westwood.

The original Globe building, pictured circa 1907, was located on Newspaper Row in downtown Boston (above left).

M

OUNT AUBURN HOSPITAL, LOCATED ON THE CHARLES River in Cambridge, is a medically advanced health center that is dedicated to providing the best possible health care. Founded in 1871 by Civil War nurse Emily Parsons, Mount Auburn today is a 300-bed Harvard Medical Center community teaching hospital.

PATIENT CARE AND SPECIAL SERVICES

The hospital provides a broad range of inpatient and outpatient services. Inpatient services include medicine, surgery, obstetrics-gynecology (ob-gyn), and psychiatry.

Unlike most other community hospitals, Mount Auburn is a referral center for the diagnosis and treatment of cardiovascular diseases. Mount Auburn provides cardiology patients and their families with comprehensive inpatient and outpatient services by a team of medical, nursing, and support staff. This continuum of care includes the Outpatient Diagnostics Center, which provides a broad range of testing and monitoring services. These include a pacemaker clinic, stress tests, EKGs, echocardiograms, and 24-hour EKG monitoring. The hospital provides sophisticated diagnostic procedures, including cardiac catheterization and coronary angioplasty. Open-heart surgery has been performed at the hospital since 1947, making it one of the first hospitals in the Boston area to provide this service. Mount Auburn recently increased its staff with the recruitment of four new cardiovascular surgeons.

To serve the needs of patients with heart disease, the hospital has a coronary intensive care unit for medical patients, an intensive care unit for surgical patients, a progressive coronary care unit for patients in the recuperative stages of heart attack, a telemetry floor for monitoring both cardiac medical and surgical patients, and an active cardiac rehabilitation program.

Other referral and tertiary services include computerized tomography (CT) scanning, hematology-oncology, nephrology, gastroenterology, neonatology, neurology, orthopedics, and vascular surgery.

For the past decade, the hospital has developed a comprehensive and high-quality ob-gyn service. A new birthing center, opened in May of 1990, includes six private birthing rooms, operating suites, a 20-bed postpartum unit with 16 private rooms and two double-occupancy rooms, a "well-baby" nursery, and a seven-bed special care (Level II) nursery. The Level II nursery is a regional referral service directed by two full-time neonatologists and staffed by hospital personnel with specialized training.

Routine ob-gyn care and menopausal management are offered by physicians located at practices in Arlington, Cambridge, Lexington, Somerville, and Watertown. Women may choose

Mount Auburn Hospital was founded in 1871 by Civil War nurse Emily Parsons (right).

Located on the Charles River in Cambridge, Mount Auburn is today a medically advanced health center dedicated to providing the best possible health care (below).

NICK NOVICK

either a physician or a certified nurse-midwife through the Mount Auburn Midwifery Associates (MAMA). Gynecological surgery procedures are performed by physicians at the hospital on both an inpatient and outpatient basis. Screening, education, and treatment of incontinence are provided by a urogynecologist.

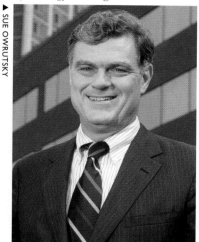

The hospital provides comprehensive cancer care, on an inpatient basis and through its outpatient Cancer Treatment Center. Experts at the center work together as a multidisciplinary team to provide medical care to patients and their families. Services include surgical intervention, chemotherapy, radiation therapy, and support groups, as well as educational sessions on pain management, nutrition, and medication.

Mount Auburn was one of the first hospitals in the area to recognize the growing need in the community for increased geriatric services. The geriatrics program includes primary care, a geriatric assessment service, a geriatric consultation service to maximize the functional abilities of older patients and minimize institutionalization, and the Care and Reassurance for the Elderly (CARE) program, which creates a postdischarge link between patients and the hospital. Mount Auburn also offers psychiatry services geared toward the needs

of older adults, provided by a psychiatrist who is board-certified in geropsychiatry and by psychologists and social workers with expertise in dealing with older patients and their families.

With the exception of second- and third-degree burn care, the hospital's emergency department provides comprehensive services. Coverage is provided by full-time, hospital-employed physicians and house staff specializing in emergency medicine.

Mount Auburn provides services to ambulatory patients through a variety of outpatient services, including those for women's health, alcohol and substance abuse, primary care, hematology-oncology, surgical

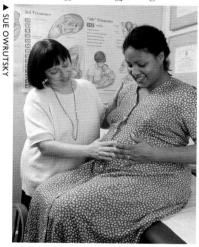

follow-up, orthopedics, psychiatry, travel medicine, occupational health, multiple sclerosis, sleep disorders, behavioral medicine, and problem gambling. The hospital also owns the Belmont-Watertown Visiting Nurse Association (BWVNA), a nonprofit, Medicare-certified home health care agency.

Mount Auburn provides a number of diagnostic and ancillary services, including magnetic resonance imaging (MRI), EEG, EMG, EKG, Holter monitoring, hyperalimentation, nutrition support services, nuclear medicine, full-body CT scanning, ultrasound, X-ray, physical therapy, occupational therapy, pathology, phar-

macy, speech pathology, blood bank, acute hemodialysis, cystoscopy, and endoscopy.

More than a Century of Care

The concept of a community hospital that offers complete care to its patients is what Emily Parsons had in mind when she first pursued the idea of a hospital for Cambridge more than a century ago. The Mount Auburn Hospital of today has matured into a complex, medically advanced health center that treats hundreds of thousands of people. But the spirit of its founding endures: to provide top-quality medical care with compassion and commitment.

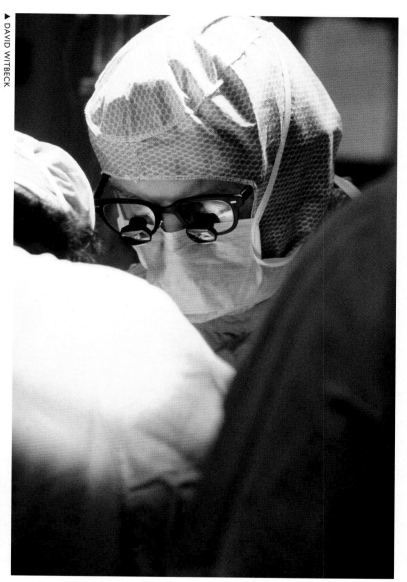

Mount Auburn Hospital President Francis P. Lynch (far left).

For the past decade, the hospital has developed a comprehensive and high-quality ob-gyn service (center).

Mount Auburn's expertise covers a range of surgical specialties, including open-heart, vascular, and gynecological surgery (above).

Sedgwick James of New England, Inc.

8

EDGWICK JAMES OF NEW ENGLAND, INC., AN INSURANCE brokerage and consulting firm, began with John Calvin Paige, a pioneer in insurance brokerage. "A competent broker is more than a friend," he once said. "The broker must provide low-cost, suitable insurance contracts through the medium of a well-balanced organization of specialists."

John C. Paige & Co., Sedgwick's local predecessor, moved to Boston in 1873 (near right).

John Calvin Paige (far right) believed that an insurance broker "must provide low-cost, suitable insurance contracts through the medium of a well-balanced organization of specialists."

Paige's insurance agency, John C. Paige & Co., got its start in 1866 in a country store in Claremont, New Hampshire. Six years after opening for business, Paige was working with the Franklin Fire Insurance Co. and was called upon to help adjust losses from the Great Boston Fire of 1872, which destroyed 10 percent of the city.

A rugged man with an exceptional personal character, Paige moved his business to Boston in 1873 and continued to practice in the city until his death

NATIONWIDE EXPANSION

John C. Paige & Co. opened offices in Portland, Maine, and New York City before merging in 1972 with Fred. S. James, Inc., a company founded in Chicago in 1858. By 1985 James had grown to more than 80 offices, with revenue exceeding $240 million.

In August of 1985 James merged with Sedgwick Group plc to form a global, full-service company with 13,000 employees in 230 offices in more than 60 countries. Less than a decade

university and school programs, and chemical companies. Besides basic programs such as workers' compensation, general liability, and property insurance, specialists within the office provide an expertise for focused products like directors' and officers', errors and omissions, aircraft products, nuclear power plant, and marine insurance as well as a full spectrum of commercial bonds.

The company's destiny is linked to the integration of its efforts with those of its clients.

in 1897. John C. Paige & Co. grew rapidly; by 1888 the firm employed 60 persons and had 120,000 insurance policies in force.

John C. Paige & Co. was known for its innovative, dynamic, entrepreneurial, and aggressive spirit. In 1900 the firm was the first broker to offer customers engineering and inspection services independent of any insurance company; thus risk consulting was born. The Paige Foundation, a subsidiary, became one of the first brokerage units to provide self-insured workers' compensation services in the United States.

later, the company, now known as Sedgwick, has achieved revenues exceeding $1.3 billion. Its 6,000 U.S. colleagues provide services to more than 400,000 clients. The Boston office, Sedgwick James of New England, is the regional headquarters for the company's business in the northeast.

21ST-CENTURY SERVICES

Boston is a principal and influential office for several Sedgwick initiatives: global markets, construction, international companies, financial institutions, utilities, health care facilities, retailers,

Sedgwick believes it is important to understand the needs of its clients and to develop programs to meet those needs. Intelligent design of a risk management strategy often depends upon intimate knowledge of the insured, the kind of knowledge only obtained through detailed study of facilities, operations, and procedures.

To ensure the uniform and high quality of its programs, Sedgwick created comprehensive client service standards that distinguish the company from other insurance brokers and risk management consultants. Sedgwick account executives establish objectives with clients based on measurable criteria. At least once a year the stewardship process requires the account executive to review progress on objectives and receive an appraisal from the client on how well the account team is performing against the agreed-upon standards.

EXPERIENCED CONSULTANTS
Sedgwick offers a broad range of consulting activities in subjects as diverse as insurance captives, structured settlements, ergonomics, environmental risk management, self-insurance, claims management, loss control engineering, and contingency planning. The Boston office has one of the best-staffed broker property conservation and safety engineering programs in the nation, providing service to clients in the region and as far away as Australia, Brazil, Iceland, Italy, Japan, and Nicaragua.

The acquisition of Noble Lowndes in 1993 allows Sedgwick to consolidate employee benefits planning for its global accounts as well as to enhance services for its domestic clients. The company offers full employee and executive plan consulting capacity, including plan design. Its benefits unit specializes in retirement plans, accident and health plans, ERISA compliance, strategic communications, executive compensation programs, and actuarial services.

RISK SERVICES
The Boston office of Sedgwick is a pioneer in the Massachusetts Quality Loss Management Program, a workers' compensation initiative designed to improve the loss exposure of insureds in the assigned risk pool.

The company performs statistical and forecasting services and assists clients with the selection of insurance and alternative risk financing programs. A publishing unit within the Boston office provides the latest risk management information to clients around the globe. Several large, local clients have formed partnerships with Sedgwick to eliminate workplace ergonomic injuries. The company's environmental focus has gained a reputation nationwide.

A CORPORATE CITIZEN
Sedgwick continues to achieve distinction as a full-service global insurance broker and risk management consultant in a client-driven environment. But the company is more than that. It supports local community programs and charities such as the American Red Cross, Walk for Hunger, United Way of Massachusetts, Museum of Fine Arts, Boston Pops and Boston Symphony, Joslin Diabetes Center, Juvenile Diabetes Foundation, Catholic Charities, Cardinal Cushing School and Training Center for Exceptional Children, the Boys and Girls Clubs of Boston, the Science Museum, and many other community service organizations. Sedgwick's employees give freely and generously of their time to local groups, participate in children support organizations, and serve with local government agencies and on the boards of nonprofit organizations. The company has hosted representatives from many countries and is a leader in bringing foreign business to Massachusetts.

What Sedgwick brings to the table is service from a highly qualified professional staff with the institutional resources of a major broker. Its personnel see

themselves as problem solvers. Sedgwick listens to its business partners and chooses resources to meet their needs. Today's operative motto might well be, "Take care of the clients and you will take care of the firm," a philosophy not too different from the one invoked a century ago by John C. Paige. Sedgwick chooses to invest in its clients and in the community in which it serves.

Sedgwick James of New England provides an important link in a worldwide network of 260 offices in more than 60 countries.

Stone & Webster Engineering Corporation

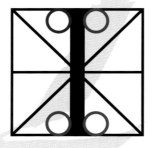

I N 1889, JUST 10 YEARS AFTER THOMAS EDISON PATENTED the incandescent lamp, two young graduates of the Massachusetts Institute of Technology (MIT) established a small electrical consulting firm in Boston's Post Office Square. At the time, some said electricity was just a fad. But Charles A. Stone and Edwin S. Webster, then both 22 years old, set out to prove the critics wrong.

Stone & Webster's first major project was the design and construction of a hydroelectric plant at the Saccarappa Dam in Maine, including a mile-long transmission line to the S.D. Warren paper mill in Cumberland Mills. The project, which proved that electricity could be transmitted for commercial purposes, established Stone & Webster as a leader in the field. By 1910 the firm had more than 100 employees and had designed and built 14 percent of the country's electrical generating capacity.

GROWING WITH AMERICAN INDUSTRY

From its roots in power production, Stone & Webster naturally moved into other areas. The company, for example, was responsible for one of Boston's most recognizable academic landmarks: MIT's domed entrance, with its distinctive columns and wide steps. Stone & Webster also built classrooms, laboratories, lecture halls, libraries, and offices for the university.

During World War I, the firm began building military bases and airfields. Over a single 10-week period, the company delivered camp facilities for 80,000 soldiers. Its famous project of that period was the expansive Hog Island Shipyard near Philadelphia. The yard held 25 acres of buildings, 80 miles of railroad tracks, and 50 boat slips. Stone & Webster also built an entire city to house the shipyard's 35,000 workers, including homes, roads, and other infrastructure.

When World War II got under way, the company was again deeply involved in the war effort. Stone & Webster designed or built all U.S. plants for the production of butyl rubber, as well as other facilities vital to the nation's defense.

After the war, the firm remained at the forefront of power technology. In 1954 Stone & Webster designed and built the nation's first nuclear power plant—charging just one dollar plus expenses in order to get a foothold in the industry. The firm went on to build 15 more nuclear power plants in the United States.

Stone & Webster was also involved in numerous projects outside the field of power produc-

From modest Boston beginnings, Stone & Webster has become a respected global engineering and construction company.

The cleanup of Boston Harbor is one of the massive, complicated projects to which the firm lends its construction management expertise (right).

tion. In 1946 Stone & Webster designed and built one of the country's largest printing plants for the publishers of the *Saturday Evening Post*. The firm's Canadian branch received widespread attention in 1968 for its major renovation and expansion of the Montreal Forum. Completed in time for the new hockey season, the entire project took just 118 days.

That kind of versatility has helped Stone & Webster grow into a global company with approximately 6,000 employees worldwide. Building on its long-time expertise, the firm today handles projects as diverse as updating power plants in Lithuania and designing an experimental driverless-car commuter system in Chicago.

DIVERSIFYING TO MEET TOMORROW'S ENGINEERING NEEDS

After more than a century, power production is still a major aspect of Stone & Webster's work. The firm designs, builds, upgrades, and maintains nuclear, coal-fired, oil-fired, hydroelectric, and geothermal power generating plants worldwide. The company also has a strong presence in the hydrocarbon process industries, particularly in petrochemicals, where it offers proprietary tech-

nologies for the production of ethylene, a basic building block in plastics manufacturing. In fact, the company's technology has been used in the design and construction of about 35 percent of the world's ethylene capacity. Stone & Webster also supplies proprietary technology to oil refiners.

Stone & Webster's diversification efforts have resulted in major environmental assignments, among them the cleanup of Boston Harbor. Environmental jobs, including consulting and remediation, now represent about one-third of its work load.

As Stone & Webster's projects have become more numerous and complex, the company has developed computer software to manage the mass of information involved. Its advanced database systems and expert systems are making industry more efficient. A company subsidiary, Advanced Systems Development Services, now markets the software and provides technical support for these systems.

Stone & Webster's progressive response to changes in the technical needs of the market has led to steady growth: In 1993 the company reported $279 million in revenues and had 30 offices in the United States and abroad. Also that year, Stone & Webster was listed in the *Engineering News-*

Record as the eighth-largest design firm and the ninth-largest contractor in the nation.

Building on its tradition of service, innovation, and quality in Boston and beyond, the company prides itself on being able to tackle virtually any challenge. That means retrofitting old, out-of-date power plants in places like the former Soviet Union. And building new petrochemical units along the Pacific Rim, where a large part of the company's business has been centered in recent years. With its longtime ability to handle complex, large-scale projects, Stone & Webster is strategically positioned to help upgrade the world's infrastructure.

Clockwise from top left:
Stone & Webster—in addition to engineering and building power plants—upgrades units to comply with clean air requirements and to increase efficiency.

Environmental projects represent the company's fastest-growing business sector.

The firm supplied construction engineering and other services to help expand Miami's state-of-the-art transportation system.

Stone & Webster provided technology, engineering, procurement, construction management, and start-up services for this Korean ethylene plant.

BOSTON CELTICS GREAT LARRY BIRD, RED SOX SLUGGER Ted Williams, and world heavyweight boxing champion Gene Tunney did not have much in common during their professional careers. But they—and thousands of other athletes, known and unknown—have all turned to New England Baptist Hospital for treatment of sports injuries.

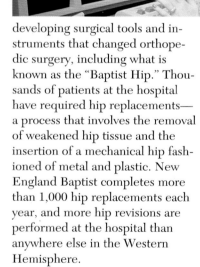

Since 1987 the Boston Celtics have looked to New England Baptist and team physician Dr. Arnold Scheller for superior care (above left).

New England Baptist uses the most sophisticated medical technology to help diagnose and treat patients (above right).

The facility, which is the official hospital for the Celtics basketball team and the 1994 World Cup in Boston, is renowned for its treatment of complex musculoskeletal disorders in both professional and recreational athletes. People come to New England Baptist from all over the world to receive care from the hospital's team of sports medicine professionals, which includes physicians, orthopedic nurses, and physical therapists, many of whom are athletes themselves.

But the hospital's expertise in sports medicine is only part of the story.

WORLD-RENOWNED SURGICAL EXPERTISE

The physicians at New England Baptist are highly skilled and widely known for their expertise in a variety of fields, including orthopedics. The orthopedic unit, where most of the sports medicine patients are seen, was founded in 1968 by Dr. Otto Aufranc. Revered by doctors who trained with him, Aufranc also was an innovator,

developing surgical tools and instruments that changed orthopedic surgery, including what is known as the "Baptist Hip." Thousands of patients at the hospital have required hip replacements—a process that involves the removal of weakened hip tissue and the insertion of a mechanical hip fashioned of metal and plastic. New England Baptist completes more than 1,000 hip replacements each year, and more hip revisions are performed at the hospital than anywhere else in the Western Hemisphere.

Another common procedure in the orthopedic unit is arthroscopic knee surgery, which relies on a tiny camera inserted into the knee. This type of minimally invasive technique is often preferable to conventional exploratory surgery because it allows surgeons to fully examine the surgical site through a small incision.

A COMMITMENT TO COMPASSION

Personalized care for all patients—from famous athletes to ordinary

citizens—has always been emphasized at New England Baptist. Patients are not numbers in the computer, but people who may be frightened or in pain when they come to the hospital. They are enveloped with a comforting atmosphere complete with homey furnishings and a nursing staff known for their dedication to providing customized, personal care. To that end, the hospital uses a primary care nursing system that assigns a single nurse to coordinate each patient's care. The system is so highly regarded that nurses at New England Baptist train nurses from other area hospitals.

"Our nurses' commitment to the patient is unquestionable, and their level of training and competency is unparalleled," says hospital President and CEO Raymond C. McAfoose.

Cardiac nurses, for example, are specially trained to care for patients with severe angina, allowing them to move out of the intensive care unit and onto a more comfortable nursing floor.

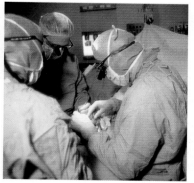

New England Baptist Hospital has grown from a single room in 1893 to a highly skilled facility providing technologically superior health care services. The hospital has an international reputation for excellence in orthopedic surgery and other procedures.

Nurses are trained to monitor heart rhythms, identify heart diseases, and treat patients connected to intravenous drip systems delivering nutrition and medications like nitroglycerin. They are also trained to perform cardioversions and defibrillations under the supervision of a cardiologist.

Superior nursing care is one of the many reasons New England Baptist was honored in 1993 by the Joint Commission on Accreditation of Healthcare Organizations with a three-year accreditation with commendation. Of the more than 3,000 hospitals the commission surveys, only about 11 percent receive such praise. "Awards like that don't come without having a compassionate, committed, talented staff," McAfoose says.

BRINGING IN THE FUTURE

Far from resting on their laurels, the doctors and researchers at New England Baptist are constantly working to develop new medical technology and procedures to help patients.

The hospital is one of five U.S. trial sites for ROBODOC, a computerized robotic drilling system that drills incredibly precise holes in bone for hip replacements. Computerized drilling allows for a better fit between implants and the bone that holds them in place.

Another example of innovation at New England Baptist is

the hospital's development of a specialized three-dimensional imaging device. This instrument converts two-dimensional magnetic resonance images or computed bone and tissue tomography scans into easily comprehensible 3-D images (holograms) of the

body's interior, providing a much more complete picture to surgeons and physicians.

Leading-edge technology is also at work in the hospital's diagnostic cardiology department, where New England Baptist cardiologists use a color Doppler imager, nuclear testing, and a state-of-the-art cardiac catheterization laboratory to diagnose and treat patients with heart disease.

In addition to technological innovation, the hospital is developing affiliations and implementing other structural improvements that deliver better care to patients. Cardiac diagnoses, for

instance, take place at New England Baptist, but heart patients who require surgery are treated at Deaconess Hospital. Deaconess, which is known for its cardiac expertise, has just joined with New England Baptist and other hospitals to form a regional health care network. The arrangement allows cardiac patients from New England Baptist to receive seamless care of the highest quality by traveling with their doctors to Deaconess.

When New England Baptist was founded in 1893, it was housed in a single room. And while it has remained committed to continuing the personalized care it delivered over a century ago, the hospital has also undergone major changes, maturing into a highly skilled provider of technologically superior health care services. This unique combination has made New England Baptist a medical institution known around the world.

The hospital's nurses take a warm, caring, and understanding approach to patient care (left).

A nursing dispensary at New England Baptist in the late 1800s.

243

New England College of Optometry

FROM ITS FOUNDING 100 YEARS AGO BY DR. AUGUST A. Klein, the New England College of Optometry has led the way in developing professional education for the eye doctors who serve patients around the world. Indeed, many credit Klein with a major role in establishing the profession itself. As the region's only college of optometry, and one of only 17

Dr. Larry R. Clausen, president, leads the first and oldest college of optometry in the United States (right).

The college's main academic building and library (below) are located in Boston's historic Back Bay neighborhood.

in the country, the New England College of Optometry has established an outstanding record of service to both the nation and the Greater Boston community.

Dr. Larry R. Clausen, president of the college, notes that even from the early days, the school provided many services to the general and disadvantaged Boston public. Today that commit-

ment is stronger than ever. For example, the New England Eye Institute, the school's clinical facility, provides a broad range of diagnostic, rehabilitation, and dispensing services to all members of the community. The New England College of Optometry also operates the nation's only eye clinic for homeless veterans, provides support to Boston's neighborhood

◀ J. D. SLOAN

◀ JAY BEEBE

health centers, and brings eye care directly to homebound individuals, low-income seniors, and handicapped city residents.

SUPERIOR TRAINING FOR KEY HEALTH CARE PROVIDERS

From an annual pool of some 600 applicants, the New England College of Optometry admits approximately 100 entering students—with an even ratio of males to females—and has a yearly total enrollment of about 400. Some 40 percent of the student body comes from New England, with an equal portion coming from other parts of the United States. The remaining students hail from Canada and several other countries. Its international enrollment is the highest among the nation's schools and colleges of optometry.

Optometry is a relatively new field; it gained formal recognition in the United States in the early 1900s and continues to observe rigorous standards. The New England College of Optometry is no exception. The school provides a four-year, postbaccalaureate program of studies leading to the Doctor of Optometry (O.D.) degree, signifying success in the school's challenging and broad-based curriculum of vision and biosciences, clinical sciences, and practical hands-on patient care. Studies in vision science provide knowledge in optics and the function of the human visual system, while studies in bioscience offer a grounding in the structure and functioning of the eye and the human body. Additional optometric instruction provides instrumentation skills and patient management capabilities, while clinical experience unifies and reinforces the curriculum as a whole.

Although helping students become outstanding clinicians is a key goal of the school's programs, Clausen says an increasing emphasis is being placed on research and on pursuing new developments in the biosciences. "The movement toward HMOs and managed care has already provided a boost to the profession," he says. "Also, most states now permit optometrists to prescribe medications for eye diseases, and we expect that all states will permit this within a few years."

To ensure that the New England College of Optometry stays in the forefront of new de-

velopments, plans are also being developed to expand research activities in the biosciences and vision sciences and, in particular, to establish a myopia research center, embracing a wide range of research disciplines.

VISION FOR THE FUTURE

While educating 70 percent of the optometrists in the New England states is a major accomplishment in itself, the New England College of Optometry hasn't rested on its laurels. Thanks to the clinical facilities and services the college has provided for community health organizations, large numbers of area residents have already received a much-needed medical service. Many of those individuals

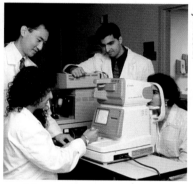

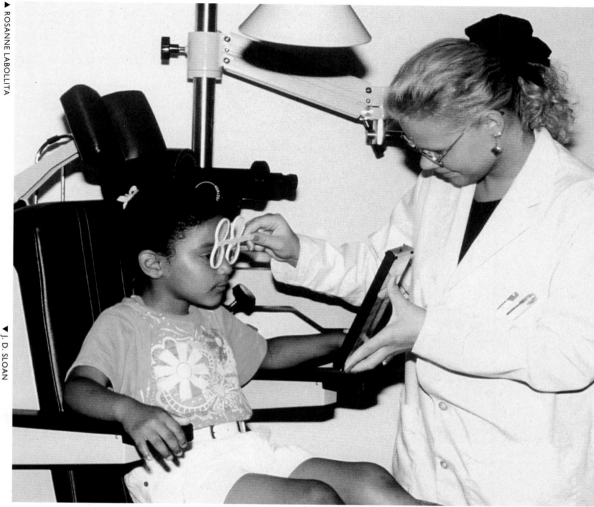

would not otherwise have had access to those services. Thousands more have also been helped through the college's external affiliations with organizations as diverse as the Perkins School for the Blind in the Boston suburb of Watertown, the Dimock Community Health Center in Roxbury, and the Veterans' Administration Medical Center in Providence, Rhode Island.

"Our local outreach programs not only provide a valuable service to the community, they also provide an opportunity for students and faculty to do research, deliver eye care, and promote a system of comprehensive eye care," says Clausen.

Reaching out internationally is a logical extension of that tradition. The New England College of Optometry is a pioneer

in international education, establishing the most diverse international program of any college of optometry. Not only do its programs attract a large number of foreign students, but the college also offers educational programs in Spain, Italy, Israel, and South Africa. According to Clausen, the school recently signed an affiliation agreement with the National Center of Optometry in Wenzhou, China.

Since assuming presidency of the institution in 1990, Clausen has overseen two-thirds of a planned $6.5 million renovation of the college's five-building, turn-of-the-century campus. During Clausen's tenure, the endowment fund also has been expanded dramatically.

Now, to ensure that the New England College of Optom-

etry will meet the challenges of its second century, the faculty, staff, alumni, and friends of the institution have defined long-range priorities and have taken steps to implement them. Specifically, the trustees of the college have commenced a multiyear campaign, called "2000 in Sight." This campaign will provide capital for facility renovations, student and faculty endowment, and program development in bioscience research, clinical programs, and international education.

"As we strengthen our programs and facilities, we will come to rely even more on our relationships with other institutions and with the communities of Greater Boston," says Clausen.

For decades, numerous college outreach programs have provided vital services to the community (above).

Students take part in clinical training at the New England Eye Institute (left), the college's primary clinical facility.

Perini Corporation

 NE HUNDRED YEARS AGO, BONFIGLIO PERINI FOUNDED a small, family-run civil works construction company called Perini & Sons. Befitting his talents as a stonemason, Bonfiglio laid the foundation of an organization that has evolved into one of the foremost construction and real estate development companies in the United States.

In 1920 Perini completed a bituminous concrete paving job in Greene, Rhode Island.

Chairman and president since 1972, David B. Perini represents the third generation of family leadership at Perini Corporation (top).

Throughout its first century, Perini has pioneered new techniques, systems, and equipment to improve the efficiency of the construction process. This spirit of innovation has enabled the company to build some of the world's most challenging projects, including a number of well-known landmarks in Boston.

BEGINNING A SECOND CENTURY

As Perini begins its second century, the company remains committed to improving and expanding its core businesses: Building Construction, and Civil and Environmental Construction.

The Building Group consists of Perini Building Company—which includes three divisions and several branch offices operating in the eastern, central, and western regions of the country—and Perini International Corporation. Perini Building Company focuses on niche building markets, including correctional facilities, hotel/casinos, and sports complexes, as well as its traditional markets of health care, education, and civic and cultural projects. Perini International Corporation has extensive experience working for U.S. government agency-sponsored projects such as the construction of embassies and consular posts in Africa, the Middle East, South America, and, most recently, the independent states of the former Soviet Union.

Perini's Civil and Environmental Construction Group is a leader in infrastructure construction. It has built some of the largest and most sophisticated heavy construction projects in North America, including major highway and bridge contracts, mass transportation projects, dams, and tunnels. As part of the Civil and Environmental Construction Group, Perland Environmental Technologies, Inc. performs environmental remediation work across the country.

HUMBLE ROOTS

Perini's position as a leader in the construction field is a long way from the company's humble roots. Back in 1894, Perini & Sons subcontracted with larger firms to build water supply projects in the Northeast, clearing land for reservoirs and building elaborate stone wall structures.

Bonfiglio Perini sought partnerships with other contractors whose talents complemented his own. He looked beyond the horses and tipcarts that were the earthmoving method of the day to steam-driven, mechanized equipment that would revolutionize the construction industry. At the time of Perini's death in 1924, daily operations were taken over by his sons Joseph, Louis, and Charles, and his daughter Ida, who renamed the company B. Perini & Sons. Lou, then only 21 years old, became president.

Under Lou's direction, the company broke new ground in construction and set new records in the industry. Throughout his life, Lou sought opportunities for the company that others might find too strenuous or difficult. His "go anywhere, do anything" spirit and capability enabled the company to diversify its operations beyond domestic heavy construction to include building, marine, pipelining, coal mining, international construction, and real estate development operations.

After Lou's death in 1972, leadership of the company was passed on to the third generation of the Perini family. As president, Lou's son David B. Perini has continued to seek projects well suited to the company's capabilities and to assume leadership roles on issues that influence the construction industry as a whole. During his tenure as president, the company has participated in many projects of historical importance, such as the Trans-Alaska Pipeline and the Negev Airbase, part of the Camp David Peace Accords between Israel and Egypt.

CONTRIBUTING TO THE BOSTON LIFESTYLE

Alone or in joint venture, Perini has been responsible for the construction of many projects that influence the quality of life in and around Boston.

Much of Logan International Airport, Boston's gateway to the world, has been built by Perini. The Callahan Tunnel beneath Boston Harbor and the Massachusetts Turnpike Extension that links Boston with its western suburbs were both milestone projects for Perini. Urban mixed-use developments such as Copley Place

Harvard Square, Davis Square, and Alewife—as well as twin-bore tunnel sections along the MBTA's Red Line Extension project, expanding service from Harvard Square in Cambridge to Somerville.

Other notable Perini projects in Boston include the renovation of the Massachusetts State House and waterfront landmarks

PARTNERS IN PROGRESS

Today, Perini is helping Boston prepare for the year 2000 and beyond. The construction of the Residual Treatment Facility at Deer Island, the Intermodal Surface Transportation Center at

Clockwise from top left: Notable Perini projects in Boston include the renovation of the Massachusetts State House.

Urban mixed-use developments such as Copley Place and the Prudential Center—built originally in 1962 and redeveloped in 1993 by Perini— have revitalized Boston's historic Back Bay.

Perini is helping Boston prepare for the year 2000 and beyond through construction projects such as the Residual Treatment Facility at Deer Island.

The company's diverse portfolio includes the rehabilitation of this historic section of Boylston Street.

and the Prudential Center—built originally in 1962 and redeveloped in 1993 by Perini—have revitalized Boston's historic Back Bay.

In the 1980s the company was responsible for the construction of three subway stations—

such as the Federal Reserve Bank Building and the piers and parking facility at Rowes Wharf. Public spaces built by the company such as City Hall Plaza and waterfront parks contribute greatly to the city's lifestyle.

South Station, and the Central Artery's I-93/I-95 interchange in Charlestown will enable the city to enter the 21st century pursuing new opportunities to improve the lifestyles of Boston residents, commuters, and visitors.

ARTHUR D. HILL WAS A REMARKABLE MAN. A LAWYER with a fiercely independent mind and a devotion to public life, Hill started a law firm in 1895 that still bears his stamp. Hill & Barlow, which today has approximately 100 lawyers, includes specialists in corporate law, construction law, taxation, commercial law and bankruptcy, labor and employment law, real estate, environmental law, litigation, trusts and estates, and family law. But it is Hill's legacy of expertly delivered and socially conscious legal services that continues to define Hill & Barlow.

A TRADITION OF INTEGRITY

Hill's most famous case was his representation of Nicola Sacco and Bartolomeo Vanzetti, Italian-born political activists accused of murder, in their final and unsuccessful attempt to escape the death penalty. By the time Hill joined the defense, the case had become a political hot potato, and his involvement put him at odds with Boston's established business community.

"Defending them was an act of great courage because the establishment in Boston was of a single mind that Sacco and Vanzetti should be drawn and quartered," says Gael Mahony, a lawyer in the firm.

Hill's explanation for why he accepted the case reveals a commitment to independent thinking and a devotion to the law that remain defining characteristics of the firm today. At the time, Hill said: "If the president of the biggest bank in Boston came to me and said his wife had been convicted of murder, but he wanted me to see if there was any possible relief in the Supreme Court of the United States and offered me a fee of $50,000 to make such an effort, of course I would take the retainer, as would, I suppose, anybody else at the bar. I do not see how I can decline a similar effort on behalf of Sacco and Vanzetti simply because they are poor devils against whom the feeling of the community is so strong, and they have no money with which to hire me."

"That case sort of put a stamp on the firm," Mahony says. "After that, Hill & Barlow gained a reputation for getting involved in issues of importance."

Even after Hill's death in 1947, the firm continued its tradition of participation in high-profile, controversial cases. Lawyer Calvin Bartlett successfully represented two Harvard professors in federal court against contempt citations issued by Senator Joseph McCarthy's infamous Senate committee. More recently, Mahony was appointed Special Assistant Attorney General in the early 1960s—during which time he successfully prosecuted indictments for corruption in connection with the building of the Boston Common underground garage.

Today, Hill & Barlow stands securely among New England's leading law firms. Recent cases include a $130 million victory in the litigation over development rights to Boston's Fan Pier; continued successful representation of major New England law firms in malpractice cases; and continued advice to the developers of International

Trial attorney Gael Mahony (near right) represents major corporate clients from across the United States. Real estate specialist Charles C. Ames (far right) represents a leading national real estate investment adviser.

PHOTOS BY JOHN EARLE

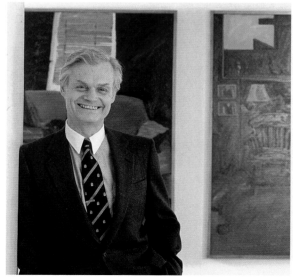

Place, New England's largest office development.

Hill & Barlow also continues its commitment to helping the community, dedicating more of its time to pro bono work than any other major firm in Boston. For example, a panel of lawyers from the firm provides representation in Dorchester's district court for juveniles, many of whom have been charged with serious criminal offenses. A similar Hill & Barlow program exists in the Middlesex County court system.

In another case that attracted national attention, the firm represented students attending public schools in 18 disadvantaged Massachusetts communities. The action challenged the constitutionality of financing public education through local property tax revenues. The Supreme Judicial Court agreed with the plaintiffs, ruling that the existing system of school financing denied equal educational opportunity.

ATTORNEYS OF SUPERIOR SKILL

Even more than the firm values service to the community, Hill & Barlow prides itself on the way it serves its clients. The firm has made a deliberate decision to stay relatively small, with only 100 lawyers compared to more than three times as many at some other Boston firms, says lawyer Penny Cobey. The smaller scale keeps Hill & Barlow clients in closer contact with senior attorneys.

"We think it is very important that there be a close connection between the chief lawyer and the client," Cobey explains. "The person whom you meet initially is the person you'll work with and the person you can call. He's not just the one who gets you in the door and sends you the bill."

Hill & Barlow's lawyers are among the best in the state, selected from the top ranks of the best schools. Between five and 10 associate lawyers are hired each year out of 5,000 applicants. The

result is a group of professionals with "a real dedication to the highest standards of legal practice," Cobey says.

Many Hill & Barlow attorneys have gone on to other high-profile careers. Three of the past six Massachusetts governors—William Weld, Michael Dukakis, and Endicott Peabody—previously were partners in the firm. Hill & Barlow attorney Reginald Lindsay was appointed to a federal district court judgeship in early 1994, and Deval Patrick became the U.S. Assistant Attorney General for Civil Rights in March of that year.

The firm that Arthur Hill started 100 years ago has retained more than his name. He emphasized commitment to clients, attention to detail, a willingness to challenge established wisdom, and service to the community. Hill & Barlow, even today, remains true to that vision of service and integrity.

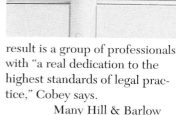

The firm is headquartered in Boston's One International Place.
PHOTOS BY JOHN EARLE

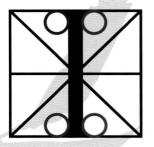

Deaconess Hospital

I N 1896, WHEN FOUNDING DEACONESS MARY E. LUNN first envisioned what is now Boston's Deaconess Hospital, she wrote of a place where "science and kindliness unite in combating disease." From its roots in a converted brownstone on Massachusetts Avenue, the Deaconess has grown into a world-renowned health care facility with a reputation

The professional and compassionate nursing staff has helped the Deaconess earn a reputation for high-quality, patient-centered care (top right).

The Deaconess is a leader among research institutions in the country and is the 14th-largest recipient of funding from the National Institutes of Health. The hospital's highly regarded program quickly brings advances from the research bench to the patient's bedside (bottom right).

PHOTOS BY LARRY MAGLOTT

for providing advanced treatment and exceptional quality care to the most seriously ill patients.

The original hospital—which primarily cared for surgical patients—expanded and enhanced the range of services available in the ensuing decades. By the early 1900s, the hospital had moved to its current location in the Longwood Medical Area, home of many of the world's preeminent academic medical centers. Here, the Deaconess flourished and broadened its mission to embrace both medical research and education, becoming a major teaching hospital of Harvard Medical School in the early 1980s.

The Deaconess is distinguished among its colleague institutions by its focus on many of today's most serious and complex illnesses. The hospital is internationally recognized as a leader in the research and treatment of diabetes, cardiovascular disease, cancer and infectious diseases, gastrointestinal problems, and behavioral or psychiatric disorders, as well as for organ transplantation.

Since its establishment, the Deaconess has been home to some of the most talented physician-scientists in the nation. Clinical highlights abound, including the first use of insulin in New England for the treatment of diabetic patients. The Deaconess Cancer Research Institute was established in 1951 to study causes and potential treatments for cancer. The first of its kind in New England, the institute remains a leader in the study of chemopreventive agents and their role in the prevention of prostate, colon, and

breast cancers. Hepatobiliary surgeons at Deaconess Hospital performed New England's first successful liver transplant in 1983. What was then considered an ex-

perimental procedure has become a widely accepted therapeutic modality and a specialty of the hospital, offering patients with liver disease an opportunity for longer, healthier lives.

Although complex illnesses have served as a focal point for new clinical developments at the hospital, programs such as the

Mind/Body Medical Institute and the Institute for Prevention of Cardiovascular Disease have promoted innovative disease prevention modalities in the region and

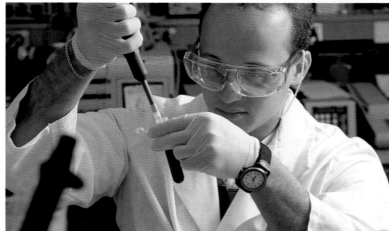

throughout the nation. The institutes examine the roles that lifestyle factors—including stress, poor nutrition, and lack of proper exercise—play in the development of hypertension, heart disease, and other life-threatening conditions, as well as studying the physical and emotional triggers of heart attacks.

The new $135 million Clinical Center (left), which will house state-of-the-art operating suites, radiological imaging equipment, and medical/surgical units, will serve as the technological hub for the Deaconess and affiliated health care institutions.

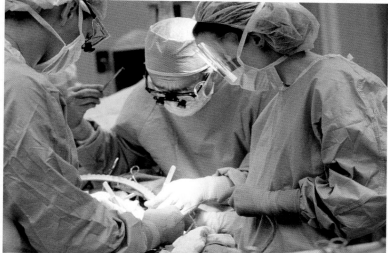

The Deaconess has a full-time staff of more than 330 physicians and 600 nurses, and provides training for approximately 200 residents and fellows each year. The hospital also has highly regarded research programs in a multitude of disciplines, which receive more than $25 million annually in funding from both government and private sources. Furthermore, the hospital has a long tradition of collaboration and maintains relationships with a number of prestigious institutions, including Dana-Farber Cancer Institute, Joslin Diabetes Center, and Har-vard's Joint Center for Radiation Therapy, as well as with community hospitals throughout the region.

As the Deaconess approaches its centennial year, the hospital continues to develop new opportunities for working with colleagues to redefine the delivery of health care services. By merging the teaching hospital agenda with that of community physicians, health centers, and hospitals, the Deaconess is building a network that recognizes the distinction between primary, secondary, and tertiary care, and provides the most appropriate care in the most appropriate setting.

This emerging network of health care providers will build a foundation of local health care services in the community that is linked to academic teaching hospitals—ensuring patient access to a comprehensive range of services from preventive care to multidisciplinary case management and treatment. As a member of this larger health care network, Deaconess Hospital's mission to provide high-quality, specialized medical services will be fostered well into its second century.

As Harvard Medical School faculty, Deaconess doctors combine highly specialized clinical practice with research and teaching responsibilities—helping to train the next generation of physicians (above).
PHOTOS BY LARRY MAGLOTT

251

GENERAL FRANCIS PEABODY AND EDMUND ARNOLD FOUNDed the law firm of Peabody & Arnold in 1899. The firm's first offices were at 10 State Street in Boston in a building that has made way for a modern office tower. In the almost 100 years since then, the firm, too, has grown and prospered. It is now the largest tenant at the prestigious Rowes Wharf

complex and occupies three floors of the landmark structure, which overlooks Boston's inner harbor and airport. Evolving from the two-man firm launched almost a century ago, Peabody & Arnold now has 100 lawyers who maintain a full-service practice, ranging

regulation, financial services, and commercial lending. The commercial lending group, as one example, frequently represents lenders and other creditors in today's highly competitive credit environment, which is marked by detailed risk analysis, changing debtor protec-

The personal law group advises clients in the areas of personal tax planning, probate, and trust administration, and assists companies in the implementation of pension and employee benefit plans. Lawyers in the department provide planning advice to clients

LEN RUBENSTEIN

RICHARD MANDELKORN

Peabody & Arnold Managing Partner Joseph D.S. Hinkley (near right).

from zoning disputes to intellectual property matters.

THE EXPERTISE TO MEET DIVERSE LEGAL NEEDS

The firm's attorneys are grouped into three general practice departments: business, litigation, and personal law. Each group is further divided into smaller practice areas where attorneys and staff with specialized expertise address clients' specific legal needs.

The firm's business department includes practice groups focusing on corporate and securities matters, international transactions, real estate, mortgage-backed securities, project finance, public finance, mergers and acquisitions, corporate trust and securities custodianship, bank

tion laws, and threats of lender liability. Peabody & Arnold's extensive experience in all areas of secured and unsecured commercial lending enables it to effectively structure and close especially complex transactions, including those with unusual collateral or time constraints.

Lawyers from Peabody & Arnold's business department also serve as general counsel to publicly and privately held corporations engaged in an array of businesses, including manufacturing, retailing, franchising, research and development, and service-related fields. The firm provides all manner of corporate legal services to these companies, ranging from securities offerings and mergers to advice on distribution and compensation matters.

on the disposition of their property after death and on the disposition of their assets and income during their lifetime. The personal law group at Peabody & Arnold seeks to understand each client's specific circumstances and family needs, and to preserve, allocate, or liquidate assets to minimize taxes. The firm strives to make estate plans simple and flexible enough to meet the client's needs for as long as possible.

The litigation group at Peabody & Arnold assists companies in general commercial litigation, loan workouts, and FDIC-related conservatorship and receivership issues. The firm has a comprehensive insurance defense practice and has earned a national reputation in major

hazardous waste and environmental litigation as well as other specialty areas such as intellectual property and admiralty. The firm's construction, surety, and fidelity law insurance practice is also nationally recognized for its cost-effectiveness.

Lawyers in the litigation department strive to avoid court action whenever prudent. They aim to minimize disputes, in many cases advising clients to accept a reasonable settlement or utilize alternative dispute resolution methods if appropriate. But when full-scale litigation is unavoidable, Peabody & Arnold's attorneys use thorough case analysis and careful strategy to fight aggressively and effectively for their clients. The firm has an outstanding record in both federal and state courts, part-

ly based on its widely recognized expertise in litigation involving fidelity and financial institution bonds, construction bonds, and environmental coverage insurance.

PUTTING TECHNOLOGY TO WORK

Peabody & Arnold efficiently runs its wide-ranging practice by using the latest technology to store and process information. The firm's custom-designed computer system uses imaging technology to file and categorize documents, providing attorneys and staff with quick, efficient access to all available expertise. The system also has sophisticated client accounting and word processing capabilities and the ability to link all company personnel with electronic messaging and calendar services. The

firm subscribes to numerous on-line databases, which lawyers can access from their desks.

Peabody & Arnold has a pragmatic business approach to legal problems and attempts to provide clients with real-world solutions. The firm is always conscious of its clients' requirements for cost containment and predictability, and meets these needs by using appropriate staffing and technology. Peabody & Arnold's professional relationships endure because the firm provides top-quality legal counsel without forgetting the specific needs of each client.

Peabody & Arnold is today the largest tenant at the prestigious Rowes Wharf complex, which overlooks Boston's inner harbor and airport.
PHOTO BY STEVE ROSENTHAL

Whittier Partners Group, L.P.

SUCCESS IN THE COMMERCIAL REAL ESTATE SERVICE BUSIness can only be assured by focusing on the needs of clients. At Whittier Partners Group, L.P., understanding client needs has literally shaped the company in a way that gives the Whittier team the incentive to be more responsive than any other commercial real estate firm in the region.

NEW ENGLAND'S LARGEST FULL-SERVICE COMMERCIAL REAL ESTATE SERVICES COMPANY

In May of 1994 Whittier Partners joined forces with The Farley Company of Hartford, Connecticut, forming the largest commercial real estate services company in New England. The union provides comprehensive market coverage of the Hartford and New Haven markets as well as the Boston, suburban Massachusetts, southern New Hampshire, and Rhode Island markets. The merger was a direct response to client requests that the firms provide services across a broader northeast territory. The combined entity, controlled through Whittier Partners Group, L.P., consists of two partnerships: Whittier Partners in Massachusetts and Farley Whittier Partners in Connecticut.

Since its inception on January 1, 1900, Whittier Partners has engaged exclusively in commercial and industrial real estate activities, servicing both local real estate owners and national institutions. Whittier Partners is the Boston affiliate of both International Commercial Realty Services (ICRS) and Valuation International, Ltd. Farley Whittier Partners is the Hartford office of ONCOR International, a professional organization servicing real estate needs worldwide. The firm is the largest commercial real estate brokerage operation in Hartford.

The combined firms maintain a staff of over 200 professionals who are committed to

Bill Farley (left) and Michael Sherman lead the two divisions of Whittier Partners Group.

excellence. Together, they manage a portfolio of approximately 11 million square feet of commercial and retail property.

DIVERSE SERVICES, IN-DEPTH KNOWLEDGE

As a full-service firm, Whittier Partners Group applies its entrepreneurial energy to a broad range of commercial real estate services. The company has expertise in the brokerage of commercial and industrial real estate, investment sales, management, construction, fee development, appraisal, consulting, and marketing of commercial properties.

The Brokerage Division is comprised of 40 brokers with expertise in office, industrial, retail, high-technology, and investment real estate. From the Boston and Hartford offices, the division can provide responsive service to virtually any type of landlord or tenant in New England. The firm's brokerage expertise is nationally recognized, and eight of Whittier's partners are members of the prestigious Society of Industrial and Office Realtors (SIOR)—more members than any other firm in New England.

Whittier's Asset Management Division provides property owners with a complete spectrum of asset and property management services from accounting, financial, insurance, and tax services to contract, engineering, construction management, and leasing services. The Whittier team of dedicated professionals uses sophisticated financial and operational programs, processes, and controls and—to meet the growing

needs of its clients—has developed its own proprietary real estate software and database systems that provide landlords with a full range of financial reports, cash flow projections, and analyses. The Asset Management Division also manages "distressed" real estate that has been repossessed by financial institutions and creates for its owners plans to resurrect the property's earning capabilities as quickly as possible, whether by sale or lease.

The Appraisal and Consulting Division is one of the oldest, largest, and most capable in New England, having provided valuations for a major portion of the existing commercial real estate in Boston. Because judgments as to value enhancement and creation are an integral part of real estate analysis, the division's 12 appraisers are skilled in market assessment, real estate economics, and understanding the competition. Further, Norman Kenny, a past chairman of Whittier Partners, was a founder of the prestigious American Institute of Real Estate Appraisers. Whittier takes pride in its continuing support of this organization's ideals and in the fact that it has more Member Appraisal Institute (MAI) members than any other firm in New England.

The Advisory Division assists individual, corporate, and institutional clients in a wide range of property acquisition, ownership, and disposition issues. Services provided include investment and market analysis, property pricing strategies, due diligence for acquisitions, portfolio analysis, development planning and management, marketing planning, valuation and disposition assistance, and expert witness testimony. In one instance, Whittier provided expert testimony on the value of the 3.2 million-square-foot Boston Fan Pier project to help determine damages in a suit brought by the land lessor.

Keeping clients informed of change is important in the real estate industry. Whittier's Research Department tracks more than 25,000 business tenants in metropolitan Boston and compiles information on their real estate needs. This group follows price and vacancy fluctuations of approximately 300 million square feet of office, retail, research and development, and industrial space throughout New England. To ensure that Whittier maintains the advantage of being the best informed in the industry, the Research and Marketing Department prepares daily, confidential, in-house reports on user activity and produces quarterly market reports for both the Massachusetts and Connecticut markets.

A COMMITMENT TO EXCELLENT SERVICE

Whittier Partners Group is a people-based company. Although the firm utilizes and invests in the most sophisticated database systems and advanced methods of analysis, it believes that people create value in real estate and that experienced people do it well. Whittier's success is a direct result of its ability to attract talented professionals in a competitive market and to inspire them to work on a collaborative basis.

Through the sharing of expertise and resources among offices, Whittier offers clients throughout the region a consistent, high level of service that creates value for their real estate investments.

▶ GARY GOODMAN

Clockwise from bottom left: The firm's corporate headquarters in Boston is located at 155 Federal Street.

Farley Whittier Partners is headquartered at 100 Pearl Street in Hartford, Connecticut.

Since its inception on January 1, 1900, Whittier Partners has engaged exclusively in commercial and industrial real estate activities in Boston's central business district and throughout New England.

OSRAM SYLVANIA

EPARATELY, WE WERE RECOGNIZED FOR INNOVATION AND quality. Together, we are setting a new standard. OSRAM and SYLVANIA—a perfect fit." These are the words that were used in business and trade advertising in early 1993 to describe the "new" company, OSRAM SYLVANIA INC., formed when Munich-based OSRAM GmbH acquired

Danvers, Massachusetts-head-quartered SYLVANIA, the second-largest lighting manufacturer in North America. The merger truly was a perfect fit.

"When the two companies came together, we found we had like approaches to serving the needs of our customers in the lighting marketplace. Our ideals and our business strategy of focusing on innovation, new products, energy savings, and the environment were common values. With all these similarities, the coming together of the two companies made sense, and the mechanics of the merger were accomplished quickly and efficiently," says Dean T. Langford, president of OSRAM SYLVANIA INC.

With annual sales of $1.5 billion and more than half the Fortune 500 companies as customers, OSRAM SYLVANIA's overall mission is to combine research and development, technical support, and innovative applications to create unbeatable lighting solutions for end users and customers. "Customer satisfaction is important in the lighting business where we come up against strong competition in all the markets we serve," says Langford.

THE ANATOMY OF A COMPANY

OSRAM SYLVANIA brings technology to light with products that illuminate the world, anywhere light is needed. All told, it adds up to over 6,000 different lighting products, most of them carrying the SYLVANIA brand name. The company also is a technology leader in such precision-engineered materials as phosphor, precious and toughened metals, high-tech electronic connectors, and hair-thin wire made of tungsten and other materials.

The core of OSRAM SYLVANIA consists of 12,500 employees, 25 manufacturing plants, and a network of sales offices and distribution centers across North America. "When you look at us in more depth, you find some fea-tures of our organization that set us apart. For example, in our Precision Materials & Components organization, we make from scratch most of the materials and components that go into the various lightbulbs manufactured by us," Langford notes. "We have an uncommon self-reliance."

The capability of OSRAM SYLVANIA employees to design and build the machinery needed to manufacture lightbulbs is another unique feature of the organization, along with an inter-dependent network of research and development facilities that are deployed across the organization. One central research center for fundamental lighting technology, located just north of Boston, inter-acts with eight research and development laboratories at selected manufacturing locations.

THE HARD-DRIVING FORCE OF R & D

Armed with the most sophisticated tools and a clear understanding of the needs of the many markets it serves, OSRAM SYLVANIA has achieved a number of "firsts" as well as some remarkable accomplishments.

In the automotive light-ing arena, the company is the industry's leading independent manufacturer of headlamps, with all of the major domestic and transplant automakers as its customers. The Hillsboro, New Hampshire-based Automotive & Miniature Lighting unit of OSRAM SYLVANIA has achieved this impressive position through total quality, product innovations, and marketing excellence.

OSRAM SYLVANIA employees observe one of the many operations at the company's fluorescent manufacturing facility where energy-efficient lamps are made.

JOHN SOARES

In the general lighting category, the list of firsts is lengthy and impressive. In recent years, most of the new products the company has brought to the marketplace have had energy-saving features, including products for the home and for industrial, commercial, municipal, and specialty applications. The company's line of compact fluorescent lamps and halogen lightbulbs is the broadest in the industry. And OSRAM SYLVANIA has won three Academy Awards for scientific or technical achievement.

A Necessity Taken for Granted

Most of the time, lighting is taken for granted, but it extends into every part of everyone's daily routine. The average home, for example, uses about 35 lightbulbs for general illumination. Then there are the other lights in the home: inside the refrigerator, stove, and microwave; miniature lights to illuminate radio dials, clocks, even toy trains and bicycles; and don't forget flashlights.

Outside the home, lighting is used to expand the living area to the yard or pool, to provide a safe and secure environment, to light streets and parks, to control traffic, and to light signs and building facades.

And specialty lighting is used by hospitals, in the doctor's or dentist's office, or by X-ray technicians. The list goes on.

Pushing the State of Technology

Ideas are taking shape as OSRAM SYLVANIA engineers and scientists work on the next generation of lighting. Whether it's a lighting product to help in the treatment of cancer or new applications for existing technology, the creative process is the lifeblood of the company.

Neon lighting for use as brake lights and turn signals, high-intensity discharge headlamps, and subminiature fluorescent lamps for interior lighting are all examples of technologies that are being perfected for the automotive industry. More efficient, longer-life products for the home and industry are being studied in the laboratory.

It is innovation like this that could evolve into the lighting technologies of tomorrow—brought to the world by OSRAM SYLVANIA.

Clockwise from top left:
The front and back sections of a Ford Mustang have been modified to display OSRAM SYLVANIA's latest automotive lighting technology, including high-intensity discharge headlamps and advanced neon lighting for brake and tail lights.

OSRAM SYLVANIA INC., the North American subsidiary of OSRAM GmbH of Germany, is headquartered just north of Boston in Danvers. The company manufactures and markets a wide range of lighting products, and precision materials and components.

Eight powerful xenon lamps from OSRAM SYLVANIA generate 56 million units of candlepower to light up Boston's landmark Prudential Center during the filming of a commercial.

WITH A BRAND NAME THAT IS KNOWN THE WORLD OVER, The Gillette Company is truly a great American success story. The story begins with the invention of one man: King Camp Gillette, a turn-of-the-century Bostonian who pioneered razors with disposable blades. According to King Gillette, "No one previous . . . had conceived the idea of

King Camp Gillette, a turn-of-the-century Bostonian who pioneered razors with disposable blades, founded the company in 1901.

The Gillette Company has long been a fixture in American culture (right).

producing . . . a blade that would be so cheap to manufacture that its cost to the consumer would permit its being discarded when dull."

Gillette's insight, combined with a flair for business, ensured almost immediate success for the Gillette Safety Razor when it was introduced in 1903. Within a few years, the popularity of the invention had led to the development of overseas sales and manufacturing operations to supplement production in Boston and to serve a growing world market. Soon, millions of blades were being sold each year. By 1926, the company's 25th anniversary, there were twice as many Gillette razors in America as there were telephones, and the company's output of sharpened steel could have encircled the globe at the equator.

The Boston company and its world-renowned name were well on their way to becoming fixtures in American culture.

MORE THAN JUST A SHAVE

Beginning in the 1930s, Gillette branched out and applied its technological and manufacturing expertise to a growing range of related products. The company entered the toiletries business in 1936 when it began manufacturing its own brand of shaving cream. In 1948 Gillette acquired The Toni Company—a manufacturer of home permanents. In the 1950s the company introduced White Rain shampoo and Adorn hair spray, and in the 1960s added Right Guard deodorants and antiperspirants to the product mix.

After more than 50 years of innovation and growth, there was no stopping Gillette, and the trend toward diversification continued with a string of successful acquisitions. In 1955 the company purchased California-based Paper Mate Company, a manufacturer of ball-point pens; in 1967 Gillette acquired a controlling interest in Braun AG, a German maker of electric shavers and other small appliances; and in 1973 Gillette acquired Jafra Cosmetics, a California skin care company.

Throughout its history, however, blades and razors have remained the foundation of the company's worldwide success. During the 1970s, Gillette introduced the Trac II twin blade shaving system (1971) and the Atra pivoting head twin blade system (1977). Both achieved immediate market success. Then in 1990, in another pioneering advance in shaving technology, Gillette introduced the Sensor razor—a product that rapidly gained worldwide popularity. The progress of the Sensor franchise has been accelerated by the equally outstanding success of the Sensor for Women and SensorExcel shaving systems.

STRENGTH AND VALUE

Today, The Gillette Company has manufacturing operations at 62 facilities in 28 countries, while its products are distributed through wholesalers, retailers, or agents in more than 200 countries and ter-

equipment, and marketing. Nearly 1,000 scientific and engineering team members continually strive to expand their knowledge of the technologies in which the company's products are based. One measure of the success of these efforts is an increasing rate of new product introductions. During the second half of 1993, for example,

For Boston, Gillette has always been a great asset, employing thousands of people and making the city the world's shaving headquarters. In addition to its extensive support of charitable causes nationally and worldwide, Gillette has made a special effort to contribute to respected local institutions such as the Boston

▼ DICK NORTON

ritories. Some of Gillette's most popular products include the Sensor, Sensor for Women, and SensorExcel shaving systems; Right Guard, Dry Idea, and Soft & Dri deodorants; Jafra skin care and cosmetic products; White Rain hair care products; Gillette Series men's toiletries; Paper Mate, Parker, and Waterman writing instruments; Braun Flex Control electric shavers, Braun Oral-B plaque removers, and Braun FlavorSelect coffeemakers; and Oral-B Advantage toothbrushes.

After rebuffing a hostile takeover bid by Revlon Corp. in the mid-1980s, Gillette has continued to be well regarded by investors, with the value of its stock increasing year after year. In 10-year total return to investors from 1983 to 1993, Gillette topped all companies with market value in excess of $10 billion. That's because Gillette keeps its eye trained on the future and constantly reinvests in research and development, facilities and

▶ STEVE DAHLGREN

the company achieved a record of 17 new product introductions, including the Gillette SensorExcel shaving system, Right Guard Pure Power clear gel deodorants and antiperspirants, and the Oral-B Advantage toothbrush. Strong consumer demand for both new and established company products boosted total Gillette sales to a record level of more than $5.4 billion in 1993.

Symphony Orchestra. That kind of community-oriented attitude, honed for nearly a century, has ensured Gillette an honored place among the region's thriving businesses. Still guided by the precepts of its founder, The Gillette Company will continue to offer innovative products that represent a good value for the consumer—in Boston, across the United States, and around the world.

Clockwise from top left: Through research, the company strives to expand its knowledge of the technologies in which its products are based.

Gillette designs and builds its own equipment to manufacture blades and razors.

Technology developed by Gillette over the years is used at the company's joint venture in India to make razor blades for this vast, growing market.

The Stop & Shop Companies, Inc.

THE STOP & SHOP COMPANIES, INC. ENTERED THE SUPER-store age in 1982 with the opening of its first Super Stop & Shop in Pembroke, Massachusetts, 25 miles south of Boston. The company now operates nearly 100 superstores, but its roots go back 80 years to a small corner grocery store and a man named Sidney Rabb.

President and Chief Executive Officer Robert G. Tobin (left) and Chairman Lewis G. Schaaneman, Jr., credit dedicated and visionary employees for the company's success.

Stop & Shop was founded in 1914 as Economy Grocery Stores Company. In 1918 Rabb, a man known as the father of the modern supermarket, joined the business and quickly set about improving operations. The company undertook an aggressive growth strategy and, in 1925, Rabb began his 60-year tenure as chairman.

In those days, food stores were typically small, specialty markets, offering customers just one type of food—bread from a bakery, meat from a butcher shop, and dry goods from the grocery.

Rabb had a vision of a large, self-service market that would offer customers convenience and lower prices, while generating larger profits for the company. In 1935 the company opened its first Stop & Shop "supermarket" on the outskirts of Boston. It was such a success that the company began phasing out its smaller grocery stores and focusing its resources on supermarkets.

In 1946, the company officially changed its name to Stop & Shop, Inc., and in 1947 it was operating 86 supermarkets, and

annual sales had risen to more than $42.5 million. Headquartered today in Quincy, Massachusetts, the company continues to be the leading supermarket chain in New England, with sales of more than $3.5 billion in 1993. The company now operates 95 superstores and 32 conventional stores in Massa-chusetts, Connecticut, Rhode Island, and New York, with plans to open 18 more superstores by the end of 1995. And now the company is making history again with its new focus on the innovative Super Stop & Shop stores.

EVOLUTION AND INNOVATION

As Stop & Shop has changed, so have its customers. The company's product mix is now as diverse as the families who walk through its doors. Customers need make only one stop to fulfill their shopping needs. Superstores offer over 52,000 products—including a wide selection of perishable, grocery, and general merchandise items—and Stop & Shop's many full-service departments save busy shoppers valuable time. In addition, all stores are customized to their locations, offering communities large selections of locally favorite items.

The Stop & Shop Pharmacy is the drugstore of the 1990s. The Stop & Shop Florist, the largest in New England, provides access to worldwide delivery services. The Stop & Shop Video Center offers up to 10,000 titles, including rentals of state-of-the-art CD-ROMs. And Stop & Shop continues to test new departments, such as in-store branch banking, to make the shopping experience even more complete.

To support the one-stop shopping environment, Stop & Shop has invested in technology for the 1990s and into the 21st century. The company's point-of-sale scanners provide quick and accurate checkout. Timesaving conveniences, such as Express Deli, allow the customer to order products by computer. Stop & Shop continually is searching for new technology to make the shopping experience more efficient for its customers and more productive for its stores.

COMMUNITY INVOLVEMENT

Since its founding, Stop & Shop has been an active member of the community. The company works closely with major food banks in its trade areas, providing product donations, assisting with transportation and warehousing, and initiating food drives and fund-raisers. In 1993, Stop & Shop donated over $10 million in products, cash, and services to feed needy families in the Northeast.

With the help of its suppliers and customers, Stop & Shop raises $1 million annually for the Jimmy Fund of the Dana-Farber Cancer Institute. Now totaling $4 million, these donations help give families hope that a cure for cancer eventually will be found. At the local level, individual Stop & Shop stores "adopt" charities within their communities and conduct a wide range of fund-raising activities. Stop & Shop also is active in its hometown of Quincy with events benefiting local charities.

The families and communities of Boston's metropolitan area will continue to change and so will their shopping needs. Stop & Shop is dedicated to serving customers with superstores that offer quality, value, variety, and convenience. The company has remained the Boston area's leading food retailer for 80 years because it listens to its customers—and responding to their needs is Stop & Shop's number one priority.

GARY GLADSTONE

M.J. MALONEY

RICK FRIEDMAN

Clockwise from far left:
The Super Stop & Shop pharmacy is one of 24 shops under one roof.

Employees kick off the Food for Friends fund-raisers at corporate headquarters in Quincy.

Super Stop & Shop offers its customers the value, quality, and convenience of one-stop shopping. The South Bay Superstore is Boston's first in-town superstore.

BOSTON

PROFILES IN EXCELLENCE

▼ RICHARD PASLEY

eScenza Diamonds has been located since 1915 in a gray stone structure much like any other in the Downtown Crossing shopping district. The building is today marked by a large marquise stating "The Diamond & Jewelers Building at 387 Washington Street" and by a handsome bronze mural in the lobby depicting the history of a diamond, commis-

sioned by DeScenza Diamonds. But take one of the elevators to the sixth floor, and the doors will open to something remarkable—15,000 square feet of floor space overflowing with a treasure trove of riches.

AN 80-YEAR TRADITION OF QUALITY AND VALUE

DeScenza Diamonds' success lies in its commitment to offering high-quality jewelry and other luxury items at a savings of 25 to 40 percent. Buying diamonds and gems direct and crafting much of its jewelry in the store, the company is able to keep its prices remarkably low without sacrificing quality. "We cut out the middleman," explains Diane DeScenza-Herth, marketing director and granddaughter of the founder. The company also keeps prices down by selling from its unassuming sixth-floor location, rather than maintaining a more expensive street-floor location.

It was a concept that Alfred F. DeScenza originated in 1915. Born in 1891 to Italian immigrants in Boston's North End, Al DeScenza left school after the sixth grade to help supplement the family income. He later worked as a page at First National Bank of Boston. During that time, DeScenza ran errands for bank executives, often in the jewelry district; he then began supplying small jewelry items to bankers, using a safe deposit box at the bank to hold his inventory. Eventually, his side career became successful enough to attract the

attention of his employer. Forced to choose between banking and jewelry, DeScenza chose the latter and began renting a portion of the company's current space on Washington Street.

Then, as now, the location was one of three "jewelers buildings" in downtown Boston that made up the center of New England's jewelry trade. There, hundreds of small wholesalers supplied jewelers throughout New England with goods and services.

"We've been knocking down walls ever since," says Hugh MacIsaac, Sr., vice president and son-in-law of the founder.

The company's growth has continued at a rapid pace. Fred DeScenza, president and son of the founder, recalls that by the mid-1960s, the crowds were such that, to maintain order, customers

were issued numbered tickets when they entered.

DeScenza Diamonds has since expanded its retail floor space and is today the largest store in the Washington Street buildings. The company sells more merchandise than most retail jewelry stores in the United States and has satellite stores in Framingham and Worcester.

In addition to jewelry, DeScenza Diamonds sells fine watches, including Omega, Tag

Heuer, and Patek Philippe lines; elegant writing pens from companies like Montblanc; crystal by Orrefors and Waterford; silver and stainless steel flatware; and china from companies like Royal Doulton, Wedgwood, and Bernardaud. DeScenza Diamonds also owns two gift shops in the historical Faneuil Hall building: Faneuil

Clockwise from top left: Alfred F. DeScenza established the company, Alfred F. DeScenza & Sons, in Boston in 1915.

"Beautiful Blues," DeScenza's sapphire and diamond jewelry.

The Rosenthal star candleholder and cobalt blue Faberge "Galaxy" bowl are beautiful gift choices at DeScenza Diamonds.

Quadrillion-cut,™ invisibly set diamond and colored gemstone rings are uniquely designed and available only at select jewelers.

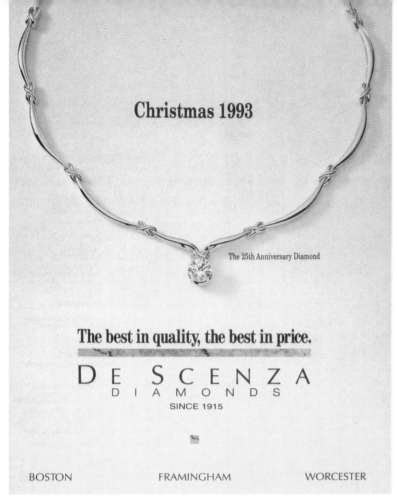

Christmas 1993

The 25th Anniversary Diamond

The best in quality, the best in price.

DE SCENZA
D I A M O N D S
SINCE 1915

BOSTON   FRAMINGHAM   WORCESTER

DeScenza's stunning 25th anniversary diamond solitaire necklace is shown on the cover of the 1993 Christmas catalog (above left).

DeScenza Diamonds offers contemporary and classic styles for the unique taste of each customer (above right).

Hall Heritage Shop, which sells colonial reproductions of such collector's items as scrimshaw, pewter, and hand-hammered copper weather vanes crafted in New England, and Job Tyler's General Store, which offers fun gifts from Boston.

A DIAMOND BUYER'S BEST FRIEND

Diamonds are the heart of DeScenza Diamonds. Couples come from throughout New England to select engagement rings. More than a few, according to DeScenza-Herth, are a little jittery, but the company's gemologists take the time to calm nerves and explain the details of diamond buying. Customers spend an average of an hour and a half in private viewing rooms learning how a diamond's quality is judged.

To ensure that all stones are accurately graded, DeScenza diamonds are reviewed by the company's gemologists, three of whom must agree on the grade of each diamond. The diamond's unique characteristics are "fingerprinted" when sold, and are filed so that the diamond can be easily

identified. Customers who want a second opinion on the quality of a stone may have it appraised immediately after purchase, since all purchases carry a 10-day, money-back guarantee. "We want our customers to be completely happy," says DeScenza.

Customer loyalty in some instances has continued through generations. "Many customers had a trust in my father, which he developed by giving very personal care," DeScenza says. "We've tried to carry that same feeling over." News of the company still travels by word of mouth. "When customers leave here satisfied," MacIsaac adds, "they go out and work for us."

INSURANCE REPLACEMENTS AND CORPORATE GIFTS

In addition to its retail business, DeScenza Diamonds has a thriving insurance replacement business, as well as a corporate gift division that produces customized gifts like rings, watches, paperweights, and trays.

Although known for its reasonable prices and value, the

company also has a reputation for its gift wrapping services. A typical gift comes secured in bubble wrap and multiple layers of tissue with the DeScenza Diamonds seal; each item is then boxed and wrapped. "It's the finest wrapping you will ever see. People are excited as they unwrap a gift purchased from DeScenza Diamonds," says DeScenza-Herth.

The company's tradition of quality and service is thriving today, and founder Alfred DeScenza would certainly be pleased to see his family's continued involvement in the business. Among its 120 employees are the founder's three children, 10 of their children, and one fourth-generation family member.

DeScenza-Herth sums it up succinctly: "We have the best in quality and the best in price." Judging by the crowds that keep DeScenza Diamonds busy, the precious treasures and rare values to be found at the store are no longer Boston's best-kept secret. This is truly a landmark not to be missed!

Ernst & Young LLP

RNST & YOUNG, ONE OF THE LARGEST PROFESSIONAL services firms in the world, has been a leading member of the Boston business community for nearly 80 years. Today's Ernst & Young was created by the historic merger of two giants in the industry, Arthur Young and Ernst & Whinney. The Boston office of Ernst & Young provides leading-edge

professional services in audit, tax, performance improvement, information technology, change management, and business planning for hundreds of clients, including individuals, corporations, and organizations in virtually every product and service category.

Area Managing Partner Jim DiStasio (above) oversees Ernst & Young's New England-area practice.

Ernst & Young's offices are located on Copley Square in the John Hancock Tower, the tallest building in Boston (right).

LEADING-EDGE SERVICE AND SOLUTIONS

Ernst & Young takes a business adviser approach toward meeting clients' needs. This approach is based on an integrated services framework that enables audit, tax, and consulting professionals to work together with clients to enhance financial and operational performance. "The satisfaction, yet challenge, of effective service results from the ongoing development of new ideas that create value for our clients. At Ernst & Young, we work together in an integrated team to develop such ideas," says Managing Partner Jim DiStasio.

The New England practice, headquartered in the John Hancock Tower in the heart of historic Back Bay, comprises more than 700 professionals with varied functional backgrounds and technical specializations. These professionals deliver highly tailored services to specific industry and functional groups, including health care, insurance, financial services, real estate, consumer products, software and electronics, life sciences, aerospace and defense, industrial products, emerging businesses, and not-for-profit, among others.

This industry specialization allows the firm to serve client needs more effectively by concentrating talent and focusing the experience, knowledge, and skills of its professionals on their areas of expertise. Consequently, the in-depth solutions that Ernst & Young provides are based on a thorough understanding of the variables affecting a client's particular industry or business segment.

ORGANIZED TO MEET CLIENT NEEDS

Organized to meet client needs, the Boston office has earned a leadership position in numerous industries. The local office reflects the status of Ernst & Young's international organization, whose manufacturing specialists have made it the leading audit, tax, and consulting firm for the Fortune 500's largest industrial companies.

Boston enjoys an international reputation for having some of the best teaching hospitals and medical facilities in the world. Ernst & Young works closely with many of these organizations, helping them respond with innovation to today's environment of sweeping health care reform. In the insurance and financial services industries, Ernst & Young has built a strong reputation, with a Boston client base that includes some of the most internationally recognized names.

Tax laws throughout the world are becoming more complex and constraining and revenue authorities even more demanding. Members of the New England business community look to Ernst & Young for assistance in implementing aggressive, forward-looking strategies to maximize their local, state, national, and international tax positions. Resident in Boston are more than 150 of the firm's most experienced and knowledgeable tax professionals.

A Focus on Business Innovation

Ernst & Young's Boston-based Management Consulting Group focuses on issues critical to a company's competitiveness and ability to create value. The firm is a leader in both knowledge and practice in the disciplines of information technology and performance improvement. The Boston information technology team provides solutions in all phases of systems—planning, analysis, design, construction, and implementation. Performance improvement consultants focus on reducing client operating costs and cycle time while improving quality and customer satisfaction.

Unique to Boston is the

firm's Center for Business Innovation, a think tank for Ernst & Young professionals worldwide. Located in a brownstone at One Walnut Street on Beacon Hill, the center brings together leaders from the firm, world-class organizations, and major universities in New England and throughout the nation to produce a greater understanding of management issues and solutions.

The center's expertise and resources allow it to combine in-depth understanding of particular approaches and technologies with a management perspective on how they contribute to business. As a result, the center is able to translate the leading edge into practical solutions that provide a competitive advantage. Research activity and output of the center include books and major articles, research reports and working papers, focused executive discussions, workshops and conferences, and constant communications with Ernst & Young client service teams and academics.

Also based in Boston are consultants who specialize in health care, employee benefits and compensation, mergers and acquisitions, international services, restructuring and reorganization, litigation services, real estate valuation, business valuation, and actuarial services.

With nearly a century of experience to shape and refine its

performance, Ernst & Young offers superior service, knowledge, and commitment to a wide variety of clients in the region. One of the largest and most-established professional services firms in the world, this organization has the vision, flexibility, and resources to provide New England businesses with the innovative solutions demanded by an increasingly competitive global marketplace.

Reaching Out to the Local Community

Ernst & Young reaches out in many ways to the Boston community, a community often in need of volunteers who can provide caring support. Some of the groups that Ernst & Young professionals join forces with include United Way, March of Dimes, Big Brother/Big Sister Association of Boston, Boston Museum of Science, Boston Public Library, Make-A-Wish Foundation, Museum of Fine Arts, Center House, Friends of the Elderly, Boston Symphony, New England Shelter for Homeless Veterans, Boston Housing Partnership, Inroads Minority Internship Program, Boston Ballet, and AIDS Action Committee, to name a few. From simply lending a helping hand to assisting in planning, implementing, and tracking the results of community projects, Ernst & Young is making a world of difference in the lives of many New Englanders.

The Center for Business Innovation, located on Beacon Hill, is a key resource for Ernst & Young professionals and clients worldwide.

The firm's library uses the most current resources in print, on-line, and CD-ROM to assist clients and staff with leading-edge, strategic, and technical information.

Ernst & Young professionals utilize state-of-the-art information systems audit software to leverage the audit efficiency, coverage, and quality provided by automated audit techniques (top).

BZ-TV IS NOW ON THE AIR!" PROCLAIMED NEWS ANCHOR Arch MacDonald on June 9, 1948. So began the tradition, innovation, and commitment to excellence of WBZ-TV4. In that first year, WBZ-TV brought new scenes to the eyes of New Englanders that until then had been found only in print: a Boston Braves-Chicago Cubs game broadcast from

Chicago, the Republican and Democratic national conventions, and the world championship boxing match between Joe Louis and Jersey Joe Walcott.

But before WBZ gave the region sight, it gave New England sound. WBZ Radio 1030AM originated in East Springfield in 1921, one of the first licensed radio stations in the United States. The station brought listeners news, concerts, lectures, sports, and a

Pictured here in front of the State House, WBZ Newsradio's mobile studio can be spotted all over New England covering news (near right).

WBZ Newsradio's Gary LaPierre and Gil Santos help deliver the most popular morning radio program in New England (far right).

PHOTOS BY ERIC ROTH

number of other "firsts": the first radio transmission of a hockey game, the first Boston Symphony Orchestra concert on radio, and the first live, on-the-scene radio transmission.

CHANGING THE WAY NEW ENGLAND SEES THE WORLD

New Englanders have come to depend on WBZ Television and Radio—especially for the stations' commitment to comprehensive news coverage and involvement in community issues.

WBZ Radio, which is heard in 38 states and in parts of Canada, became an all-news station in 1992. It is the number one radio station in New England, providing news all day, talk at night, and sports all weekend. WBZ-TV, the first station in the country to have an investigative news unit, continues to actively uncover stories of local and national importance. Using the combined resources of both sta-

tions, WBZ has a distinct advantage in providing New England with the best coverage of breaking news and the most comprehensive weather coverage.

WBZ delivers information with a remarkable team of reporters and anchors, many of whom have been with the station for decades. The main anchors on WBZ-TV—Liz Walker, Jack Williams, Bob Lobel, and Bruce Schwoegler—have been together since the early 1980s, bringing continuity, experience, and regional familiarity to WBZ News 4.

Liz Walker, anchor of WBZ News 4 at 6:00 p.m. and 11:00 p.m. with Jack Williams, joined WBZ-TV in 1980. One of New England's most admired and respected anchors, Walker is actively involved in many community projects, especially WBZ's "Stop the Violence" public service campaign. She also spends her time speaking to young people around the region about the importance of education and

setting goals.

Jack Williams, also a New England favorite, has been with WBZ-TV since 1975. Throughout his career, he has been honored by numerous organizations for his reporting skills and his unmatched commitment to the community for his efforts on behalf of his weekly news series, "Wednesday's Child," which he created in 1981.

Bob Lobel, WBZ-TV's sports director, joined the TV 4 news team in 1979. His popular "Sports Spotlight" series and his talk show "Sports Final" make him

The WBZ News 4 team includes (from left) Bob Lobel, Liz Walker, Jack Williams, and Bruce Schwoegler.

WBZ's efforts are backed by talented staff and state-of-the-art equipment.

PHOTOS BY ERIC ROTH

a favorite of New England sports fans. Throughout his career, Lobel has covered the entire spectrum of New England sports, including anchoring the station's Boston Marathon coverage since 1982.

Bruce Schwoegler, WBZ-TV's chief meteorologist, has been forecasting and analyzing the weather on WBZ since 1968. An expert in earth science, his reports have regularly covered such environmental problems as acid rain, drought, and air and water pollution. He is active throughout the region, visiting schools to present earth science programs.

WBZ Newsradio 1030's morning anchor team of Gary LaPierre and Deb Lawler, with Gil Santos on sports, delivers the most popular morning radio program in New England. Between these native New Englanders, there are over 65 years of radio broadcasting experience and over 30 awards garnered for excellence in reporting. LaPierre and Santos have been a team for 24 years—longer than any other radio or television team in the region.

Well-known talk show host David Brudnoy takes to the airwaves each weeknight, providing New Englanders with one of the most popular talk radio programs in the region. Each week, the entire WBZ radio team of highly respected news anchors and reporters, along with Brudnoy and the extensive WBZ sports team, provide exceptional radio broadcasting that continues the tradition of serving New Englanders for over 70 years.

MAKING A DIFFERENCE IN THE COMMUNITY

The charitable work and community involvement of WBZ Television and Radio are a New England tradition. The station has a long history of community service, beginning with the first public service campaign on television, launched in 1948. Since then, WBZ has initiated campaigns on a wide variety of community concerns, from AIDS to the arts. The station was the originator of the country's first nationally syndicated campaign, "For Kids' Sake." The latest campaign, "Stop the Violence," puts the breadth of station resources behind efforts to increase awareness of issues surrounding

violence in the home, in the schools, and on the streets.

The tradition continues at WBZ—bringing New England the most comprehensive news coverage and an ongoing commitment to the community. "We intend to remain intensely involved in the community," says WBZ-TV Vice President and General Manager Deb Zeyen. "Not just reporting on issues like violence, but acting aggressively to solve the problems that face us."

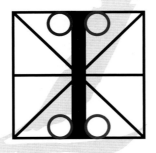

Rollins Hudig Hall of Massachusetts, Inc.

I N THE LATE 1970S, WHEN THE FIRST SPACE SHUTTLE was being developed and tested, finding adequate and appropriate insurance coverage for such a major project was a very difficult assignment. In a historic first, global insurance brokerage giant Rollins Hudig Hall rose to the occasion, amassing nearly all of the world's available insurance capacity to create a policy with a $1 billion limit.

That is the kind of international expertise a firm as large and experienced as RHH can bring to a professional assignment. The company's local arm, RHH Massachusetts, is the largest full-service insurance brokerage and consulting company in New England, with 240 employees. RHH Massachusetts' services include the placement of all commercial lines of insurance, employee benefits, actuarial services, proprietary risk management information systems, captive insurance company management, development and administration of new products and programs, and risk management and loss control consulting.

What that means is that RHH helps companies design ways to manage risks to human and physical assets. That can include anything from workers getting hurt to potential damage from accidents and litigation involving third parties. RHH Massachusetts designs comprehensive risk management solutions for Fortune 1000 companies, governmental entities, and charitable organizations, using a wide variety of insurance and financial mechanisms to treat and manage such hazards.

AN OLD COMPANY WITH A NEW FACE

Rollins Hudig Hall's roots run deep in the region. The company's oldest ancestor, the Fred C. Church Company, was started in nearby Lowell in 1865. The small insurance firm became a regional power in 1928 when it merged with two others and changed its name to Boit, Dalton and Church. Over the next four decades the insurance industry changed dramatically. Increasing governmental regulation and the globalization of the marketplace put new demands on insurance brokers. Insulating

The RHH executive committee includes (from left) Executive Vice President Michael E. Toner, President and COO Webster B. Brockelman, Jr., Chairman and CEO William J. Tvenstrup, and Executive Vice President Charles W. Furlong.

business from the impact of loss became an integral function of financial management. The field of risk management was born, and Boit, Dalton and Church was at the forefront of the new industry.

In the 1960s many of the company's clients went international, and Boit, Dalton and Church responded by expanding services around the world to meet their needs. Today, RHH has offices in places like Russia, Mexico, and Denmark that are staffed with people native to the area who know the regional languages, laws, and customs.

Boit, Dalton and Church merged in 1972 with the Frank B. Hall Company and took its name. In 1992 Aon Corporation, a $17 billion conglomerate based in Chicago, bought the company and changed its name to Rollins Hudig Hall. "We're an old company with a new face," says company President and COO Webster B. Brockelman, Jr.

The affiliation with Aon gives RHH the stability of a major corporation while allowing it to maintain the entrepreneurial spirit of a smaller firm, says Chairman and CEO William J. Tvenstrup. RHH's mission statement reads: "We will aggressively pursue opportunities on all fronts, finding creative solutions for our clients. Our culture encourages all employees to actively participate in building RHH. Together we will accomplish our goals by placing our clients' needs first at all times."

A PROUD HERITAGE

RHH Massachusetts is proud of its New England heritage and its strong regional identity. The company values thrift, strong client

relationships, and a commitment to the community. In a time when many corporations have lost touch with their origins, RHH Massachusetts draws strength and direction from its New England roots. "We have been able to retain and build on a value system that generated our early success," Brockelman says.

The company does more than just draw from the region; it also gives back. "We are good corporate citizens," Tvenstrup says. Senior members of the firm are active on the boards of hospitals and cultural and business organizations. RHH also has a sizable annual budget set aside for charitable contributions to educational, medical, and cultural organizations.

Building on more than a century of growth and success, RHH has become one of the largest insurance brokerage firms in the world. While its size is certainly one of its greatest assets, the company strives to stay dynamic and in touch with its clients' needs. The RHH vision statement reads, in part: "Our people are our most valued resource, and our clients are the focus of our work. The RHH company culture is characterized by caring, entrepreneurialism, integrity, professional accountability, openness, localness, and teamwork."

Throughout its history, RHH has managed to retain the values of its humble Lowell origins while growing into a global insurance brokerage powerhouse. Says Tvenstrup, "We have converted ourselves from a company steeped in history to a modern, international organization."

Lahey Clinic

WITH AS MANY AS 2,400 OUTPATIENT VISITS TO ITS Burlington campus each day, Lahey Clinic has long been internationally renowned as a leader in specialty medicine. But as the health care field is changing to respond to advances in technology and industrywide reform, so is this clinic of more than 300 physicians. With its specialists still at

the core, Lahey is expanding its boundaries both geographically and in terms of the services it provides to patients.

Through affiliations and partnerships with community-based primary care physicians, practices, and hospitals, as well as the construction of a regional medical center north of Boston, Lahey has positioned itself as a

"Our approach emphasizes practitioners at all levels joining together to provide a continuity of care—whether in terms of patients visiting an internist for a sore throat in a community-based office, or undergoing traditional gallbladder surgery at an affiliated community hospital, or receiving a hip implant at Lahey's main center in Burlington."

under one roof to pool their knowledge and work as a team to solve medical problems.

The clinic began with just four physicians. But its reputation and staff grew as Lahey doctors became pioneers in such fields as thyroid, liver, and bile duct surgery; radiation therapy for cancer; neurosurgery; urology; and diagnostic imaging. By the mid-1960s, the Lahey staff had grown to 70 physicians. The clinic had expanded to a handful of buildings spread over several city blocks, and inpatient services were provided by area hospitals located at least one mile away. It was clear that a new facility was needed to consolidate these diverse activities in one location.

The result was the Lahey Clinic Medical Center in Burlington, which opened in 1980. The seven-story facility houses the outpatient resources of the Charles A. Dana Ambulatory Care Center, provides inpatient services through the 272-bed Mary and Arthur R. Clapham Hospital, and offers care without an appointment for routine health problems at the Walk-In Center. Lahey today enjoys a national reputation in such diverse specialty areas as urinary and colon/rectal surgery, aortic surgery, neurosurgery, ophthalmology, and renal artery bypass surgery.

The seven-story Lahey Clinic Medical Center opened in Burlington in 1980.

◀ WEBB CHAPPELL

health care leader in eastern Massachusetts. These new affiliations form the growing Lahey Health Care Network, which provides primary care services backed by the specialty capabilities of the Burlington clinic.

"Lahey's affiliations and partnerships represent an extremely positive trend for the future of health care in the United States," says Chief Executive Officer Bruce W. Steinhauer, M.D.

A PIONEER IN THE 1920S

The clinic was established in 1923 when prominent Boston surgeon Frank H. Lahey left the Harvard and Tufts medical school faculties to concentrate on specialty patient care. Located in cramped quarters in the heart of Boston, his new clinic was something of a pioneer for its time. While most physicians worked alone, referring difficult cases to area medical schools, Lahey brought specialists together

EXPANSION FOR THE FUTURE

Responding to more recent changes in the health care environment, Lahey has expanded to locations as much as 40 miles away from its Burlington headquarters.

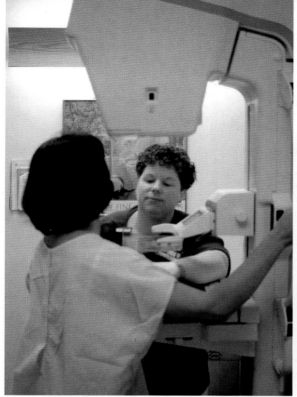

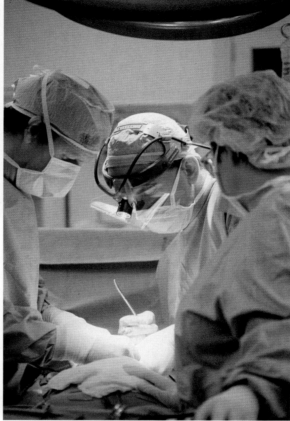

Clockwise from top left:
The Breast Imaging Center is part of Lahey's comprehensive Breast Care Program.

A team approach by doctors representing virtually every medical specialty is a key element of Lahey's practice.

The clinic's reputation for surgical excellence dates back to its beginnings.

Physician expertise and advanced technology are combined in Lahey's practice.

PHOTOS BY CHUCK KIDD

For example, in 1994 a five-member physician practice in the suburb of Lexington became the first group to join a system of community-based primary care practices jointly owned by Lahey and its health maintenance organization partner, Harvard Community Health Plan.

Lahey also has affiliated with AtlantiCare Medical Center, located north of Boston in Lynn, and with Wing Memorial Hospital and Medical Center, based in the central Massachusetts town of Palmer. In both cases, these community hospitals will remain independent but take part in cooperative programs, including making some of Lahey's specialty services available at their own facilities and referring patients for complex specialty care at the Burlington clinic. In addition, AtlantiCare is an active partner with Lahey in the development of Lahey Clinic North, a regional

medical center that opened in the fall of 1994 in Peabody.

Lahey also has forged an agreement with Boston's Joslin Clinic to share resources and services in the treatment of diabetes. And in the suburb of Arlington, Lahey recently acquired Symmes Hospital in partnership with AdvantageHEALTH, one of the Northeast's largest operators of skilled nursing and rehabilitation facilities.

These new affiliates and members are a part of the Lahey Health Care Network, which was launched in 1993 when two multi-physician practices in suburban Boston joined Lahey to provide primary care services throughout Massachusetts. The Lahey Health Care Network is intended to provide patients with easy-to-access resources for every level of health care—locally based primary care physicians, community-level hospital services, and specialty

services at the clinic in Burlington.

Steinhauer says that the new affiliations and partnerships offer patients an unparalleled continuity of care. And he stresses that the network is necessary as the medical marketplace is required to be increasingly more efficient.

"It is popular to say that the health care community is making these changes to position itself in anticipation of national health care reform," he says, "but that largely misses the point.

"The health care field is already reforming itself in response to the changing economics of health care insurance, as private employers and federal programs such as Medicare, which together pay the great bulk of health care costs, increasingly move to approaches that reward and require more efficient management of care."

BayBank

BOSTONIANS KNOW BAYBANK AS THE BANK ON ALMOST every street corner. Nationwide, the company is consistently recognized as one of the most innovative leaders in the banking industry. Throughout the Commonwealth of Massachusetts, BayBank has more than 200 full-service offices and over 350 automated banking facilities serving

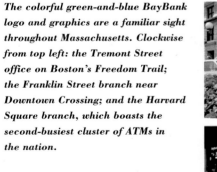

William M. Crozier, Jr., chairman and president of BayBanks, Inc., in the company's 24-hour telephone sales and service center.

158 cities and towns.

BayBank traces its roots back to 1928. Over the past 20 years, under the leadership of Chairman and President William M. Crozier, Jr., the bank holding company known as BayBanks, Inc. has become one of New England's largest, with two separately chartered BayBanks in the Commonwealth: BayBank Boston, N.A. and Burlington-based BayBank. The organization is more commonly known to the public simply as BayBank. The ubiquitous green-and-blue BayBank logo and graphics have become closely identified with Boston and all of Massachusetts. They appear more often—in big cities and small hamlets—than the identification of any other business.

BANKING ON CONVENIENCE

Over the years, the BayBank name has become inextricably linked with convenience. Indicative of the bank's commitment to consistently bring convenience and

value to customers is the number of times it has been first to offer banking innovations. In 1977 Bay-Bank was one of the first banks in the nation to install ATMs. This vision of the future launched an expansion of the BayBank distribution network unparalleled in the company's history. The key elements were the BayBank Card and the X-Press 24® banking machine network—one of the most successful electronic banking programs ever introduced in the country.

Today, BayBank has the 11th-largest deployment of ATMs in the nation. Forty percent of eastern Massachusetts households have at least one BayBank Card. The proprietary X-Press 24 ATM network—including ATMs at other franchise banks—processes more than 134 million transactions per year.

Through the X-Press 24 network, BayBank was the area's first bank to move into point-of-sale, allowing ATM card holders to use their BayBank Cards at gas

stations, supermarkets, and other retail locations. Moreover, BayBank was the first bank in the United States to develop and distribute a catalog of its products and services. Through the BayBank Catalog, customers can order more than 160 products and services by phone or mail, 24 hours a day, seven days a week.

All BayBank customers have the freedom to stop into any one of the company's more than 200 branches, many with extended hours. Banking by phone is another convenient option. BayBank's 24-hour telephone sales and service center is staffed by 400 highly trained people on nearly an acre of floor space. The center handles close to 10 million sales and service calls per year, offering customers a wide range of banking products and services, from account opening to investments to applying for many different kinds of credit. BayBank telephone banking saves precious time for customers who lead busy lives.

The application of tech-

The colorful green-and-blue BayBank logo and graphics are a familiar sight throughout Massachusetts. Clockwise from top left: the Tremont Street office on Boston's Freedom Trail; the Franklin Street branch near Downtown Crossing; and the Harvard Square branch, which boasts the second-busiest cluster of ATMs in the nation.

nology has played an important role in most BayBank innovations. "Our mission for consumers," says Lindsey C. Lawrence, president and chief executive officer of BayBank Systems, Inc., "is to consistently deliver value and convenience through the use of technology, superior quality products and services, and highly reliable operations."

Among the many BayBank innovations related to convenience is the idea that customers generally need a range of financial services. With this in mind, BayBank created Value Packages. These bundled product and service packages include the Premium, Classic, Student, and Starter Value Packages. Typically included are savings, checking, and credit products; the BayBank Card; and other options tailored to meet the needs of a variety of customers. The Bay-Plus account offers even greater advantages. It is BayBank's most powerful combination of checking, savings, and investment products, with exclusive benefits and special savings.

Another BayBank innovation is X-Press Link. Every customer with a variety of BayBank accounts has the option of linking up to 16 different accounts through the BayBank ATM card. This gives customers the ability to use their cards to transfer funds between most BayBank accounts—including savings, money market, credit card, and credit line accounts—at X-Press 24 banking machines or through telephone banking. To make this feature easy to use, BayBank customers select custom names for linked accounts, making it unnecessary to memorize account numbers.

A GOOD NEIGHBOR
Demonstrating its belief in the viability of Boston's neighborhoods, BayBank introduced the Neighborhood Banking Program in 1990. This program has been one of the most aggressive initiatives in the nation to open inner-city branches. BayBank took another leadership role under the program by expanding its services, lending, credit, and basic banking products for ethnically and economically diverse consumers.

Since 1990, as part of BayBank's neighborhood master plan, six new offices have opened in Boston's neighborhoods, including an in-supermarket branch— the first in eastern Massachusetts. Furthermore, nearly 30 cash machines have been added in the neighborhoods. BayBank serves an ever-growing population of inner-city residents with educational programs, and with products and services—many in foreign languages—designed to meet the unique needs of Boston's diverse population. The Neighborhood Banking Program has been so well received that it was recently extended to cities across the Commonwealth.

BUSINESS BANKING
BayBank's business customers can be found in many different industries, including health care, retailing, manufacturing, wholesaling, trading, and services. BayBank also services a large group of nonprofit organizations and institutions, including some of the finest universities and charities in the nation. Moreover, BayBank is the state's leading public finance bank serving municipalities.

BayBank has a leading market position serving businesses because of its strong commitment to these customers, as well as an innovative line of products and services designed to meet their needs. For small businesses, Bay-Bank offers a full line of packaged products that includes checking and savings accounts, the BayBank Business ATM Card, and credit services. For larger companies, the range of services includes cash management, information report-

ing, credit services, investments, international services, trust services, and employee benefits.

All BayBank business customers have access to the convenience of 24-hour telephone banking, as well as a dedicated team of corporate customer service representatives.

THE NEW HORIZON
Throughout its history, BayBank has applied innovation, creativity, and determination to all of its endeavors in an ever-changing world. In this respect, BayBank and the city of Boston are, indeed, kindred spirits. As BayBank approaches the new century, it will continue to be an illuminating element within the broad beacon of light shining on Boston.

For five consecutive years, BayBank has been the presenting sponsor of Boston's world-renowned Head of the Charles Regatta, which attracts nearly 250,000 spectators annually.

BACK IN 1929, THE YEAR OF THE GREAT WALL STREET stock market crash, farsighted aviation pioneer Sherman Fairchild created a holding company that linked a number of small airlines in a coast-to-coast network. As the Great Depression took hold, though, Fairchild decided to separate his airline and his aircraft manufacturing interests.

In preparation for the future, American Airlines is upgrading its terminal facilities in Boston. The result will be faster service for departures and arrivals, as well as increased comfort along the way.

The result was the formation of American Airlines, which had become the nation's dominant air carrier by the end of the 1930s.

When American Airlines began flying passengers in and out of Boston's Logan Airport in 1926, the facilities were little more than a simple landing strip. Access to the downtown area was by way of ferryboat, and passenger planes flew to the roar of piston-powered engines and whirring propellers.

Since then, the airport has expanded enormously and now offers hundreds of flights daily. Downtown Boston can be reached through one of two—soon to be three—tunnels connecting it to Logan International Airport. And American Airlines still flies in and out of Boston—now with its fleet of giant, sophisticated jet aircraft.

TRULY AN AMERICAN CONNECTION

With 36 jet departures each day, as well as eight commuter flights, American Airlines lives up to its name for Boston—providing both the city and the region with extensive connections to the rest of the United States and beyond. Regular flights leave the American terminal bound for Miami, Dallas, San Juan, Chicago, Los Angeles, and Orlando, among other destinations. Systemwide, American services some 160 airports in more than 40 states.

Although most of the airline's traffic is business related, students attending the Boston region's many colleges and universities represent a major market share. "We also get quite a few tourists, especially for the fall foliage season," says James G. Nobles, general manager of American Airlines in Boston.

The airline also moves its share of freight in and out of the New England region. In recent years, up to 7 million pounds of freight a month has been handled, as well as 1.5 million pounds of mail. But at American Airlines, people come first, and the company focuses its growth and improvements on developing ways to better serve passengers.

FILLING SPECIAL ORDERS

Most airline customers want one thing—to get to their destinations quickly and without delays. According to Nobles, though, more and more passengers are choosing American for its special services in addition to its established on-time record.

"We can provide special help to individuals traveling for medical reasons—even if they must be transported on a gurney," he explains. And for VIP passengers who have special needs for security or privacy, the airline can also be accommodating. "We've provided hospitality for former President George Bush several times on his way to Maine," Nobles notes. And when Olympic skater Nancy Kerrigan suddenly found herself thrust into the international limelight, American Airlines helped her get where she was going with minimal disruption and inconvenience.

"We can provide people with a special number to call if they have unique requests like this. It is just another way of serving their travel needs," Nobles says.

FLYING INTO THE FUTURE

As times have changed, American Airlines has been ready, providing an expanding number of services and extra conveniences demanded by the flying public. In preparation for the future, Nobles says, a comprehensive effort is now under way to upgrade American's terminal facilities in Boston. "We are spending $14 million to renovate, add ticket counters, double the size of baggage-handling areas, increase the size of the concourse, and add three gates to the existing six," he explains.

The result will be faster service for departures and arrivals, as well as increased comfort along the way. Nobles notes that the expanded American Airlines facility will be state-of-the-art and will also include expanded and upgraded dining opportunities.

Of course, being a state-of-the-art company is nothing new to American Airlines, which helped specify the design of some of the nation's first commercial passenger aircraft, including the DC-3. In the 1930s, this fast and comfortable plane, a favorite of the airline, became the first aircraft type to achieve profitability on its passenger revenues alone. Later, American provided the technological basis for today's modern air transportation industry when it created the SABRE computerized reservation system in 1964. American set the pace for the industry once again when, in the 1970s, it became the first airline to offer frequent flier discounts to its customers. By the late 1980s, American was the largest airline in the nation in terms of passenger miles flown.

It is this longtime commitment to innovative services that continues to make American Airlines one of Boston's vital links to the rest of the world.

Blue Cross and Blue Shield of Massachusetts

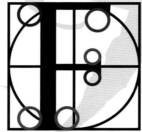

FOR WELL OVER A HALF CENTURY, BLUE CROSS AND Blue Shield of Massachusetts has held a unique position in the health care marketplace. Founded in 1937, the company was the first to offer statewide health insurance, and as the state's largest health services company it remains today the insurer of last resort for the citizens of Massachusetts, ready to help

anyone who applies for coverage.

The company is no less committed to providing universal health care today than it was at the time of its founding. However, as the health care environment has undergone dramatic changes in recent years, the company has transformed itself and its businesses accordingly. Beyond its traditional fee-for-service insurance programs, Blue Cross and Blue Shield of Massachusetts is now a fully integrated health services company, offering an array of managed care products while also being directly involved in the delivery of health care.

As a diversified provider of health services, Blue Cross and Blue Shield is a company devoted to the delivery of high-quality, cost-effective health care solutions; a company dedicated to understanding and serving the needs of its diverse customer base; and a company committed to playing a leadership role in its service to the community, as well as in helping shape the next generation of health care.

DELIVERING HEALTH CARE ACROSS THE COMMONWEALTH

With 2.1 million members statewide, Blue Cross and Blue Shield of Massachusetts is by far the largest health services company in the Commonwealth, providing a full range of services to meet a broad cross section of customer

health care needs.

Blue Cross and Blue Shield became New England's leading managed care company in the early 1990s. It assumed this position with the successful launch of *HMO Blue*, the first statewide health maintenance organization ever established in Massachusetts, and its merger with Bay State Health Care.

Today, managed care is a cornerstone product for the company. It consists of affiliated physician and hospital networks, as well as Blue Cross and Blue Shield health centers, all dedicated to providing high-quality, affordable health care solutions. *HMO Blue* was the state's fastest-growing HMO in both 1992 and

Patricia Anderson (left) and Francine Babachicos discuss one of the educational programs presented by the Health Information Service Center.

▼ JET PHOTOGRAPHY

and information-sharing networks, Blue Cross and Blue Shield is taking important steps to connect all participants in its sphere of business, which will simplify many operations, improve service, and reduce costs. For instance, the company has developed an electronic network called StatLink, which links thousands of physicians via personal computer, allowing them to share information, reduce paperwork, and streamline medical claims processing.

ASSERTING ITSELF AS A LEADER

Blue Cross and Blue Shield of Massachusetts is not only a leader in the health services field. As a major employer in the Commonwealth, the company is leading the effort to celebrate diversity in the workplace through its internal awareness programs, as well as its hiring and employment practices.

The company also demonstrates its leadership in the many communities it serves throughout the Commonwealth, striving in all of its outreach initiatives to project a philosophy of caring and compassion.

That philosophy is expressed in many different forms—from the company's involvement in the Caring Program for Children initiative to provide preventive health care services to uninsured children, to its active role in helping improve the quality of education in the public schools, to its support of public awareness campaigns combating prejudice in the workplace and the neighborhoods.

Whether striving for improvements in the health services delivery system of tomorrow or maintaining a healthy social environment in which to live and work, Blue Cross and Blue Shield of Massachusetts is committed to asserting itself as a leader—one that can help make a difference.

1993, with membership approaching 500,000.

Blue Cross and Blue Shield also continues to offer a variety of traditional medical insurance products. These fee-for-service products allow members to visit the doctor of their choice, and they provide the most extensive medical coverages. They are, however, a more costly alternative to managed care plans like *HMO Blue*.

Blue Choice, the newest product offered by Blue Cross and Blue Shield, is a hybrid health care plan that provides its members with the best features of both previously mentioned products: the lower cost of managed care and the broader range of choice offered through fee-for-service plans.

A COMMITMENT TO QUALITY AND SERVICE

Differentiation within the health services industry is now being driven by two principal factors: the quality of care and outcomes that are delivered, and the level of service that is demonstrated to the consuming public. Blue Cross and Blue Shield of Massachusetts is constantly striving to assure that its quality and service excellence are always at levels that set the industry standard.

Blue Cross and Blue Shield has taken a leadership role in establishing quality measurements as a valid and universal means for the health care industry to gauge its performance. The company is one of only a few organizations nationally that are actively working to develop measurement techniques and data sets on various health care issues. The information that is assembled will ultimately help the industry set quality standards for itself, which, in turn, will help consumers decide where and from whom they will receive the best quality care.

To continue being more responsive to the needs of members and providers, the company has made a strategic commitment to build its own up-ramp onto the "information superhighway." By constructing new communications

RICH IN HISTORY AND TRADITION, THE ELIOT, BOSTON'S luxury suite hotel, combines the style and elegance of Old World charm with the sophistication of contemporary Europe. The atmosphere of a luxury European hotel can be felt in the intimate suites of this historic building located on one of Boston's most beautiful residential streets.

The nine-story structure, which faces north onto the famed Commonwealth Avenue promenade, is the last of a once-flourishing breed of grand hotels that dotted the prestigious Back Bay neighborhood of stately brick town houses. Built in 1925 adjacent to the Harvard Club, The Eliot was designed for retired alumni of Harvard University. "Elderly Bostonians would retire and live here in comfort," explains

The Eliot, which faces north onto the famed Commonwealth Avenue promenade, is the last of a once-flourishing breed of grand hotels that dotted Boston's Back Bay neighborhood of stately brick town houses.

co-owner Dora Ullian, whose father-in-law bought the property in 1939.

Up until a few years ago, The Eliot existed as a residential and extended-stay hotel. But starting in 1990, Ullian and her husband renovated the property and transformed its rooms into 91 luxurious suites that are now typically used for one- and two-night stays.

The Eliot, named for a former president of Harvard University, Charles W. Eliot, is today making a new name for itself in Boston. The hotel has found a niche between the luxury chain hotels and more moderately priced hotels. Modeling her business on the small, urban hotels of Europe, Ullian provides guests with all the elegance of a luxury hotel, but for far less money. "We try to give guests the intimacy, grace, and elegance my husband and I found in European hotels," she says.

Because The Eliot does not offer some facilities traditionally associated with large hotels, such as banquet rooms, expansive lobby areas, and multiple bars, Ullian can pass on the savings to her guests. "We have spared no expense when it comes to our guests' comfort. Our well-appointed suites offer every important amenity," she says.

COMFORT AND CONVENIENCE IN AN INTIMATE SETTING

The hotel's scale is intimate throughout. The lobby is small and comfortable, with armchairs and sofas arranged under ornately

detailed moldings and a sparkling five-foot chandelier. A huge flower arrangement blooms against one wall, while historical documents and photographs from The Eliot's past line the other.

Also on the first floor is a cozy breakfast room that serves a full morning menu, including freshly made baked goods. Guests can choose from a stack of newspapers outside the door and enjoy their meal to the soft sound of classical music.

The building's exterior was recently updated, and a stunning wrought-iron and glass portico was added as part of the renovation. The portico was made by Italian artisans who labored for more than 2,000 hours before the structure was shipped to The Eliot and installed by crane. Around the new entrance, the grounds have been tastefully landscaped.

Each suite includes a bedroom and a living room divided by French doors, as well as a small, well-stocked private pantry. Even the bathrooms, covered from floor to ceiling in rich Italian marble, reflect European elegance. Unique in appearance, the rooms are decorated in subtle pastels and floral patterns by German-born designer Klaus Fuchs, whose work is also found in the Ritz-Carlton

and Four Seasons hotels. Fuchs filled the suites with antique-style furniture and paintings, making them feel less like hotel rooms and more like posh apartments in the Back Bay.

While the suites at The Eliot reflect the luxury and life-style of early Boston, they are completely equipped for the 1990s. Each room has a two-line telephone, modem capability, and two televisions, making the hotel ideal for business travelers.

Thus far, Ullian's all-suite approach has enjoyed a positive response. In a city with an average hotel occupancy rate of 71 percent, The Eliot boasts an average occupancy of over 80 percent.

ELEGANCE WITH A PERSONAL TOUCH

Guests of The Eliot come from all over the world and are often academics, artistic performers, or parents visiting their children at nearby universities. Within easy walking distance are Boston University, Massachusetts Institute of Technology, Symphony Hall, the Hynes Auditorium, the Museum of Fine Arts, and the fine shops of Newbury Street. The hotel's guests, according to Ullian, are loyal: Many return to The Eliot every visit and often request their favorite suite. As further evidence of its popularity, The Eliot was recently named one of "The World's 100 Most-loved Hotels" by the Japanese travel magazine *Gulliver's Travels*.

Most important to Ullian, however, is that all of the hotel's services are provided in the most congenial way. "We keep guests coming back by offering an atmosphere of kindness, thought-fulness, and concern," she says. "Our staff is dedicated to serving our guests, whatever the request."

That dedication is often mentioned on comment cards by departing guests. As one visitor put it in a recent letter to Ullian, "I have stayed in many hotels around the world. The elegant, marvelous suites and building are complemented by the most courteous, helpful staff, who made my visit a real pleasure." Ullian maintains that it's The Eliot's personal touch that really makes the difference.

FROM ITS HEADQUARTERS IN BOSTON'S PRESTIGIOUS 60 State Street office tower, adjacent to historic Faneuil Hall and the financial district, ITT Sheraton Corporation manages a worldwide hospitality network of nearly 400 properties in 61 countries. Long a Boston institution, ITT Sheraton—a subsidiary of ITT Corporation—traces its

Headquartered in Boston's prestigious 60 State Street office tower (below), ITT Sheraton manages a worldwide hospitality network of nearly 400 properties in 61 countries.

Clockwise from top right: Sheraton Cancun Resort & Towers, Sheraton Grande Tokyo Bay Hotel & Towers, Sheraton Sofia Hotel Balkan (Bulgaria), and Sheraton Boston Hotel & Towers.

roots back to the 1930s. Company founders Ernest Henderson and Robert Moore acquired their first hotel, the Stonehaven, in Springfield, Massachusetts, in 1937. Two years later they acquired three additional hotels in Boston. One of the three bore the name Sheraton, from which the corporate name was derived.

Further acquisitions from Maine to Florida helped the company grow. Within 10 years Sheraton became the first hotel chain to be listed on the New York Stock Exchange. In 1949, ITT Sheraton began expanding internationally with the acquisition of two Canadian hotel chains.

later, the company launched the Reservatron system—the first automated electronic reservation system in the hotel industry. Later, the company was the first to pioneer a toll-free 800 number for direct consumer access to reservations at any location.

All the while, the business grew—acquiring locations in Canada, Hawaii, South America, and the Middle East. Sheraton also began building its own hotels, starting with the Philadelphia Sheraton in 1957. Another avenue for growth was opened when the company formed its franchise division, Sheraton Inns, Inc., in 1962.

But the company's success does not rest solely on its property base. ITT Sheraton has gained its reputation as an industry leader through a series of customer service and technological innovations as well. In 1948, Sheraton became the first hotel operation to utilize a telex system for room reservations. A decade

A fitting milestone was logged in 1965 when the company opened the Sheraton Boston—its 100th property—in the new Prudential Center.

GROWING HORIZONS
In 1968, Sheraton was acquired by ITT Corporation, a multinational enterprise with 1993 annual

revenues of nearly $23 billion. With the further strength afforded by this union, Sheraton forged ahead with plans for international expansion, including establishing a cruise ship operation on the Nile River in Egypt. The 1980s saw the introduction of the "new Sheraton" under the leadership of current Chairman and CEO John Kapioltas. By then, Sheraton had become a worldwide company with a global reputation for service, excellence, and quality. Milestones during the decade included the introduction of a special 800 number for travel agents; introduction of the first computerized hotel reservations service in the Middle East; opening of the Great Wall Sheraton in Beijing, the first hotel in China to bear the name of an international hotel company; the introduction of Sheraton Club International (SCI), the industry's most global frequent guest program; and the launch of the Sheraton Guest

Satisfaction System (SGSS), a unique employee training program to ensure consistent and measurable responsiveness to guest needs.

As the 1990s began, ITT Sheraton turned its focus to further improving the quality and service standards of its U.S. operations. To that end, the company earmarked more than $1 billion for construction and renovation at properties in key cities, including New York, Los Angeles, Chicago, Dallas, Toronto, and New Orleans. ITT Sheraton also began a project in 1988 to restore classic hotels, including The Carl-

ton in Washington, D.C., the Sheraton Moana Surfrider on Waikiki Beach, and the Sheraton Palace in San Francisco. That effort culminated with the grand reopening of The St. Regis in New York City in 1991. ITT Sheraton has far surpassed its first $1 billion in improvements since 1992, with additional renovations completed on such properties as the Sheraton Bal Harbour near Miami, Sheraton

Universal in Los Angeles, and Sheraton Harbor Island in San Diego.

Today, ITT Sheraton is also looking at new markets. The company has entered the growing all-suite hotel business and operates a total of 12 all-suite properties in the United States. ITT Sheraton recently entered the U.S. gaming industry by acquiring the Desert Inn in Las Vegas and by opening the Sheraton Casino in the growing northern Mississippi gaming district near Memphis.

LOOKING AHEAD

With more than $3 billion in annual revenues, ITT Sheraton Corporation has a worldwide network of nearly 400 owned, leased, managed, and franchised properties operating in 61 countries. Its departments include the Gaming Division, as well as separate divisions for North America, Latin America, Europe,

Africa and the Middle East, and Asia-Pacific. And each is growing. The Asia-Pacific division, for example, plans to open 20 additional hotels by the year 2000, bringing its total number of properties to 65.

According to ITT Sheraton's corporate mission statement, the organization is "committed to becoming the number one hospitality company." To that end, the

company has embarked on a number of programs to ensure that guests find the services and products they need and want at ITT Sheraton. For business travelers, key business services have been added to guest rooms, including voice mail, computer hookups, coffeemakers, and innovative ways to streamline or eliminate the check-in and check-out processes. Other programs include the reintroduction of ITT Sheraton Club International to include a new currency of ClubMiles, transferable to airline frequent flyer programs, and a North America initiative to upgrade the quality of food and beverage served in hotels in that division.

ITT Sheraton's goals for the years ahead are to extend operations to 90 countries by the end of the decade and, most important, to be the worldwide leader in hospitality and service.

Clockwise from bottom left: Sheraton Moana Surfrider (Honolulu), Sheraton Abu Dhabi Hotel & Resort, Sheraton Mirage Port Douglas Resort (Queensland, Australia), The St. Regis (New York), Sheraton Desert Inn (Las Vegas), The Phoenician (Scottsdale), and Sheraton Brussels Airport Hotel.

Jung/Brannen Associates, Inc.

DEEP HUES, WARM TEXTURES, AND ENGAGING GEOMETRIC patterns characterize a recent Jung/Brannen Associates project. The office space, designed and built for Massachusetts Financial Services, features elevators that open into a vaulted reception area and mahogany-paneled walls and ceilings. The floor is covered with black and gray marble

Jung/Brannen designed Massachusetts Financial Services' 325,000-square-foot office (below right).

Among the company's many high-profile Boston projects are 125 High Street (background, center) and the adjoining Hotel Meridien and One Post Office Square (foreground, left).

tiles, and soft light glows from recessed fixtures. The overall effect is sophisticated and professional.

Jung/Brannen Associates has been translating client needs into functional, elegant, and modern environments since its founding in 1968 by Yu Sing Jung and Robert Brannen. Jung/Brannen is now one of the largest architectural and design firms in Massachusetts, employing 77 people and handling projects worldwide, including Europe, the Middle East, and Asia. Along the way the company has designed, built, or renovated some of the most significant buildings in the Boston area.

FUNCTION AND BEAUTY

One of Jung/Brannen's best-known Boston projects is One Post Office Square—a 40-story downtown office tower with ground-floor retail space and a connection to the 330-room Hotel Meridien. The mixed-use development incorporated the restoration of the historical Federal Reserve building, with its intricate interior detailing and famous murals.

Another high-profile Jung/Brannen accomplishment was the design of 125 High Street, which features two linked high-rise office buildings, retail space, and

the Boston Fire Department's Division One headquarters. Although the fire station is constructed of the same materials as the rest of the structure—pink and gray granite and ornamental aluminum painted a dusty green—it is distinct because of its gently bowed second-story bay crowned with a bronze medallion

bearing Boston's city seal.

In addition to office-building design, Jung/Brannen is well known for its contract design expertise, from planning a small office renovation to laying out the infrastructure for an entire building site. Another recent job involved taking a seldom-used pedestrian plaza and transforming it into a landscaped area with a fountain and an indoor/outdoor cafe.

DEFINING CLIENT NEEDS

Jung/Brannen works closely with clients to define their needs and find solutions. According to Director of Interior Design Duncan Pendlebury, the firm "translates a company's corporate culture into a business environment." For some, that means large corner offices for executives and smaller interior offices sized and arranged by seniority. For others, offices might be open and clustered around communal areas. "It's all about serving the client," Pendlebury emphasizes.

Jung/Brannen also tries to create environments that serve as uplifting places to work. "There's a subconscious comfort level to moving through and working in spaces that are organized. It's very subtle," says Pendlebury, adding that well-designed space reflects positively on a company's corporate image.

Clearly, the team at Jung/Brannen Associates understands that the attitudes of clients and employees alike are shaped by the corporate environment. With that philosophy as a guide, the firm continually proves its ability to create attractive, functional designs.

PETER VANDERWARKER

NICK WHEELER

HERE IS A TREE IN THE JAPANESE GARDEN AT FIDELITY Investments' Boston headquarters that appears to be healthy—even thriving. But not very long from now it will be removed and replaced—as it is periodically—as a symbol of change. ■ "The idea is not to get too used to looking at one thing," says Fidelity Chairman Edward C. Johnson 3d.

"We are always challenged by seeing something new."

Indeed, much of the company's success throughout nearly five decades in business has been based on change and innovation. Fidelity, which today is one of America's largest financial services companies, embraces a Japanese concept called "Kaizen" as its cultural core. Through Kaizen, the company encourages innovation by giving employees the power to evaluate and constantly improve their work and the products they provide to customers.

"If there aren't a lot of people being innovative in many different areas, the whole system eventually freezes because there aren't enough new things happening," says Johnson. "Creativity has to be encouraged at every level within an organization."

Nurturing innovation and continuous improvement has created a strong entrepreneurial spirit within Fidelity Investments, and helped to fuel the company's rapid growth. With more than $350 billion in customer assets, Fidelity today is the country's largest mutual fund company and the second-largest discount brokerage firm. It is also the number one provider of 401(k) retirement plan services to corporations and a leading manager of 403(b) retirement plans for not-for-profit institutions. The firm employs about 13,000 people— roughly 6,000 of whom work in the Boston area.

But Fidelity Investments is impressive for much more than its size and leadership in the fi-

SETH RESNICK

nancial services industry. The company is also successful at making money for its customers. For the three years ending in December 1993, Fidelity funds outperformed 84 percent of all other mutual funds, and the company's stock funds outperformed 90 percent of their competitors.

Founded in Boston in 1946, Fidelity Investments is today headquartered in the city's financial district.

FIDELITY'S BEGINNINGS
This commitment to excellence in money management is deeply rooted in Fidelity's history. The firm was founded in Boston in 1946 by Edward C. Johnson 2d, father of the current chairman, to serve as an investment adviser to the $10 million Fidelity Fund.

Fidelity has made it extremely easy for almost anyone to invest. The company operates walk-in Investor Centers around the country where investors can talk with a Fidelity representative in person.

Johnson managed the fund himself and, at the same time, began developing the concept for the Fidelity Puritan Fund, another growth and income fund that was launched in 1947. Over the next 10 years, Johnson and his associates created a number of other funds with a variety of investment approaches, forming the Fidelity Group of Funds.

In 1957 Edward C. "Ned" Johnson 3d joined the company as portfolio manager of Fidelity Trend Fund. Fidelity's assets under management rose quickly in the 1960s—led by the popularity of Fidelity Trend Fund and another growth-oriented fund called Fidelity Capital. By 1972, the year Ned Johnson took over leadership of the firm from his father, Fidelity's assets under management had grown to $3 billion.

The early 1970s were a difficult time for the mutual fund industry. Declining stock prices and rising interest rates caused growth-oriented mutual funds to become less popular than they had been in the previous two decades.

But this change also offered a tremendous opportunity. Johnson, an innovator like his father, helped to create a new category of mutual funds that offered an attractive yield and a stable share price: money market funds. In 1974 Fidelity became the first company to offer check writing on money funds. And the firm, which previously had distributed its products exclusively through independent brokers, began experimenting with direct-response advertising and toll-free telephone lines as a way to sell directly to the public.

Developing this direct communication channel with customers allowed Fidelity to better understand investors' needs, and to assume a leadership role in offering them the information and assistance they need to make sound investment choices. "Fidelity's business," says Johnson, "is based on two goals: to help people invest successfully and to offer them the tools they need to do so. We believe that given the right tools, individuals make their own best investment decisions."

Fidelity's commitment to providing timely, educational information is reflected in the publications it offers customers. Investors automatically receive an investment magazine and newsletters designed with their specific needs in mind. They also enjoy access to a wealth of materials—such as brochures on topics like "Saving for Your Child's Education" and "Planning for Retirement"—that are available upon request. To help investors keep track of their investments, Fidelity provides transaction confirmations, regular account statements, and fund reports.

Fidelity has made it extremely easy for almost anyone to invest. It operates walk-in Investor Centers around the country where investors can talk with a Fidelity representative in person. The firm's representatives also are available by phone 24 hours a day, 365 days a year. More than 100,000 people call Fidelity every day to request information, make a transaction, or discuss their investments with a knowledgeable representative. Almost 300,000 more callers take advantage of Fidelity's state-of-the-art automated information lines, accessing information with their Touch-Tone phones.

Another way Fidelity brings consumers closer to the investment process is by giving them direct access to the financial markets through their personal computers. Using a comprehensive software package, customers can obtain real-time price quotes, carefully monitor their accounts, perform research and analysis, and trade stocks, options, and mutual funds.

AN EXPANDING PRODUCT LINE

Fidelity currently offers more than 200 mutual funds that meet a variety of financial objectives. Over the years, the company has expanded its business in other areas. The firm launched its discount brokerage business in 1979. In 1986 Fidelity began offering its own line of credit cards. The company entered the annuity

business in 1987, and in 1989 created "Spartan funds," which are designed as low-cost funds for long-term investors.

Fidelity is also a leader in providing retirement services to individuals and institutions. The firm began offering 401(k) retirement plans to corporations in 1985 and now manages about $60 billion in employee retirement assets for more than half of the Fortune 500 companies. It is also one of the nation's top five providers of retirement plans to nonprofit organizations, including colleges, universities, health care institutions, foundations, and other charitable organizations.

CUSTOMER FOCUS AND COMMITMENT

Fidelity's focus on customer satisfaction is strongly tied to its extensive customer research. The firm uses a variety of methods to keep one step ahead of its clients' needs. Everyone at Fidelity pays careful attention to letters from customers, for example, and managers frequently attend customer round-

tables and focus groups. The firm also conducts regular phone and mail surveys, and even documents informal conversations with clients.

The result of this intense customer focus has been an ongoing expansion of the types of investments the firm offers, as well as continuous improvement in the quality of the services it provides. After learning that investors needed help deciding how to allocate their money among different types of mutual funds, for example, Fidelity created a comprehensive workbook called *Fidelity FundMatch*. Now, with more investors becoming comfortable using personal computers, Fidelity has developed asset allocation software for customers to use on their home PCs.

"We strive to provide the level of service that sets the standard for other firms," says Johnson. "I believe there's always an opportunity to do our job a little better than we're doing it today."

The firm employs about 13,000 people—roughly 6,000 of whom work in the Boston area. Shown here is Fidelity's Fixed Income Trading floor.

DeWolfe New England

EWOLFE NEW ENGLAND HAS BEEN PROVIDING RESIDENtial real estate services to the Greater Boston area for more than four decades, and during that time the company has earned a reputation for integrity, leadership, and innovation unequaled in the industry. Under the energetic leadership of Ann L. DeWolfe and then her son, current Chairman and CEO Richard B. DeWolfe, the company has gained regional acclaim for its professionalism, fairness, and civic involvement—principles that have remained with the company into the present.

Today, DeWolfe New England is a full-service home-ownership company, conducting operations from 46 sales centers throughout eastern Massachusetts and New Hampshire with a service area that extends into Rhode Island and Maine. In addition to representing home buyers and sellers, DeWolfe New England provides mortgage financing and relocation management services to its customers.

Richard B. DeWolfe (right) is chairman and CEO of The DeWolfe Companies, Inc.

ADAPTING TO MEET THE NEEDS OF BUYERS AND SELLERS

Founded in 1949 by the DeWolfe family, the company began operations in the Boston suburb of Quincy and quietly built a solid reputation for integrity, service, and professionalism.

In 1974, when Richard DeWolfe assumed leadership, the company entered a new era of growth and development. Adopting an aggressive acquisitions strategy, DeWolfe quickly expanded the company's presence in the Greater Boston market. Equally important, he redefined the company's mission, moving beyond the limited scope of a traditional real estate agency that represented only sellers of property, to a diversified home-ownership enterprise offering a full range of services home buyers and sellers require.

"We wanted to distinguish ourselves from the traditional real estate brokerages by providing a package of home-ownership services," DeWolfe says. "Our goal was to convince consumers that if they were looking for a product or service related to the home, they could come to DeWolfe and either find it or be provided with a direct link to it."

The first major step in this direction occurred in 1976 with the addition of a relocation

A traditional New England Cape-style home. DeWolfe New England assists in more than 7,000 home sale transactions each year.

▼ JERRY HOWARD

The company's Westford, Massachusetts, sales center is located in a converted New England farmhouse (left). DeWolfe operates 46 sales centers situated throughout eastern Massachusetts and New Hampshire.

services division. Within a decade, the relocation division had formed alliances with major corporate clients, and its reputation for quality service began to spread outside New England. In 1988 DeWolfe Relocation joined a national relocation services network, linking the company to more than 300 major market areas across the country. Today, the company provides both national and international relocation services.

The next major addition to the home-ownership concept occurred in 1986 when the company added a mortgage banking division. "Virtually every community in this country has been abandoned by banks and S&Ls—the institutions that were the major components of the home mortgage infrastructure," says DeWolfe. "In their place, private mortgage companies have come on the scene, filling the gap but at the expense of personal service and product flexibility. We hope to give consumers more choices and better service."

In 1993 DeWolfe New England continued its trend of responding to the changing demands of consumers by becoming the first major New England firm to offer buyer representation to its customers. Traditionally, real estate agents represent only sellers in home sales transactions. But increased consumer awareness has created a demand among home buyers for representation in what

is typically the single most important purchase they will make. Now, home buyers can contract with DeWolfe sales associates to represent their interests in every aspect of the home-buying transaction.

GROWING INTO THE FUTURE

The result of DeWolfe New England's commitment to meeting diverse consumer needs has been a steadily increasing market share. With a continually expanding staff of dedicated real estate professionals—today numbering more than 1,000 associates—the company each year sets new sales performance records.

In 1986 and 1987, *Inc.* magazine named DeWolfe one of the "500 Fastest Growing Companies in America." And, according to industry surveys, DeWolfe New England was one of only 34 companies nationwide to record home sales totals of over $1 billion in 1993.

In 1994 *The Boston Globe* named DeWolfe one of Massachusetts' top 100 firms. The *Globe's* annual rankings, based on composite scores of key business performance indicators, placed DeWolfe in the top 50 percent of this select group. In addition, *Real Trends*, a real estate industry journal, ranked DeWolfe 29th out of the top 250 real estate firms in the country.

In the fall of 1992, The DeWolfe Companies, Inc. became the first publicly traded residential

real estate firm in the country. Access to public capital markets enabled DeWolfe to continue its aggressive growth strategy while adding increasingly sophisticated administrative, training, and marketing systems. By 1994 the company had become one of the largest real estate service firms in New England, a respected industry leader both within the region and nationally.

Although DeWolfe has changed dramatically from its early days in Quincy, the company's guiding principles have remained constant. Each year, DeWolfe associates donate thousands of dollars and dedicate thousands of hours to local charities and community projects. From walkathons to parades to dunking booths, DeWolfe associates can be counted on to participate in a worthy cause.

In 1994 the company moved its headquarters to a new facility in the western Boston suburb of Lexington, a historic community known for its role in the opening battles of the American Revolution. DeWolfe honors the region's heritage and is committed to playing a worthy role in its future. "There is a real enthusiasm among the people who are part of this organization that the region is something special and that our company is something special," DeWolfe says. "And it shows—we treat our clients the same way."

The Stubbins Associates, Inc.

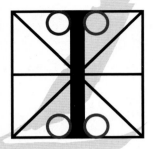

IN YOKOHAMA, JAPAN, A 73-STORY BURNISHED GRANITE building stands, visible in Tokyo 25 miles away. Commissioned by the Mitsubishi Estate Corporation, the project was designed by The Stubbins Associates, a Cambridge-based architectural firm. ■ The building is not only a visual wonder but a technological one as well. To counteract the

Among the firm's three design projects for Vanderbilt University is the Psychology Building (below right).

The aluminum skin and distinctive shape of the Stubbins-designed Federal Reserve Bank of Boston have made it a local landmark.

natural swaying of the 1,000-foot structure, the firm employed an innovative counterweight system that uses two 170-ton weights to dampen the building's shifts from high winds or small earthquakes.

The Stubbins Associates is known worldwide for visually striking and technologically innovative projects. Founded in 1949, the firm has designed such well-known buildings as Citicorp Center in New York City, with its distinctive triangular top, and the Federal Reserve Bank of Boston, whose aluminum skin and distinctive shape have made it a local landmark.

BRINGING EXPERTISE TO PROJECTS OF EVERY SIZE

While skyscrapers and other large, mixed-use urban projects are among the firm's most high-profile designs, The Stubbins Associates devotes a considerable amount of its time to smaller projects, such as the new U.S. Embassy and the American ambassador's residence in Singapore, a sprawling, Asian-style building on a gentle slope. Other projects on a smaller scale

expectations of the owner, the users, and the public at large.

Design is also tailored to client needs. The firm does not impose a set of preconceived design solutions or stylistic inclinations on its clients. Instead, The Stubbins Associates evaluates each building program in its specific context and devises a unique solution. That approach results in a range of designs—from the stately Ronald Reagan Presidential Library to the futuristic, cylindrical Singapore Treasury Building. "Design character is derived from the unique circumstances of the project at hand," Green says. "We don't espouse a dogma about

▲ NICK WHEELER

▲ TIMOTHY HURSLEY

have included the Biological Sciences Learning Center and Jules F. Knapp Medical Research Complex at the University of Chicago.

Regardless of size, all of the firm's projects share the intangible quality of design excellence. According to CEO Richard Green, the best design fits the building into its environment, relies on quality ideas, and fulfills or exceeds

design, and the variety of our practice keeps us fresh."

In addition to architectural design, The Stubbins Associates offers many other services, including feasibility studies, programming, master planning, interior and landscape design, construction administration, and computer-aided design drafting.

This commitment to meeting customer needs with

comprehensive service and striking, high-quality designs has allowed the firm to create some of the most notable buildings in the world. The Singapore Treasury Building, for example, rises 52 stories—a huge cylinder wrapped in aluminum. Located in the city's central business district, the 1.4 million-square-foot structure houses office space, retail shops, and an underground garage. The tower's rounded form minimizes its exposed surface area, which reduces energy consumption. Since its completion in 1986, the building has become a national landmark now pictured on some of the country's paper currency.

The Stubbins Associates recently designed a 60-story building for the Commission of Foreign Economic Relations and Trade of Anhui Province in China. Located on the edge of the Two Mile River overlooking the old city of Hefei, the building will contain exhibition, conference, retail, entertainment, office, and hotel facilities. The design incorporates Chinese motifs: the roof echoes local architectural style, and the actual construction will utilize Chinese-made materials and equipment whenever possible. The Stubbins Associates was chosen for the project because of its international expertise in the design and construction of state-of-the-art, high-rise, steel-framed structures.

The firm's reputation has provided opportunities to design a variety of other projects, from a 400-room hotel at the World Trade Center in Boston for Fidelity Capital and the John Drew Company to a series of projects for Lotus Development Corporation. The broad expertise of The Stubbins Associates is also apparent in the diversity of interior design projects it has completed. In Boston, the firm recently designed the executive offices for two international publishing companies, Harcourt General and Houghton Mifflin, each with different goals.

The Stubbins Associates provided both clients with an innovative design solution reflecting their distinct program, priorities, image, and technological needs. The firm continues its interior design expertise with assignments for the Bank of Boston and other local corporate, institutional, and developer clients.

COMMITTED TO QUALITY

The Stubbins Associates is recognized as one of the world's premier design organizations. Among its more than 150 design awards is the coveted American Institute of Architect's Firm Award, which is presented annually to only one architectural organization in the United States. The Stubbins Associates was one of the first architectural firms recognized for its "consistent work of the highest quality both in design and detailed execution."

The quality of the firm's work is also illustrated in the amount of repeat and referral business it receives. Approximately 75 percent of its clients have either worked with the company before or were referred by someone who has. Harvard University, Prudential Property Company, Hewlett-Packard, Harcourt General, Bristol-Myers Squibb, Cushing Academy, and BayBank are among the firm's repeat customers. In addition to completing its seventh assignment for The MITRE Corporation in 1991, The Stubbins Associates is currently designing its third project for Vanderbilt University—a new Learning Technology Center for Education.

For more than 45 years, The Stubbins Associates has given poetic expression to pragmatic concerns. Today, the firm continues its longtime commitment to design excellence and technical innovation.

The 73-story Landmark Tower in Yokohama, Japan, is a visual and technological wonder designed by The Stubbins Associates.

The firm has designed such well-known buildings as Citicorp Center in New York City, with its distinctive triangular top.

Dunkin' Donuts

WILLIAM ROSENBERG, WHILE WORKING AT A BOSTON-AREA shipyard during World War II, came up with an idea for a new business. He realized that workers preferred not to leave the site and would buy their meals and snacks at the factories if they could. To meet this demand, he launched a lunch-truck business that grew into a fleet of 250 trucks.

But it was his second idea that made business history.

Rosenberg noticed that a large part of his sales were in coffee and donuts, so in 1950 he started another business selling just those two products. The shop, called Dunkin' Donuts, was almost instantly successful. Rosenberg expanded, opening more shops and becoming more and more well known in Boston and throughout its suburbs. His innovative spirit still at work, Rosenberg began franchising the shops—a new

current size of more than 3,500 shops in 28 countries.

Today, Dunkin' Donuts is the largest coffee and donut shop chain in the world, with annual sales of nearly $1.5 billion. The company sells more than 4 million donuts per day, enough to circle the globe twice. But as well known as Dunkin' Donuts is for its donuts, coffee is actually the company's biggest seller. Half a billion cups of it are sold each year, and the company buys 20 million pounds of coffee beans

LISTENING TO CUSTOMERS

The company has grown steadily because it gives customers what they want: reasonably priced, high-quality products in convenient locations. New customer desires have emerged over the years, and Dunkin' Donuts has sought to meet them. The original product line, for example, now includes muffins, bagels, cookies, and croissants.

But Dunkin' Donuts still owes its success to William Rosen-

Since 1950, Dunkin' Donuts has built a reputation for serving the world's finest coffee and donuts. The company now sells more than 4 million donuts per day and half a billion cups of coffee each year.

idea at the time—and by 1963 Dunkin' Donuts had spread to 100 locations.

His son Robert, who was raised sweeping donut shop floors and learning the business from the ground up, took over the company in 1963. A graduate of Cornell's restaurant school and the Harvard Business School, the younger Rosenberg guided the firm to its

annually for its U.S. shops alone. These beans are specially selected, roasted, and tested for Dunkin' Donuts and are freshly ground just before being brewed. The coffee itself is always fresh—a new pot is made every 18 minutes. In a recent poll, 60 percent of Bostonians surveyed voted Dunkin' Donuts coffee the best tasting in the city.

berg's 44-year-old, simple idea: coffee and donuts. As people's idea of coffee has become more sophisticated in recent years with the proliferation of gourmet coffees, Dunkin' Donuts has responded to the demand with the recent introduction of Dark Roast, the first new Dunkin' Donuts coffee in the company's history. The coffee, which costs the same

Dunkin' Donuts has grown steadily because it gives customers what they want: reasonably priced, high-quality products in convenient locations.

as the traditional brew, is roasted longer at higher temperatures, giving it a more full-bodied, European taste.

To keep tabs on customer needs, Dunkin' Donuts relies on its franchise operators—all but 11 of the 3,500 shops are operated by individual shopkeepers who interact with customers and can determine their reaction to products and policies. These franchisees are encouraged to communicate with management, and the company takes their input seriously. Dunkin' Donuts has local, regional, and national advisory councils made up of franchisees who are elected annually by their peers and who meet with senior management quarterly to make suggestions and address concerns. "We have a great deal of input into the direction the company takes," says franchisee Jason Dubinsky.

This partnership keeps Dunkin' Donuts a perceptive, responsive organization. "We can't survive without them, and they

can't survive without us," says Bill Chiccarelli, director of public relations. "We're in it together, and it's made us successful."

The franchisees who are keeping Rosenberg's dream alive are doing it the same way he did— through hard work and dedication to customer service. Dubinsky bought his first Dunkin' Donuts franchise in 1971. "I worked it, and worked it hard," he says, adding that his wife and two young sons put in a lot of hours to help make the shop succeed. But the effort paid off. Dubinsky and his sons, now grown, own and run seven stores. Franchisee John Boujoukos is another example. He worked in Dunkin' Donuts' corporate office for 15 years before

finally buying a franchise of his own. He now owns three shops outside of Boston.

It seemed like a simple idea, selling such inexpensive, everyday products as coffee and donuts. But by sticking to the basics of hard work, high quality, and customer service, Dunkin' Donuts has become a successful American institution.

Franchisees are encouraged to communicate with management, and the company takes their input seriously (above).

Bull Electronics

A S A $5 BILLION GLOBAL OPERATION, PARIS-BASED BULL Worldwide Information Systems is one of the world's top information technology firms. The company, which first established a manufacturing presence in Boston in 1957, today works in more than 100 countries. Its 10 divisions develop, manufacture, market, and sell a complete line of

integrated information technology products, services, and solutions. One of those key divisions is Bull Electronics, a high-tech contract manufacturing business that gives clients comprehensive "copper to carton" service.

designation means that Bull Electronics is capable of managing all aspects of a product's delivery to market—from designing the product and building the raw board to shipping it in its final form.

each innovative new microchip or operating system, computer companies feel the pressure to keep pace," he explains. "So today's state-of-the-art computer assembly can quickly become yesterday's news. Contract manu-

Bull Electronics is a full-service, ISO 9002-certified contract manufacturing business providing "copper to carton" services (above left).

Joel H. Beck, president, Bull Electronics (above right).

FOCUSED ON CONTRACT MANUFACTURING

Established in Boston as part of Bull Worldwide's business in 1993, Bull Electronics leads the planning and implementation of the company's "merchant" business. Also known as "contract manufacturing" or "inloading," the division's services involve performing specific jobs or manufacturing tasks under long-term contracts with other corporations, many of which previously handled the tasks themselves. The "copper to carton"

While contract manufacturing has been used by electronics manufacturers and automakers for years, the concept is experiencing a revitalization in the computer industry. As product lines continue to grow more diversified and sophisticated, many companies are realizing that it is actually more cost-efficient to rely on contract manufacturers for many parts or services, according to Joel H. Beck, president of Bull Electronics.

"With the emergence of

facturing helps companies avoid such obsolescence by allowing them to contract for the latest production technologies without making a substantial capital investment."

Contract manufacturing has also given Bull Worldwide a new lease on life in what has become an increasingly competitive computer manufacturing industry. With the creation of Bull Electronics, the company put its existing competitive advantages, like its worldwide purchasing power and extensive distribution capabilities, to work for its customers.

"Bull has more than 60 years of innovation behind it," says Beck. "But you could argue that the contract manufacturing division is a two-year-old start-up."

The success of the new business division has also allowed Bull Worldwide to maintain a flourishing manufacturing plant within Boston. Once home to a number of large computer companies, the city has been abandoned by many of those industry giants, which have migrated to suburban

33 percent of Bull's corporate-wide manufacturing business. The company expects that figure to double in 1994. Customers of Bull Electronics currently include industry giants like Packard Bell, Hewlett-Packard, and Zenith Data Systems.

THE CORNERSTONE OF SUCCESS

If meeting quality, delivery, and pricing requirements is the foundation of Bull Electronics, then the cornerstone of its success is its diverse workforce, according to Beck. Salaried employees

rowing in the same direction."

He adds, "We are very people-oriented. We believe that the way to make a successful business is to focus on your people; the bottom line will take care of itself."

To that end, Bull Electronics currently supports several employee training and education programs aimed at preparing its workforce to meet the challenges of the next century. They include ongoing, aggressive job training, and traditional classroom and on-line instruction. The company also sponsors classes in English

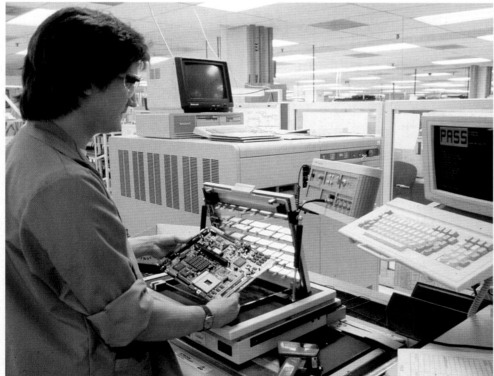

plants or West Coast facilities. "We are the last computer company in Boston," says Beck. "And we are committed to staying here. Our location gives us excellent access to excellent people."

From a 257,000-square-foot facility in Boston and a second 1.2 million-square-foot facility in the suburb of Lawrence, Bull Electronics has become a critical component in the company's manufacturing strategy for the next several years. In 1993 the new division generated

include 40 percent minorities, with 24 separate minority groups and a large percentage of women, Vietnam veterans, and disabled staff members. More than 20 languages are spoken at Bull's manufacturing plants, including American Sign Language and Khmer, the official language of Cambodia.

"As corny as it may sound, we put the focus of our company on our people," says Beck. "What we've benefited from is the uplift of 1,000 people

as a second language for its employees, as well as a self-paced general education curriculum that includes reading, writing, math, and GED preparation.

"Some of our programs enhance job skills; others enhance the individual," Beck says. "We're convinced that in either case both Bull Worldwide Information Systems and its employees benefit."

Highly trained technicians use the latest equipment and leading-edge technologies (above left).

Paying particular attention to cost, quality, delivery, and service, Bull Electronics can help customers gain a competitive advantage (above right).

HE WORLD'S FASTEST MICROPROCESSOR — OR COMPUTER on a chip—isn't built in California's Silicon Valley; it's made in Massachusetts. Only 35 miles west of Boston is one of the best-kept secrets in the state. Here on a hilltop, a brand-new, $450 million facility is turning out microprocessors with capabilities that boggle the imagination. Hardly bigger than

a thumbnail, Digital's Alpha AXP chips contain over 9.3 million transistors and process information at up to 1 billion instructions per second.

These chips are not only faster than anything else on the market, but they handle a larger amount of data with each cycle. Conventional microprocessors handle 32 bits, or units, of infor-

For example, cable television companies are using Alpha-Generation technology to create "commercial channels" on their existing cable networks. Businesses are using these ready-made multimedia networks to communicate with their customers and suppliers. Other cable operators are now test marketing new video-on-demand services that give cus-

the growth of this Massachusetts-based company.

When Digital was founded in 1957, computers were million-dollar machines locked in glass rooms and attended by a priesthood of data processing specialists. Scientists, engineers, and other users had to take their work to the data processing center.

The minicomputer changed that.

Digital's first computer system, the PDP-1, featured a startling innovation. It was the first commercially produced system to feature a video screen that, together with a keyboard, enabled the user to interact directly with the computer. This was very different from the IBM punched card technology of the time.

The PDP-1 was the first computer that allowed the user to play video games. Users could even write their own programs and get an immediate response from the computer.

Interactive computing caught on.

And the small, inexpensive systems that made it possible became known as minicomputers, a concept that Digital pioneered. These easy-to-use systems brought computing out of the data processing center and into offices, departments, and laboratories where accountants, business analysts, engineers, scientists, and laboratory technicians could access and process information at their desks and "network" with colleagues.

The minicomputer was the driving force behind Digital's growth from the 1960s through

Hardly bigger than a thumbnail, Digital's Alpha AXP chips (top) contain over 9.3 million transistors and process information at up to 1 billion instructions per second. The Alpha-Generation family of products is playing a key role in the development of new applications that require the added capacity that only a 64-bit system can provide.

mation at a time. Alpha AXP chips handle 64 bits of information at a time. Where a 32-bit system can process or track enough data to fill 98 file cabinets, a 64-bit chip can manage enough information to fill 422,315,569,369 file cabinets.

With the best price/performance in the industry, Digital's AlphaGeneration systems have already accounted for more than $1 billion in sales and are playing a key role in the development of new applications that require the added capacity that only a 64-bit system can provide.

tomers instant access to whole libraries of motion pictures that they can view whenever they want.

AlphaGeneration systems provide a key capability needed to implement these video-on-demand services. While the current generation of computer systems can memorize just 45 seconds of uncompressed full-motion video, AlphaGeneration systems can track 50 million hours.

DECADES OF INNOVATION

Innovation is not new to Digital. It has been the driving force behind

the 1980s. PDP-8, PDP-11, and later VAX systems became standards against which other computer manufacturers measured performance.

Largely on the success of the minicomputer and Digital's ability to integrate computers into open, enterprise-wide networks, the company grew from a three-man operation in an old woolen mill in Maynard, Massachusetts, to become one of the largest companies based in the Bay State. With over 50 percent of its revenues coming from overseas, Digital is today a $13 billion company with facilities throughout the Greater Boston area and the world.

Digital now does business in over 100 countries and develops and manufactures products in the Americas, Europe, and the Pacific Rim. Building on its core competencies in software, systems, networks, and services, Digital—working with its business part-

ners—provides a complete range of information processing solutions from personal computers to integrated worldwide networks.

A NEW STYLE OF COMPUTING

Capitalizing on these strengths, Digital is emerging as a world leader in client/server computing. This new style of computing answers two very different customer needs.

First, there's the need for personal productivity, the need to access and process information—a need that was met originally by timesharing and later by personal computers. Second, there's the need to gather, organize, and process large volumes of data—a need that was met first by the mainframe and later by peer-to-peer networks and clusters of mid-range systems.

This new style of computing reflects the culture and

values that have made Digital the company it is today. Digital was founded on the belief that computers should be approachable and easy to use—that they should make it easy for people to work together.

Teamwork is particularly important in building open client/server computing environments. Because these environments almost always include hardware and software from a number of different vendors, no company can implement client/server computing by itself. It is a concept that only can be implemented in partnership with the customer and with other computer companies.

Digital is building those partnerships. They are key to the company's future growth, to the continued growth of the computer industry, and to finding new ways to use computer technology to create a better, more productive, and more informed society.

Digital's wafer fabrication facility in Hudson is turning out microprocessors with capabilities that boggle the imagination (above left).

The company provides a complete range of information processing solutions for a variety of application areas (above right).

With the PDP-1, Digital's first computer, the company pioneered interactive computing (below left).

Spacewar, the first interactive video game, was developed on a PDP-1 in 1960 (below right).

The Prudential

WITH ITS SOARING GLASS CEILINGS, STOREFRONT-LINED promenades, sidewalk cafes, inviting benches, and quaint pushcarts, the newly renovated Prudential Center resembles a comfortable town center. Along its avenues, families window-shop, workers hurry to lunch, and tourists take in the atmosphere. ■ The bustling scene is a far cry

Built in 1965, the Prudential Center tower was Boston's first skyscraper. Newly remodeled, it features soaring glass ceilings, storefront-lined promenades, sidewalk cafes, inviting benches, and quaint pushcarts.

from the Prudential Center of just a few years ago. Built in 1965, the complex was the city's first skyscraper and—at the time— on the cutting edge of mixed-use development. It combined retail, office, hotel, residential, and underground parking space in a way that was revolutionary. But by

the early 1980s, "The Pru," as the complex is locally known, had become something of a 1960s relic, retaining the look and characteristics of a bygone era at a time when Boston's retail and office space was becoming more and more sophisticated.

The recent renovation, which is the first phase of a five-part project, expanded the building's retail space to 200,000 square feet and included the installation of a glass arcade ceiling that rises

◄ BRUCE T. MARTIN

◄ WILLIAM HUBER

two stories above ground. The project has brought the amount of retail, office, hotel, and residential space at the Prudential Center to more than 7 million square feet. Future plans for the 26-acre site include two new office towers, three residential condominium buildings, a commercial center, and new streetscapes and open spaces.

The Center is the local flagship property of The Prudential Realty Group, a division of The Prudential Insurance Com-

pany of America. The New Jersey-based company, which began operations in Boston in 1958, is today one of the world's largest financial institutions, employing more than 100,000 people worldwide and managing $373 billion in assets.

The Prudential Realty Group is among the leading real estate investment management organizations in the United States, with a portfolio that includes office, retail, hotel, warehouse, and research-and-development space, as well as land. It oversees 205 office buildings across the country, which contain 61 million square feet of office space, 21,200 hotel rooms, and 19.3 million square feet of retail space.

DIVERSE SERVICES FOR A CHANGING NATION
In addition to The Prudential Realty Group, The Prudential has three other major divisions in Boston: Prudential Insurance and Financial Services, Group Operations, and The Prudential Real Estate Affiliates.

The company was founded in Newark, New Jersey, in 1875 by John Dryden. Then called The Prudential Friendly Society, the organization initially sold industrial insurance. For pennies a week, the policies helped pay the funeral expenses of the insured. Today, The Prudential is the largest insurance company in North America.

Prudential Insurance and Financial Services is the company's oldest operation and is also its largest retail business, providing

7 million American households with life, property, casualty, and other insurance products, as well as annuities. The division also receives mutual fund management through Prudential Securities Inc., the fourth-largest brokerage firm in the country.

The Prudential Group Operations handles a wide range of employee benefits products and services, including a full spectrum of managed health care products. In 1951 The Prudential pioneered major medical insurance, which quickly became the industry mode. Today, the company's full range of group health insurance products includes PruCare (its managed care program), as well as major medical, dental, vision, prescription drug, life insurance, and long- and short-term disability plans, which cover more than 20 million people. In 1973 the division expanded into the health care delivery field, assuming management responsibilities for the Rhode Island Group Health Association, one of the nation's first federally qualified health maintenance organizations (HMO). Soon thereafter, The Prudential developed its own HMO and then branched out to offer a range of health care services.

The Prudential Real Estate Affiliates, which is represented by more than 30,000 residential and commercial real estate brokers nationwide, was founded in 1987. Evidence of its rapid growth is the $46.8 billion in property sales the division achieved in 1993. Currently, The Prudential Real Estate Affiliates has 34 offices located throughout Massachusetts, providing residential and commercial sales and leasing services. This subsidiary is a member of Prudential's Residential Services Corporation of America, which also includes Prudential Home Mortgage, Prudential Resource Management, and Lenders Services, Inc.

MAKING A DIFFERENCE IN THE BOSTON COMMUNITY

Although The Prudential is impressive in size and accomplishment, the company has also distinguished itself in its charitable activities throughout Greater Boston.

The Prudential Center, for example, has dedicated itself to helping the city's children. The Center's support of the Summer Jobs for Youth Program of the Private Industry Council has resulted in a number of innovative programs like the multilingual Pru Rangers, who offer information to Boston's international visitors. The Prudential also works with the Grow Clinic for Children at Boston City Hospital, which provides food and counseling for families of children who suffer from malnutrition.

Over the past several years, PruCare has been an annual premier sponsor of the Massachusetts Special Olympics Summer Games, which are held each June in the Boston area.

Social Investments, an area of the company that invests in community social needs, has helped fund low- and mixed-income housing in Boston's Roxbury and South End neighborhoods, as well as the rehabilitation and expansion a community health clinic in Worcester. Among the activities of The Prudential Foundation is the awarding of grants to nonprofit organizations across the country. The Boston area, for example, benefited recently from grants to fund a student health center at Boston High School and to support the Boston Ballet School of Dance.

As diverse as The Prudential's services are, the company is unified by its heritage of solidity and trust. It is a reputation that has been nurtured through more than 100 years of providing financial products and services that respond to the changing needs of people everywhere.

The Prudential Center Christmas tree lighting, attended by thousands of people every year, has become a tradition in Boston.
PHOTOS BY FAYFOTO

Teradyne, Inc.

WHEN ALEX D'ARBELOFF AND HIS PARTNER NICK DeWOLF launched their new electronics company in 1960, they chose an unlikely location: Summer Street, in the heart of downtown Boston, a stone's throw from Jordan Marsh and Filene's. "We lived on Beacon Hill and wanted to be able to walk to work," explains d'Arbeloff. Growth soon forced the new

company, called Teradyne, out of its Summer Street loft and eventually to its present headquarters on Harrison Avenue, still very much downtown. Along the way, Teradyne has become a true force in the electronics industry as the largest manufacturer of the automatic test equipment (ATE) other manufacturers depend on to ensure product quality.

INNOVATIVE TECHNOLOGY AND ENGINEERING EXCELLENCE

The first Teradyne product tested diodes automatically—a revolutionary concept in the early 1960s. A few years later, Teradyne gave the world its first computer-operated transistor and integrated-circuit test systems. In the late 1960s, Teradyne launched a connector

division, which has since become the world's largest merchant supplier of backplane systems. In the 1970s the company expanded its product line to include circuit-board test systems, and it entered the telecommunications business with a revolutionary new system for testing telephone lines. Today about 50 million of the world's telephone lines are tested daily

Teradyne's headquarters is located near the hub of Boston's highway and mass transit networks.

with Teradyne equipment.

Although Teradyne is hardly a household word among the general public, every major electronics manufacturer in the world recognizes the name as synonymous with engineering excellence, for Teradyne's test systems must stay a step ahead of the devices they are called on to test. The accurate, economic testing of a "computer on a chip," for example, requires some of the most demanding technology found in electronics.

As a charter member of a cooperative industry effort to improve quality, Teradyne has taken a leading role in establishing a culture of continuous improvement. To date, more than 1,000 Quality Improvement Teams have been formed at Teradyne, and most of the company's employees have been trained in the methodology of Total Quality Management. The company's dedication to quality has earned it a number of industry awards, as well as several ISO 9000 certifications.

In Teradyne's core business, the production of integrated-circuit test systems, the company is in an enviable position as the only supplier with major market positions in all three sectors: VLSI logic, memory, and linear/mixed-signal testing. The company's best-selling system, the A500 series of linear/mixed-signal

testers, commands a 40 percent share of its market. The A500 is produced by Teradyne's Industrial/Consumer Division, based in the Harrison Avenue headquarters building in Boston.

AN INNER-CITY COMPANY WITH A GLOBAL PERSPECTIVE

Through its direct sales force, Teradyne conducts business in every region of the industrial world. Company Vice President Fred Van Veen notes that, unlike many other companies, Teradyne has never had a separate export division. Instead, the whole organization has maintained a global perspective, an approach that matches the multinational character of Teradyne's major customers. Teradyne has a strong presence in Europe, Japan, and the Pacific Rim. Overall, almost half of the company's sales come from outside the United States.

Yet, despite its global reach, Teradyne's headquarters remains anchored in downtown Boston. The company's two large downtown buildings are near the center of Greater Boston's highway and mass transit networks, and Teradyne has been able to recruit a stable and dedicated workforce from both urban and outlying areas. Proximity to Logan International Airport is an added convenience for Teradyne's well-

traveled employees, while it also facilitates the swift shipment of the company's products to the far corners of the world.

Teradyne's long commitment to Boston has pumped billions of dollars into the region over the years, helping thousands of families pay mortgages, educate children, and enhance their lives. Teradyne has also played its part in supporting various charitable and civic organizations.

Looking to the future, strong market positions, a heavy commitment to research and development, and an emphasis on Total Quality Management are seen as the keys to the continued success of this pioneering company that has chosen to make its home in downtown Boston.

The combinational circuit-board test system was a Teradyne innovation in 1980. The latest edition of the Boston-produced system is the L300 series.

Abt Associates Inc.

WHAT DO CONTACT LENSES, FOOD STAMPS, AND EARLY childhood education have in common? Ordinarily very little, except that Abt Associates Inc. has worked on aspects of each during its nearly 30-year history. As one of the nation's largest for-profit government and business research and consulting firms, Abt Associates offers practical solutions to problems encountered by a wide variety of clients, including U.S. and foreign government agencies, corporations, foundations, and international organizations. The company is built on the belief that sound information and empirical analysis are the best foundations for decision making in business and government.

OFFERING DIVERSE EXPERTISE

Founded in 1965 in Cambridge by Dr. Clark Abt, the company has achieved an international reputation for using scientific methods of measurement to help solve social and business problems and guide government policy decisions. Since its early focus on government agencies, Abt Associates has grown by diversifying into the business sector. From its Cambridge roots, the company has also expanded geographically, establishing corporate offices in Amherst, Massachusetts; Chicago, Illinois; Bethesda, Maryland; and Moscow, Russia. In addition to its work in the United States, Abt Associates has completed projects in more than 80 countries and currently has projects under way in the former Soviet Union, the Middle East, Latin America, Africa, and Asia.

Today, the company's staff of more than 600 applies its problem-solving expertise to governmental organizations as well as a variety of industries, including financial services, health care, pharmaceuticals, biotechnology, information technology and telecommunications, and agribusiness. Abt Associates offers its government clients a number of services, such as program evaluation, policy analysis, and technical assistance, as well as quality measurement and management. For private-sector clients, it provides quality measurement and management, strategic planning, management consulting, human resources consulting, market research, and new product development services.

The company researches ongoing problems and experimental programs that affect people's daily lives. During its history, Abt Associates has helped design programs that cover the entire

span of human development, from prenatal care and early childhood development to effective classroom teaching techniques, employment programs, and Medicare policy.

"We focus on major social, business, and societal issues,

Appreciation of the environment is reflected in the award-winning design and landscaping of Abt Associates' Cambridge office park facility (below left). The firm has a significant practice in environmental economics and risk analysis.

The firm not only conducts research in child and family development, but also pioneered on-site day care over 25 years ago (below right).

PHOTOS BY LINDA BRYANT

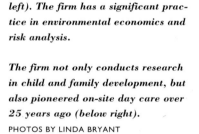

Both the management of the firm and client engagements are carried out by multidisciplinary teams of researchers and consultants (left).

Abt Associates, an employee-owned firm, is a leader in public policy research and strategic business consulting (opposite).

PHOTOS BY LINDA BRYANT

working on the leading edge in both the public and private sectors," says Abt Associates President Wendell Knox. "We are unique not only in scope but also in the depth of our expertise and ability to meet our clients' needs."

PROVIDING INFORMATION THAT GETS RESULTS

Abt Associates is involved in a variety of important projects, from helping pharmaceutical companies license new products to helping government agencies evaluate the feasibility of disseminating welfare benefits electronically. The company continues to be involved in two studies of the long-term effects of silicone breast implants, one for an industry client and the other for a government client. It also has been engaged to manage domestic field trials of AIDS vaccines and other preventive approaches to the disease.

Abt Associates has applied its expertise to studying and evaluating options for health care reform in the United States. "As the nation's health care delivery system becomes increasingly tangled, we are looking to devise solutions to improve it," Knox says. To that end, the company

has performed seminal work on guidelines for pricing hospital and physician services and on options for national health care reform.

Abt Associates has undertaken assignments for many major banks, mutual fund companies, and insurance companies. For these financial services firms—located in New England, throughout the United States, and overseas—Abt has assisted in the development of strategic marketing, developed customer satisfaction programs, and performed a variety of other services that have added measurably both to the effective functioning of the client firms and to their bottom lines.

The company's expertise in fields like financial services and health care delivery systems, along with its competence in the areas of economic development and agriculture, have made its input valuable to emerging economies throughout the world. Abt Associates was awarded a major contract to undertake health care finance and service delivery reform in the New Independent States of the former Soviet Union. "We are helping with the conceptualization and implementation of innovative, market-oriented

financing, management, and organizational initiatives in five demonstration sites," Knox explains. "The goal is to rapidly learn what new approaches achieve the desired improvements, so that lessons may be disseminated broadly in the New Independent States." Abt has additional assignments to help privatize other aspects of this region's economy.

Over the next few years, Abt Associates expects its business to grow globally, as the company increasingly develops clients in reemerging economies like Mexico and South Africa, the newly democratized countries of central and eastern Europe, and the Middle East. And as new industries and technologies emerge, the company will expand its breadth of expertise to consult with decision makers in those fields. Regardless of the client, its specialty, or location, Abt Associates is consistent in the advantages it offers. Whether providing policy guidance to a foreign country or technical assistance to a U.S. start-up, the company's strength lies in its ability to translate information into practical solutions that produce results.

303

BOSTON
PROFILES IN EXCELLENCE

1969	AdvantageHEALTH Corporation
1972	WCVB-TV Boston
1973	Bain & Company, Inc.
1974	Gannett, Welsh & Kotler, Inc.
1980	Stratus Computer, Inc.
1981	GCC Technologies
1981	Le Meridien Boston
1981	Tufts Associated Health Plans, Inc.
1982	Boston Back Bay Hilton
1983	Chipcom Corporation
1983	Voice Systems, Inc.
1984	Preferred Temporaries, Inc.
1984	Viewlogic Systems, Inc.
1985	Avalon Partners, Inc.
1986	Office Environments of New England, Inc.
1986	The Registry, Inc.
1987	Lynch Murphy Walsh & Partners
1987	Wainwright Bank & Trust Company
1988	Fallon Hines & O'Connor, Inc.
1988	High Street Capital Partners, Inc.
1988	Sterling, A Division of Olsten Staffing Services
1989	McFarland Associates, Inc.
1989	Molten Metal Technology
1991	Cambridge Technology Partners

▼ DAVID COMB

WHEN THE FIRST ASTRONAUTS ON THE MOON ANNOUNCED their "one small step for man," it marked a significant moment for modern technology. While less celebrated, the founding of Optronics less than a year before also marked an important milestone in an emerging series of remarkable technology successes.

In 1968 Optronics shipped its first high-resolution scanner for the scientific community. Soon after, the company began manufacturing high-tech film writers and supplied the LandSat satellite with writers that record mapping information beamed to Earth. In the years since that breakthrough, Optronics film writers have produced more than half of all the images sent back to Earth by satellites. Like the many products that have followed, the scanner and the film writers were part of the company's 25-year tra-

The company is headquartered at 7 Stuart Road in the Boston suburb of Chelmsford (near right).

James "Jamie" P. Jacobs is general manager of Optronics (far right).

dition of precision and innovation.

In 1986 Optronics was acquired by Intergraph Corporation of Huntsville, Alabama, the world's largest company dedicated to developing and manufacturing interactive computer graphics and computer-aided design systems. The merger was a win-win situation for both companies: it created greater opportunities to combine Optronics' advanced imaging technologies with Intergraph's efforts in new, untapped markets.

Today, as a division of Intergraph, Optronics is continuing that tradition. Located in the Boston suburb of Chelmsford, Optronics now offers a wide range of products, including laser image-

setters, scanners, photo plotters, and hardware and software options serving the graphic arts market.

TECHNOLOGY FOR THE PRINTER'S ART

Through the mid-1980s, the company continued to apply its film

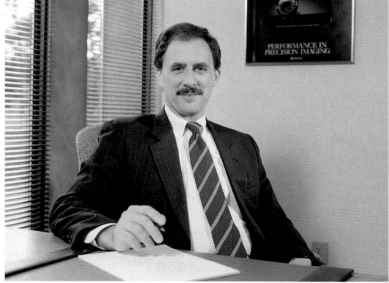

imaging expertise to the production of high-resolution photo plotters for use in digital cartography and computer-aided design and engineering systems.

Starting in 1988, Optronics began applying that same expertise to developing high-precision imaging technology to improve many of the processes used to create high-quality printing. Focusing on the complex, labor-intensive phase of printing known as "prepress," Optronics introduced its ColorSetter 2000 laser imagesetter. For the first time, a product was available that permitted high-quality film separations—the elements needed to create vibrant colors in the

finished printing—directly from computer-generated files, saving both time and money. Today's ColorSetter imagesetting products are PostScript compatible, the de facto standard for sharing graphic arts data via computer. Each ColorSetter features an

external, rotating-drum, laser imagesetter that uses a blue argon-ion laser to place up to 4,000 dots per linear inch, creating precise and accurate halftone images for the printing process on medium- to large-format imaging areas. A drum imagesetter product line consisting of two internal-drum imagesetters, the DeskSetter 3000 and the DeskSetter Express, completes Optronics' product offerings for the small-format market.

The newest addition to the ColorSetter line is IntelliProof, a high-resolution, large-format digital color proof system. Setting a new technology standard, this innovative product produces color separation films and fully screened

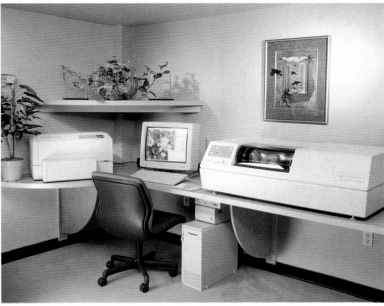

has introduced DP/Studio, a workstation for image manipulation, page assembly, color correction, and retouching. Optronics also produces the Client Object Storage and Management Server (COSMOS) to help customers organize text, images, video, and business information using industry-standard computer technology and advanced relational databases.

In May 1994, history was made—thanks largely to Optronics and its technological breakthroughs—when the first issue of *Sports Car International* magazine rolled off the presses in Kentucky—printed entirely "computer-to-plate."

In the decades since the historic moon walk, new technology has continued to bring about events previously thought impossible. Thanks to a longtime commitment to innovation, Optronics and its parent company, Intergraph, have helped make many of these breakthroughs a reality, changing the computer imaging and printing worlds forever.

color proofs. Quality screened color proofing is essential to the success of any computer-to-plate technology.

Optronics also set a new standard in 1990 when it introduced ColorGetter—the world's first tabletop, rotating-drum, photomultiplier tube (PMT) scanner for desktop color prepress. Just as advanced is today's ColorGetter 3 family of scanners. With over 8,000 lines per linear inch of resolution, the products provide customers with the performance and dynamic range of conventional, high-end scanners at a more affordable price. Optronics also has developed unique software to enhance the productivity of ColorGetter.

In addition, the company

WCVB-TV HAS BEEN HAILED BY MANY AS THE BEST local television station in America. It is a perennial ratings powerhouse in Boston and has, over the years, become the country's most honored television station. ■ But there's more to this New England institution than top-rated newscasts and award-winning programs. Since it first went on the air in 1972, WCVB-TV's goal has been to serve the needs of the community. In fact, everything Channel 5 does can be traced back to the guiding principle of its founders—a group of citizens who believed strongly in the station's responsibility "to serve the public interest." WCVB-TV is supported in this philosophy by its owner, The Hearst Corporation, an international media industry leader with a diversified array of television, cable, print, and radio interests.

WHERE THE NEWS COMES FIRST

The core of the station's commitment to the community has always been NewsCenter 5, widely recognized for its outstanding news coverage. Always a source of comprehensive coverage of late-breaking news and local events, NewsCenter 5 has been honored with broadcasting's most prestigious awards, including the national Edward R. Murrow award for overall excellence, the DuPont-Columbia University Silver Baton, and several George Foster Peabody awards, often called the "Pulitzer Prize of broadcasting."

Over the years, WCVB-TV's quality news programming has been expanded significantly. Each weekday begins with two hours of the top-rated "EyeOpener" newscast. NewsCenter 5 "Midday" broadcasts a half hour of news, followed by an hour and a half of news in the early evening and an additional 35 minutes at 11:00 p.m. Even on the weekend, News-Center 5 provides coverage at noon and at 6:00 and 11:00 in the evening. WCVB-TV provides national and international coverage to New England viewers through ABC News, America's most watched, most respected news organization.

A pioneer in American television, Channel 5 became the first in the nation to closed-caption broadcast its news for the deaf and hearing-impaired in 1986. Stations around the country quickly followed suit.

GOING THE EXTRA MILE

Also unique to Channel 5 is "Chronicle," which premiered in 1982 and is New England's only locally produced nightly newsmagazine. Through the years, "Chronicle" has continued to win awards and viewership and has been shown nationally on cable's A&E and Travel networks. Segments include an interesting mix of local, national, and international stories. A perennial favorite with viewers is the "Main Streets and Back Roads" feature, which cele-

Dick Albert, Natalie Jacobson, Chet Curtis, and Mike Lynch deliver the day's news, weather, and sports to New England viewers each weeknight on NewsCenter 5's top-rated newscasts from the station's state-of-the-art studio.

brates the local landscape and people of New England. And, when the day's top news story warrants extended coverage, "Chronicle" responds with more perspective.

At a time when few stations dedicate their resources to local programming, Channel 5's commitment to producing local documentaries and specials remains as strong as ever. For example, the station created "In Dark Houses," an in-depth documentary on the Massachusetts prison system, and "Beside the Golden Door," an insightful look at U.S. immigration policy. In addition, WCVB-TV produces and broadcasts a host of other local programming specials on topics ranging from politics to sports, from "town meetings" to music.

Channel 5 has also originated special programming for children, including the award-winning, wonderfully creative "A Likely Story," which emphasizes reading through storytelling. "Jabberwocky" (which went on the air shortly after the station was founded), "Crumpet Corners," "Use Your Smarts," "Catch a Rainbow," and "Captain Bob" are also examples of WCVB-TV's award-winning programs for young people.

WCVB-TV also has a proud tradition of outstanding public affairs programming, with weekly shows such as "Cityline," a forum for Boston's diverse urban communities. "In Good Faith" offers wide-ranging discussions of religious and moral issues, while the political and social trends of the day are the focus of "Five on 5."

COMMUNITY LEADERSHIP AND OUTREACH

Channel 5's commitment to the community also includes supporting organizations like the Muscular Dystrophy Association, the Massachusetts Coalition for the Homeless, the United Cerebral Palsey Association, the Genesis Fund, and many others. Also, the station's 90-minute telethons for the Boston Symphony Orchestra, the Boston Ballet, and the Boston Public Library have raised hundreds of thousands of dollars for these important New England institutions.

WCVB-TV is also known for its extensive public service campaigns, which have gone on to national syndication and are now reaching millions of American homes in cities across the country. Three of its most successful efforts include "Great Expectations: The Education Project"; "Family Works!," which supports and celebrates family values; and "A World of Difference," a campaign to combat prejudice.

Each of these projects included program specials, some featuring nationally known stars such as Shelley Long, Christopher Reeve, and Tyne Daly. Other components of these campaigns included news segments, public service announcements, and special events. The legacy of "A World of Difference" was a study guide that was distributed throughout public and private schools in Massachusetts. When originally broadcast, this program was declared an exemplary private-sector initiative by the White House.

Other community outreach programs at the station have included "Don't Be Pushed," an anti-drug campaign, and "Project Shelter," an effort to help the homeless.

SPECIAL EVENT SPECIALISTS

Special event coverage is also a hallmark of Channel 5's programming. For example, the station broadcasts the world-famous Boston Pops Fourth of July concert to local audiences and simulcasts the event nationally on the A&E Network. WCVB-TV also broadcasts the Holiday at Pops concert, the Boston Marathon, the Boston Sleigh Bell Parade, and the New England Airshow.

The Hearst Corporation has based Hearst Broadcasting Productions at WCVB-TV's Needham studios. This full-service television and corporate video production company develops and produces high-quality programming for a wide range of broadcast, cable, corporate, and commercial clients.

Through quality newscasts, local programs, and public service campaigns that matter, WCVB-TV enjoys an unrivaled standing in its community and in its industry.

Over the years, WCVB-TV has been honored with numerous local and national awards for its distinguished news operation, its unprecedented array of local programs, and its heralded public service efforts. It has been called the best local television station in the country.

THE OFFICES OF BAIN & COMPANY, A LEADING INTERNAtional strategy consulting firm, buzz with excitement. People move quickly. Conversations are to the point. And employees talk about an addictive energy in the office. A fast-paced organization owned by its officers and employees, Bain is in relentless pursuit of excellence for its clients,

employees, and community. This has held true since 1973, when the firm was founded by Bill Bain. He chose Boston as the home for his new company because of the city's vibrant academic community and its attractive quality of life. The firm has remained headquartered in Boston throughout its global expansion to 23 offices in 18 countries.

Bain's corporate mission—"to help our clients create such

client interactions," says Bain Chairwoman Orit Gadiesh, "is Bain's commitment to discovering the truth, looking it square in the eye, and sticking to it even when it is unpopular."

A PARTNERSHIP WITH CLIENTS

Bain & Company does far more than simply present its recommendations and move on. The company

Worldwide Managing Partner Tom Tierney. "Then we roll up our sleeves and do whatever we can to help them succeed."

The professionals at Bain are passionate "crusaders," untiring in their efforts to achieve three key objectives for their clients: improving bottom-line results, creating a significant increase in market value, and enhancing organizational capability. "The quality of our commitment and its extent are rare in this industry," adds Gadiesh. This partnership method toward problem solving is extremely creative and rewarding for all involved. Not only do the client employees assume ownership of the collaborative plans, but they also support and participate in the implementation process.

A PARTNERSHIP OF EXTRAORDINARY TEAMS

The success of the Bain approach is hard to miss. The firm believes in experimentation, innovation, and risk taking. Most of all, it believes in its people. The entrepreneurial, high-energy culture of talented and diverse individuals is the engine that helps drive the success of Bain's clients. The firm's people work as teammates and friends, dedicated to building a unique business and a very special organization.

Through practice specialty assignments in areas such as financial services, telecommunications, manufacturing, and consumer products, they benefit from industry and functional exposure. Through training and client experience, they become experts in

In addition to its headquarters at Two Copley Place in Boston (above), Bain & Company operates 23 offices in 18 countries.

high levels of economic value that together we set new standards of excellence in our respective industries"—has also remained constant. This focus on creating tangible results for its worldwide clients has been Bain's guiding principle for more than two decades and has kept client relations fresh and lines of communication open. "What comes through in our team and

prides itself on working in partnership with clients, using a team approach to help design, integrate, and implement strategic insights that create lasting economic value. This practice of working *with* clients—not just for them—continues to be a cornerstone of the firm's philosophy. "We look for client partners who truly want to win in the marketplace," says

A fast-paced organization owned by its officers and employees, Bain is in relentless pursuit of excellence for its clients, employees, and community.

designing strategies and creating value for the client.

Knowing that its people are responsible for the company's outstanding success, Bain is continually supporting the personal and professional development of its team members. The company invests in many progressive initiatives and social activities for its employees, and realizes the importance of staying in touch with former employees through its active Alumni Program. This investment creates a very intense level of loyalty and has been instrumental in the development of a consulting and administrative staff who are among the most skilled, experienced, and dedicated professionals in the industry.

A PARTNERSHIP WITH THE COMMUNITY

Bain has always been committed to enhancing the community. One of the many exciting organizations

the firm has been privileged to work with is City Year. This unique public/private partnership has enjoyed enormous success and is now cited around the country as the model national service program. Launched in 1988, the program is made up of a diverse corps of young adults between the ages of 17 and 23, each devoting nine months to full-time community service and leadership development. The corps meets every morning and fans out in teams to nonprofit organizations, schools, and government agencies across the city. Bain was a founding sponsor of the City Year initiative and has contributed to its growth in many ways by donating teams of volunteers to help design and implement strategic consulting concepts, by participating in the annual day of community service called Serve-a-Thon,™ and by providing financial assistance to help enable the future develop-

ment of the City Year program.

Bain has also invested thousands of professional hours over the last four years in a large-scale volunteer effort with the Boston Public Schools. Many people have participated in the program by working after hours analyzing student performance, calling parents and teachers to collect feedback on current and future school programs, and assessing opportunities to create a better environment for educational development. Those who have contributed to this process have found their efforts to be extremely rewarding.

For over two decades, Bain & Company has been delivering extraordinary results and providing excellent service for its clients. But in its endeavors, the firm has never forgotten its strong commitment to its employees and to the community at large.

Gannett Welsh & Kotler, Inc.

HE PAST DECADE HAS BEEN A TUMULTUOUS ONE FOR investors: big gains in the stock market coupled with the crash of 1987, the late-1980s recession, and a drop in real estate prices. But the Boston investment firm of Gannett Welsh & Kotler, Inc., by combining years of excellent investment performance, experience, and disciplined

investment strategy, has maintained consistent results for its clients.

"By investing with perspective and reason over the years, we have avoided unnecessary volatility and have maximized the long-term benefits of good investment ideas," says President Harold Kotler. "This approach has resulted in excellent performance for our clients."

Senior Vice President Edward White, director of the equity department, states, "An important ingredient of our success is something that we call thoughtfulness. In a rapidly changing en-

vironment, markets tend to behave erratically. The results are often unpredictable in the short term. Clients can react hastily to external events. As a thoughtful adviser, we view each market condition in the context of long-term fundamentals." That means an overall investment strategy emphasizing

Combining years of excellent investment performance, experience, and disciplined investment strategy, the firm and its staff work diligently to ensure consistent results for clients.
PHOTOS BY RICHARD MANDELKORN

balance and diversification. "While each of our investment programs stands on its own," Kotler adds, "we add value to our clients' portfolios by working with them to develop balanced investment strategies to meet their objectives."

FOUNDED TO FILL A NEED

Since 1974, Gannett Welsh & Kotler has been committed to providing investment products and quality service to high net worth individuals and families.

Big investment companies too often neglect individual investors in favor of larger corporate clients. But Gannett Welsh & Kotler has earned its reputation by paying close attention to individuals and families. "We recognize that a critical part of our success has been the close personal relationships that we have established with our clients," states Executive Vice President Benjamin Gannett, cofounder of the firm. "We believe that our brand of service will, in the coming decade, be increasingly valuable. Personal service will decline as bank trust departments consolidate and mutual fund companies become more efficient at serving the masses, not the individual."

The company prides itself on the quality of service it provides. "We are dedicated professionals, and our primary objective is achieving our clients' goals," says Nancy Angell, director of the municipal bond department. To that end, the firm's principal executives—Gannett, Kotler, White, Jackson Welsh, and Angell—are deeply involved in the business and are always readily available for consultation.

CONSISTENT RETURNS

Through careful research and commitment to quality investments, Gannett Welsh & Kotler has had superior results. Since 1988 the company has outper-

formed industry indexes in the taxable bond and equity markets. And in the municipal bond market, it has outperformed its benchmark since 1980.

Such success has not gone unnoticed. When Gannett Welsh & Kotler started 20 years ago, it managed $8 million for 10 clients. Today, the company manages approximately $1 billion for 675 clients throughout the United States. As a result of its relationships and exposure in the consultant community, the firm has expanded its client base in other areas like foundations, endowments, pensions, and profit-sharing plans. But its main focus has been—and continues to be—the management of individual accounts.

Gannett Welsh & Kotler achieves consistent returns by doing its homework. According to White, rigorous research is used to uncover opportunities and limit volatility. "We think it's very important to understand the characteristics of the businesses we invest in," he says. "A lot of people base investment decisions on numerical indicators, but too few people spend the time getting to know the companies they invest in. We believe that, in the long run, if the company is healthy, it will be able to withstand economic difficulties and create value."

The firm's investment decisions emphasize balance and stability. "We're always straddling our position to maximize the consistency of returns," says Welsh, director of the taxable bond department. The firm does not make investments based on speculation, or by thinking it knows something nobody else does. Instead, Gannett Welsh & Kotler looks at the long-term viability of each investment and then makes its decision based on a disciplined approach. "By taking the long view, we think we can enhance returns without compromising capital," Kotler adds.

GIVING SOMETHING BACK

A big part of the company culture at Gannett Welsh & Kotler is philanthropic involvement in the community. Members of the firm are encouraged to participate in charitable organizations, and most of them do. The Wang Center, the Jewish Big Brother and Big Sister Association of Greater Boston, the New England Home for Little Wanderers, and the Special Olympics are just a few of the programs and organizations that benefit from company donations and employee involvement.

It is all part of a company philosophy that emphasizes close relationships with clients and the community. In a time of industry consolidation, with personal service often taking a backseat to efficiency, Gannett Welsh & Kotler believes that its proven business style will better serve clients in the coming decade and beyond.

The firm's management team includes (standing, from left) Jeanne M. Skettino, senior vice president operations; Edward B. White, senior vice president equities; Nancy G. Angell, senior vice president municipals; (sitting, from left) Benjamin H. Gannett, executive vice president, treasurer; Jackson O. Welsh, senior vice president corporates; and Harold G. Kotler, president.

Stratus Computer, Inc.

CHARGE A MEAL OR A HOTEL BILL. MAKE AN AIRLINE reservation. Use the phone. File a medical claim. Trade stock. Buy a lottery ticket. ■ You could be in Boston or Las Vegas, Tokyo or London, but chances are your transaction will be handled by a Stratus computer system. ■ Stratus Computer, Inc., founded in 1980, designs, manufactures,

It might be a single, multimillion-dollar electronic funds transfer, or a rush of trading at the close of the business day. Banks, brokerages, and other financial services companies look to Stratus to keep the money moving (right).

markets, and services a broad range of continuously available computer systems and application solutions. These systems and solutions give Stratus customers the ability to run the most important parts of their businesses while maintaining the highest level of computer and application uptime, which in turn helps them give better service to their own customers.

Since 1980 Stratus has turned its exclusive focus on the critical end of business to the advantage of companies around the world and in a wide range of industries. The 2,600 Stratus employees—based in company headquarters in the Boston suburb of Marlborough and at other sites worldwide—are uniquely trained and experienced to work with customers in developing solutions for industries as diverse as financial services, hospitality, health care, telecommunications, travel/transportation, manufacturing, government, and others.

Telecommunications companies around the globe rely on Stratus solutions to give their customers a new range of reliable services.

The company's focus on this growing and crucial segment of the business world has fueled steady growth even while the rest of the computer industry has struggled through difficult financial terrain.

"Our industry is still in a period of very difficult change," says William E. Foster, chief executive officer and a founder of Stratus. "The importance of keeping up technologically has now been equaled by the importance of increased efficiency in designing, manufacturing, and selling our products. We've already taken a number of steps that will maintain

our technological leadership even in the face of rapid change."

SETTING NEW STANDARDS
Stratus offers a high-performance, flexible product family that has brought a new standard of availability to businesses. Stratus

systems are designed to enable businesses to bring operations on-line quickly, protect their investments in other vendors' equipment, run critical operations 24 hours a day, 365 days a year, and expand or enhance them as market or business conditions demand.

A new day begins at Stratus' corporate headquarters, located in Marlborough, a western suburb of Boston.

PHOTOS BY STEVE DAHLGREN

The company also offers a choice of operating systems, industry-standard communications, networking, and distributed computing capabilities. Through its own subsidiaries and third-party partners, Stratus provides a portfolio of industry-specific application software, development platforms, and messaging middleware.

But even the most foolproof solutions need safeguarding. To assure that customers' operations stay in business, Stratus pioneered a worldwide network of Customer Assistance Centers. The centers are run by service professionals who can resolve system and application software problems and dispatch replacement parts, which customers can easily insert into their systems without interrupting operations.

And Stratus' remote on-line service—where the computer system itself diagnoses any problems and "phones home" to the Customer Assistance Center to alert Stratus—was the first of its kind.

The company maintains manufacturing facilities in Marl-borough and in Dublin, Ireland, and markets its products in more than 50 countries through direct sales operations from the Asia-Pacific region to Europe and North America, and through value-added resellers, systems integrators, and distributors.

COMMUNITY PRIDE

Stratus' involvement in Marlborough and Greater Boston community events and programs has long been a source of pride to the company. Its programs for local suburban and inner-city high school interns and its donations of computer systems and software to local schools underscore the company's commitment to education. Stratus sponsors cultural events, donates money and time to charity, and participates in the United Way and in chamber of commerce activities. It has long fostered a spirit of volunteerism among its employees.

Stratus has also taken the lead in corporate recycling through groundbreaking and dynamic recycling initiatives. The company recycles half of the total waste at its Marlborough headquarters and its manufacturing facilities, diverting 401 tons from the waste stream. Stratus recycles nearly 300,000 pounds of paper annually, has reduced total waste by nearly 11 percent, and has established an environmental park on company property, where trees and landscaping have been paid for by a small percentage of the savings realized from the total recycling effort.

"If corporate America doesn't take the initiative, we'll never solve the problem," says Gary Haroian, president of Stratus. "We believe that we have a responsibility to make a contribution to the environment. And we've proved that you can save money at the same time you're fulfilling your responsibilities."

Wherever there's a critical need, Stratus will be there. The company's systems, for example, assure that 911 calls get through 24 hours a day.

PHOTO BY PETER KASKONS

Le Meridien Boston

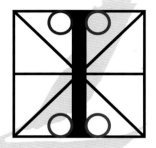

IT WAS ONCE THE PROVERBIAL SMOKE-FILLED ROOM— an inner sanctum for one of Boston's most important financial institutions. But since 1981, the governor's reception room of the Federal Reserve Bank has housed the award-winning Julien restaurant at Le Meridien Boston. And though the grandeur of the historic building remains, today's inhabitants are more likely to be young couples out for an elegant evening than cigar-smoking financial barons.

A SUCCESSFUL BLEND OF OLD AND NEW

The Meridien Hotel Company, based in France, was assigned the management of the 1920s Renaissance Revival-style building in 1981. Prior to that, developers transformed the nine-story granite and limestone structure into a 326-room luxury hotel that adds fresh elements to an old style.

The hotel's Café Fleuri is a good example of the artful mix of old and new. The 180-seat restaurant adjoins the historic part of the structure, but sits beneath a soaring, six-story atrium that connects the hotel to the contemporary One Post Office Square tower. Le Meridien also has added three new floors at the top of the hotel. Enclosed by a glass mansard roof that rakes back from the street, the addition is barely noticeable from

below. The design includes slanted glass walls that provide natural light and downtown views in many of the hotel's rooms.

While Le Meridien is certainly known for its history and beauty, it is perhaps better known for its food. The hotel houses the popular French restaurant Julien, which sits beneath gilded, 18-foot coffered ceilings. Julien is overseen by consulting chef Marc Haeberlin, whose restaurant in Illhaeusern, France—L'Auberge de L'Ill—has held the *Michelin Guide*'s coveted three-star rating since 1962.

Le Meridien's Café Fleuri serves a Sunday brunch that is renowned throughout Boston. Patés, omelets, seafood, baked goods, mimosas, and dessert crepes are just a few of the delights included in the buffet-style meal. *Boston Magazine* has named the brunch "Best in Boston" every year since 1985. Café Fleuri also offers an all-you-can-eat "Chocolate Bar" on Saturday afternoons from September to May that features cakes, tortes, mousses, cookies, brownies, pies, fondue, and other dessert items.

SERVING BUSINESS AND LEISURE TRAVELERS

The majority of Le Meridien's weekday guests, however, are not there solely for the food. For business travelers, the hotel provides a variety of room types with a full range of business amenities. Each room, for example, has a phone with two lines, voice mail, and a computer hookup. Le Meridien also staffs a business center that offers telex and fax machines, computers, photocopiers, and secretarial and translation services.

On weekends, the hotel is populated largely by tourists and families who enjoy its proximity to such attractions as the New England Aquarium, the Children's Museum, Faneuil Hall, and Boston's waterfront area. Le Meridien offers many services to make family travel easier, like its children's brunch station with pizza, tacos, popcorn, and other "kid-friendly" foods. Children's games, infant toys, cribs, and strollers are also available from the concierge desk.

While Le Meridien's reputation as one of Boston's premier luxury hotels is well established, management and staff are not resting on their laurels. Instead, they keep a critical eye on the hotel and its services, always striving to refine what they offer their guests.

Formerly the Federal Reserve Bank, Le Meridien Boston is today a 326-room luxury hotel that adds fresh elements to an old style (right).

The hotel houses the award-winning French restaurant Julien, which sits beneath gilded, 18-foot coffered ceilings (below).

PHOTOS BY RICHARD MANDELKORN

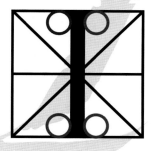

Chipcom Corporation

N THE NOT-SO-LONG-AGO DAYS BEFORE "INTELLIGENT switching hubs"—only the 1980s—managing a sea of personal computers and moving workers and their computers from one office to another was a tedious task. Generally, it involved a technician venturing into a tangle of wires in an out-of-the-way closet, locating the appropriate cable,

and physically reconnecting it to a new port.

Such a scenario is no longer the case. A local area network (LAN) built on Chipcom Corporation's hubs makes linking and moving personal computer and workstation users as easy as double-clicking on an icon and dragging it to a new location—a technology the company refers to as "port-switching."

That simple innovation has brought 11-year-old Chipcom great success. Established in the Greater Boston area in 1983, the company went public in 1991 and has since been on an upward trajectory, finishing 1993 with an impressive $160.5 million in revenue. Also that year, *Inc.* magazine named Chipcom to its list of the 100 fastest-growing public companies. *Forbes* called it one of the 200 best small companies. And *Business Week* included Chipcom on its list of the 100 best "hot growth" companies in America.

In the early part of 1994, the business press accolades continued for Chipcom. The company was ranked number 16 on *Financial World* magazine's list of "America's Best 200 Growth Companies" and number 81 on *Fortune* magazine's list of the 100 fastest-growing companies in the United States.

DESIGNED FOR EASE AND FLEXIBILITY

Chipcom designs, manufactures, and markets "fault-tolerant" intelligent switching hubs and related products that offer unparalleled flexibility. The company's products are sold worldwide to large

organizations in a variety of industries and are designed to let people who work together—either in a single building or spread out in different locations—connect and manage their computers easily. Even systems that use different network protocols, such as Ethernet, Token Ring, or Fiber Distributed Data Interface, may be linked with the Chipcom system.

Chipcom's versatile hubs can be used by a variety of customers, ranging from large, single-building organizations to huge companies with multiple locations. The company's products also are designed to be upgradable so that customers are not forced to abandon their previous investments in existing technology when they need to expand.

Another important aspect of all Chipcom systems is that they are "fault-tolerant." That means they will continue to function even if one part of the system goes down. As an example, a Chipcom representative recalls one time a visitor asked the company's net-

work manager what would happen if a key cable were unplugged. With characteristic confidence in Chipcom's products, the network manager responded by pulling the cable and showing his startled visitor that the system was indeed still running.

Throughout the company's operation, its 700 employees take pride in the quality of their work and, in fact, helped author Chipcom's values statement. It reads, in part, "We strive to set the highest standards for delivering quality products and services by knowing our customers and valuing their needs . . . We show respect for our customers, our business partners, and each other by being ethical, open, honest, and fair."

In a competitive industry that is constantly growing and changing, it's that level of dedication that has brought Chipcom Corporation more than a decade of success.

Rob Held is president and CEO of Chipcom Corporation.

The company's corporate headquarters is located in Southborough, Massachusetts (top left).

The ONcore Switching System is a next-generation intelligent "super hub" that provides customers with a graceful migration to high-speed switched networks, while protecting existing investments in hardware, software, and wiring (top right).

GCC Technologies

GCC Technologies manufactures high-resolution monochrome laser printers for business and graphic arts applications. Known throughout the computer industry for the quality of its products and service, GCC's real expertise is its ability to assess customer needs and fulfill them with innovative products.

GCC's SelectPress Printer line offers high-resolution, large-format printing to graphic arts and electronic prepress customers. The company's Elite monochrome laser printer product line is designed for office work-group customers. All GCC laser printers are fully networkable and support PostScript and PCL emulations for cross-platform office applications. GCC's standard EtherTalk solutions offer high-performance networking for high-speed printing. In addition, GCC offers a variety of specialty printers, including WideWriter 360, a large-format ink jet; WriteMove II, a portable printer for the Apple PowerBook portable computer; and ColorFast, a digital film recorder for color presentations.

From its origins as a small start-up company that developed video games to the multi-million-dollar enterprise it is today, GCC has demonstrated repeatedly its ability to design and deliver innovative products.

GCC was founded in 1981 by (from left) Chief Operating Officer John Tylko, Chairman Doug Macrae, and Chief Executive Officer Kevin Curran.

From Video Games to Computers

Headquartered in Bedford, Massachusetts, GCC was founded in 1981 by Chief Executive Officer Kevin Curran and his MIT classmates Doug Macrae and John Tylko. GCC started as a video game manufacturer, developing an enhancement for Atari's "Missile Command" and selling it as an upgrade kit to arcade operators. The company's next product was the coin-operated video game "Ms. Pac-Man," which was produced by Bally Manufacturing in 1982 and became the best-selling

arcade game in history. GCC went on to develop a total of 58 innovative consumer electronics products over the next three years that generated over $800 million in revenue for Atari and Bally. Among these was the Atari 7800 game system and related software introduced by Atari in 1984 and marketed successfully for several years.

In 1984, demonstrating the strong market-driven instincts that have made it successful, GCC decided to change its strategic direction. The company began to design products for the newly introduced Apple Macintosh computer. Although Curran, Macrae, and Tylko appreciated the computer's graphical user interface and believed it had a strong future,

they felt that the original Macintosh had serious limitations in speed and performance, which hindered its acceptance in the business world. Capitalizing on this drawback, GCC introduced the first internal hard disk drive for the Macintosh in 1985. This innovative product, named Hyper-Drive, was wildly successful and, according to many industry observers, helped save the Macintosh from oblivion.

Another of GCC's firsts was the personal laser printer (PLP), the first QuickDraw laser printer for the Macintosh. The PLP and its software were so well designed that, toward the end of the PLP's life and over six years after its introduction, it received an award for being the best low-

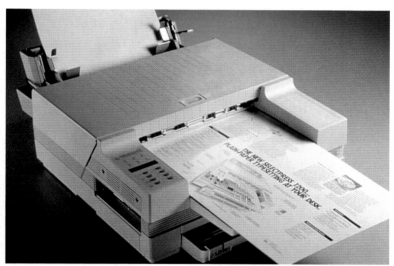

end Macintosh printer in the marketplace. These products helped GCC establish its reputation as a developer of well-engineered, high-quality, and high-performance products in the computer peripheral market.

TOP-OF-THE-LINE COMPUTER PRINTERS

GCC soon began to use that spirit of innovation and commitment to quality to develop and manufacture a full product line of printers for Macintosh computers. These new products provided users with more features than comparable Apple machines—but at the same or lower cost. Today, GCC offers state-of-the-art, award-winning PostScript printers that operate in complex networking environments, allowing them to be used simultaneously by Macintosh, Windows, and UNIX users.

GCC's printers are particularly popular in the desktop publishing, graphic arts, and electronic prepress markets. The unique capabilities of the company's printers, such as edge-to-edge printing, make possible a variety of new applications. With a GCC SelectPress 1200, a marketing department can produce a prepress proof of a brochure before sending the final version to a print shop.

And for customers with smaller budgets, GCC offers the SelectPress 600 and 600 Pro—600 dpi versions of the SelectPress 1200 with fewer features and a more affordable price. These printers have received industry-wide recognition, and the Select-Press 600 Pro was recently rated "Best of Class" in the product review in September 1994's issue of *MacUser* magazine.

GCC's Elite product line is designed for office work-group environments that demand efficient, reliable printing over networks. Its excellent paper-handling capabilities make the Elite printer an ideal candidate for the business community. The Elite line provides true cross-platform connectivity for outstanding performance in almost any network environment.

GCC's commitment to the customer does not end with the manufacturing of high-quality products. The quality of the service offered by GCC to its customers, dealers, and end users is top-notch in the industry. *MacUser* reviewed GCC's technical support and reported that "it's a pleasure to have calls handled by sales reps who are customer-friendly and know their company's products inside and out . . .GCC's reps answered all of our questions quickly and correctly."

The basis for GCC's success is a talented and creative workforce skilled in all areas of the business. Drawing upon the many outstanding universities in the Boston area, the company continues to recruit highly trained employees to help achieve its future growth. In the United States, GCC products are sold through a network of resellers complemented by factory-direct sales and service offered from the company's headquarters. GCC has an installed base of more than 300,000 users worldwide and operates subsidiaries in Great Britain, France, Germany, the Netherlands, and Canada. The company has thrived for more than a decade by setting the industry standard for innovation and by offering its customers a superior product at a reasonable price.

The SelectPress 1200 (left) produces smooth, sharp type and graphics with resolution of 1,200 dots per inch on paper sizes up to 12 inches by 19 inches, allowing users to print "full bleed" on tabloid-sized pages with crop and registration marks.

Quality and customer satisfaction are key words at GCC.

◄ WEBB CHAPPELL

Tufts Associated Health Plans, Inc.

UFTS HEALTH PLAN WAS FOUNDED AS A HEALTH MAINtenance organization (HMO) in 1981 by Dr. Morton Madoff, dean of the Tufts University School of Medicine. On its founding, Tufts became the first managed care company to involve all constituents—doctors, hospitals, and consumers—in its governance. This innovative spirit has

continued through the organization's history and has placed it as a leader in the delivery of health care. In 1986 Tufts reached another milestone when it became the first HMO in the nation to offer a fitness benefit that automatically enrolls members in the participating fitness center of their choice.

Recently, Tufts played a pioneering role as the first in eastern Massachusetts to offer a zero-premium health plan for people with Medicare. Called Secure Horizons® Tufts Health Plan for Seniors, the plan arranges for health care services to senior

Tufts Health Plans is committed to the private practice physician and is unique among health care organizations in the amount of involvement physicians have in making decisions.

LOU JONES

citizens. According to Dr. Harris Berman, president and CEO of Tufts Associated Health Plans, Inc., "We recognized the need for a health plan that offers comprehensive coverage with minimal out-of-pocket cost."

Tufts was also the first HMO in Massachusetts to establish a point-of-service (POS)

plan, called Total Health Plan, which allows members to choose between two levels of coverage each time they need care. Total Health Plan members can opt for the highest level of benefits when care is provided or directed by their Tufts primary care physician. Alternatively, members can go to any other doctor and receive traditional major medical benefits, subject to coinsurance and deductibles. However, by encouraging members to stay within Tufts' provider network, the plan helps control costs.

TAKING A
◄ LEADERSHIP ROLE

Since its founding, Tufts has been a leader in developing innovative ways to serve its members while making the best use of financial resources. Recently, the company initiated a series of steps to reduce paperwork by performing more record-keeping transactions electronically. These efforts speed claims processing while reducing administrative costs. A new, centralized customer relations department has reduced the number of calls being internally transferred by some 30 percent. As a result, members get the answers they need in a timely fashion, and frustration is kept to a minimum.

Tufts has also developed the Medical Outcomes Management Program to control costs and enhance the quality of care. One facet of the program is the Diabetes PORT (Patient Outcome Research Team) Study, conducted through the New England Medical Center with federal funding from the Agency for Health Care Policy

Research. Its goal is to find ways for physicians to better treat those with adult-onset diabetes. Another innovative aspect of the Medical Outcomes Management Program is the Breast Health Promotion Study. Funded by the National Cancer Institute, it looks at how physicians and patients can better interact to increase cancer detection rates.

Tufts also funds and conducts the Cesarean Section Awareness Program, as well as the Healthy Birthday Program, which is for women at risk for delivering preterm babies. In addition, Tufts is looking at ways to improve child immunization rates and to identify the health care needs of adolescents.

Through its ongoing medical management programs, Tufts has been able to reduce the use of hospital inpatient services significantly in recent years— helping to hold the line on premium increases for subscribers and employers. According to the annual member satisfaction survey, 97 percent of HMO members and 95 percent of POS members are satisfied overall with Tufts. A similar percentage of members are pleased with Tufts' customer relations service and rated Tufts' personnel as "knowledgeable."

A COMMITMENT TO
PRIVATE PRACTICE

Tufts is unique among health care organizations in the amount of involvement physicians have in making decisions. For example, one-third of the organization's board members are Tufts participating physicians. Furthermore,

most participating physicians are members of independent practice associations (IPAs), which elect representatives who provide input to Tufts' monthly Central Physician Committee meetings. Tufts even offers help to physicians in improving their office administration and conducts a continuing medical education program.

MEETING A NEED FOR COST CONTAINMENT

In recent years, businesses across the country have been faced with rising workers' compensation insurance costs. Responding to that trend, Tufts created ManagedComp,® an alternative workers' compensation product that is now a key element in the company's plans for the future. Since the product's introduction

in 1989, hundreds of employers have joined ManagedComp, which is currently available in five states.

So successful is Managed-Comp that 99 percent of clients renew each year, and annual premiums managed now total more than $60 million. Furthermore, ManagedComp has topped the industry, boasting the most savings and one of the highest customer satisfaction ratings in the field. In practice, ManagedComp embraces six distinct services: injury prevention, management systems, medical delivery systems, case management, claims management, and information management to control rising workers' compensation costs.

Thanks to Managed-Comp's focus on prevention, employees are injured less often.

But when an employee is injured, the plan arranges for quality care in a monitored setting to ensure that no unnecessary procedures are performed. ManagedComp also focuses on helping employees get back to work. The result is that the average Tufts Managed-Comp client suffers loss ratios of only about 40 percent—compared to a national average of some 70 percent.

When Tufts Health Plans gets involved in health care issues, everybody wins. The biggest winners of all, though, are the families and individuals who know that the Tufts team is working around the clock to promote quality, cost-efficient, professional care.

Tufts Health Plans recently installed state-of-the-art imaging technology to reduce paperwork and put the company on the road to achieving a "paperless" environment (above right).

Helping injured workers return to work and their normal lifestyles is one of the pillars of ManagedComp,® the Tufts Health Plans workers' compensation product (above left).

PHOTOS BY LOU JONES

Boston Back Bay Hilton

ALTHOUGH THE BOSTON BACK BAY HILTON OPENED IN 1982, making it one of the city's newest and most modern hotels, the Hilton name is actually one of the oldest and most respected in the hospitality industry. Founded by Conrad Hilton in 1919 with $5,000 in savings, a $20,000 investment by friends, and a $15,000 loan, the Hilton organization had

In its current configuration, the Boston Back Bay Hilton offers 330 guest rooms, which feature either a king-size bed or two double beds.

grown by the 1950s to a well-known chain of hotels nationwide. Before beginning to accept franchise operators in 1965, the company took over operations of the famous Waldorf-Astoria in New York and also acquired its first properties in Europe.

Today, the company has interests in nearly 100,000 rooms worldwide, making it one of the largest players in the hotel business.

IN THE HEART OF BOSTON

The Boston Back Bay Hilton is continuing the Hilton tradition of service and luxury from the heart of Boston. Located in downtown's historic Back Bay area, next to the recently renovated office and retail space of the Prudential Center, the Boston Back Bay Hilton is the perfect place to stay during business and pleasure trips to the area. In addition, the adjacent John B. Hynes Convention Center makes the Boston Back Bay Hilton a primary host for attendees of major trade shows and meetings. The 860,000-square-foot, state-of-the-art center is the cornerstone of the city's booming convention industry.

The vibrant technology companies of the Route 128 and Interstate 495 beltways are minutes away from the hotel via the Massachusetts Turnpike, which can be accessed only a block away. Also nearby are the research companies and educational institutions of Cambridge, including the Massachusetts Institute of Technology and Harvard University.

Within easy walking distance are other key academic insti-

tutions such as Boston University, Simmons College, New England School of Law, Emerson College, Berklee College of Music, Northeastern University, and New England Conservatory. Some of Boston's most famous hospitals,

such as Brigham and Women's, Beth Israel, Children's, Massachusetts General, and New England Medical Center, are within a two-mile radius—some are even closer. And the financial district, John Hancock Tower, and Copley

Place are easily accessible, as well. Even Logan International Airport is a short four miles away.

Boston's famous Museum of Fine Arts and Symphony Hall are close to the Boston Back Bay Hilton, as are the Isabella Stewart Gardener Museum and the Institute for Contemporary Art. For sightseeing, the Newbury Street area—with its international flavor in retail establishments and restaurants—is a mere two blocks away, as is the elegant turn-of-the-century residential charm of the rest of the Back Bay.

For the convenience of guests, the Blue Trolley sightseeing tour originates at the Boston Back Bay Hilton, providing an easy and convenient way to see the city. Public transportation is also readily accessible. Within a short walking distance are three subway stations, and streetcars provide connections to all parts of Greater Boston. Also close by is Back Bay Station, which provides access to suburban commuter rail as well as Amtrak passenger trains bound for points across the nation.

WORTH THE VISIT

For guests, the Boston Back Bay Hilton is a destination in itself. In its current configuration, the hotel offers 330 guest rooms—16 to a floor—which feature either a king-size bed or two double beds. Thanks to the triangular shape of its 26-story tower, each room has the maximum possible privacy, enhanced by extensive soundproofing. Approximately one-third of all rooms have balconies—more than any other hotel in Boston—and all rooms have windows that can be opened for a breath of fresh New England air. For relaxation, the hotel is equipped with a year-round pool and adjacent sun deck and fitness room.

Business travelers will find the hotel well equipped for their needs. Corporate Class rooms include personal business centers—desks, IBM-compatible

personal computers with Microsoft Windows and other software, laser-quality printers, modems, and fax machines.

Ken Parfitt, the hotel's director of sales and marketing, notes one reason guests can rely on having a positive experience each time they visit the Boston Back Bay Hilton is the consistency of service levels and guest room inventory. He adds, "We have a very committed staff of hospitality professionals and very little employee turnover."

For frequent business travelers, the hotel offers the Preferred Business Traveler Program. For companies using as few as 10 nights per month or 120 nights throughout the year, special room rates are available. Business travelers taking advantage of the program enjoy upgrades to the best room available at check-in—or access to a room with a personal business center for a small additional charge. Companies participating in the Preferred Business Traveler Program are also assured of a consistent room

rate for the year and increased discounts with volume. To make business trips even more productive, a total of 14 meeting rooms are located on the second and third floors of the Boston Back Bay Hilton.

Other advantages for guests include participation in the Hilton Honors program—the most popular frequent travel program in the industry—as well as free 800-number calls and calling card access, free Continental breakfast, and a complimentary morning newspaper delivered to the guest's room.

Although the hotel is located near a number of the city's finest restaurants, many Boston Back Bay Hilton guests choose to dine closer to home—at the Hilton's own Boodles Restaurant & Bar, which serves breakfast, lunch, and dinner. Known throughout the city as a classic American grill, its specialty foods—such as mesquite-grilled items—have built a loyal following. Boodles is also a favorite with beer connoisseurs, as it features

The hotel is continuing the Hilton tradition of service and luxury from the heart of Boston.

more than 100 varieties of "micro-brewed" specialty beers from across America. Once a month the fun is enhanced by inviting beer experts and beer makers to a special dinner. A presentation by a brewery, such as Boston's own Samuel Adams, follows. A Continental breakfast in the morning and cocktails and light fare in the evening are also available in the hotel's Rendezvous Lounge.

Of course, it is often the little things that make a hotel stay truly pleasant. The Boston Back Bay Hilton strives to provide many of those conveniences, including currency exchange, a multilingual staff, nonsmoking rooms, handicap accessibility, and even a provision that allows small pets to stay with guests.

A LANDMARK FOR THE 1990S

Since its opening, the Boston Back Bay Hilton has established an enviable business record, attracting thousands of loyal travelers and a significant volume of repeat business each year.

Indeed, in just one recent year, the hotel had 50,000 more requests for lodging than it could accommodate. So it's no surprise the Boston Back Bay Hilton is now embarked on an expansion and renewal program that will more than double its guest capacity. The $40 million effort will create a total of 700 guest rooms, several new meeting rooms, and a ballroom with a view of the Charles River basin. Seven new elevators will also be added, including glass elevators designed to rise dramatically along the building's exterior. When completed, the new Boston Back Bay Hilton will be the largest Hilton franchise in the world.

Looking to the future, James A. Daley, owner of the Boston Back Bay Hilton, expects to have no trouble filling all of this new space. "The recent efforts by the Commonwealth of Massachusetts to attract more international tourists have begun to bear fruit," he says. "Tourists from Europe and the Far East prefer Boston to New York because it is cleaner,

safer, and still provides cultural opportunities and great shopping."

In addition, expansion of the city's convention facilities is under way. "We are the third-ranked destination city in the United States," says Daley, "yet we have had the 41st-ranked convention center." Daley, who serves on the boards of many nonprofit and charitable groups, including the Boston Convention and Visitors Bureau and the Massachusetts Convention Center Authority, is confident that any new facilities will enhance the ability of the Hynes Convention Center to host the city's major events. With the Hynes directly across the street, that's good news for the expanded Boston Back Bay Hilton and its guests.

"There is a demand for many more hotel rooms in the city today," says Daley. "Already Boston is a destination that attracts one-third more visitors for a given event than would attend if the event were held elsewhere." Furthermore, with expanded facilities, the Boston Back Bay Hilton will be a destination in its own right—able to attract small and mid-size meetings as well as special groups.

Living up to its prestigious Hilton name in more and more ways each day, the Boston Back Bay Hilton continues to offer superior service in a luxurious, comfortable, and convenient setting.

James A. Daley (right), owner of the Boston Back Bay Hilton, expects the expanded hotel to become a destination in its own right—able to attract small and mid-size meetings as well as special groups.

The adjacent John B. Hynes Convention Center (below) makes the Boston Back Bay Hilton a primary host for attendees of major trade shows and meetings. The 860,000-square-foot, state-of-the-art facility is the cornerstone of the city's booming convention industry.

Looking to the future, the hotel has embarked on a $40 million expansion and renewal program that will create a total of 700 guest rooms, several new meeting rooms, and a ballroom with a view of the Charles River basin.

Voice Systems, Inc.

VOICE SYSTEMS PROVIDES "VOICE TRANSPORTATION" FOR the information superhighway. That's a simple but powerful statement of purpose that distinguishes this Canton-based telephone systems company and positions it prominently as a leader in the New England telecommunications industry. From its beginning as a start-up company selling

telephones to small businesses in 1983, Voice Systems has grown to be ranked second in total sales among phone companies in New England. Recently featured on the business television show "New England Today," the firm has seen its client base grow to just over 3,000.

The company's success is due in part to its association with Comdial Corporation, a major American telephone equipment manufacturer. Pictured above is Comdial's digital "Impact" voice terminal.

Comdial's newest digital product is designed with open architecture, which provides the platform of integration linking E-mail, voice mail, and a client's database (near left).

Voice Systems' installation and customer service staff provide client companies with as much support and follow-up as necessary—both during and after the installation (far left).

According to Executive Vice President Karen Schneider, Voice Systems' success is due in part to its association with Comdial Corporation, a major American telephone equipment manufacturer. Comdial is the current leader in the integration of PBX and Novell networks. Its newest digital product is designed with open architecture, which provides

the platform of integration linking E-mail, voice mail, and a client's database.

VOICE OF THE FUTURE

This open architecture design also allows an integrated PC to control the functions of the PBX. Even more exciting is the fact that there are hundreds of thousands of software developers that can design new features and applications, which can be added to existing systems in the future. "In other words," says Voice Systems President Richard Medeiros, "this puts an end to telephone system obsolescence."

Many customers, for example, have already adapted to new caller identification technology. In addition to showing the origin of the call, this technology can bring up a data screen on the caller before the phone is even answered. If the call is transferred

to another extension, so is the information on the computer screen. "Ideally," says Medeiros, "we recommend the best combination of features and technology in a telephone and voice mail system to fit the customer's needs and not the other way around."

This strategy also helps clients effectively reduce costs, increase efficiency, and enhance

growth. To successfully achieve these results, Voice Systems offers a strong blend of industry knowledge, technological expertise, and many years of experience in telecommunications. "We cannot rely on innovative technology alone," says Schneider. "We still believe in old-fashioned customer service."

Voice Systems provides its client companies with as much support and follow-up as necessary—both during and after the installation. Extensive telephone training is always provided for a client's new telephone system and voice mail. After installation, the same highly skilled team of certified technicians provides 24-hour service when needed. Voice Systems' service features cellular telephone dispatch for rapid response and computerized remote diagnostic techniques to expedite troubleshooting and repairs.

▼ ED CHERRY

According to Medeiros and Schneider, the company will continue to find unique and creative solutions to better manage the flow and delivery of "Voice Transportation." That commitment, combined with the latest telephone technology, will ensure Voice Systems a position of leadership on the information superhighway.

Preferred Temporaries, Inc.

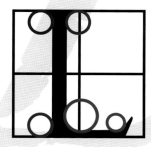

L OCATED IN GOVERNMENT CENTER'S HISTORIC OLD Scollay Square area, Preferred Temporaries, Inc. has been providing temporary employees to the Greater Boston business community for more than a decade. Preferred has established lasting relationships with numerous companies and institutions within the Boston and Cambridge areas,

and its diverse client base includes many of the top local companies and organizations in the fields of radio, television, advertising, publishing, banking, financial services, insurance, education, consulting, medicine, and biotechnology. Clients of Preferred Temporaries are also loyal—the company boasts a 93 percent retention rate.

SERVING THE CITY'S STAFFING NEEDS

Preferred Temporaries has become a fixture in the local business community. Founder Charles Orcutt, an 18-year veteran of the temporary employment industry, has kept Preferred at the top by making sure the company keeps its finger on the pulse of area business. Preferred's offices, for example, are in the heart of the downtown business sector in the Sears Crescent Building adjacent to the Government Center plaza. And although Orcutt advertises, he depends heavily on his strong personal relationships with businesspeople in Greater Boston to spread the word about his firm. These contacts also help Preferred stay in touch with the needs of the ever-changing business community.

But location, advertising, and involvement have only played minor roles in the company's success. According to Orcutt, it is Preferred's skilled and dependable temporaries who have made the company a popular source of staffing solutions.

Thanks to the wide range of skills, interests, and experience possessed by its employees,

Preferred can meet almost any client need. Businesses, for example, are frequently in search of fast and reliable temporary office support to assist when regular employees are out of the office or during periods when business volume is especially high. Preferred comes to the rescue with office support professionals who have specialized training and experience in areas such as word processing, computers, secretarial skills, medical duties, accounting, customer service, and data entry. Preferred is also constantly embracing new technology to ensure that its temporaries remain

on the leading edge of workplace technology.

In addition to being skilled, Preferred's temporaries are dependable. At least three reference checks are made on all applicants. Each employee also undergoes skills testing to measure his or her exact level of training. These processes ensure that all Preferred temporaries are capable of meeting client expectations.

In 1994 the company proudly celebrated its 10th year of staffing success in the Boston area—a testimony to its valued employees and the faith placed in them by local businesses. Preferred's goal for the 1990s, according to Orcutt, is to maintain an outstanding level of service while keeping overall costs low for clients. To that end, Preferred Temporaries will continue to operate on the belief that quality at a fair price blended with excellent service is the foundation for a successful temporary service.

Founder and President Charles Orcutt, an 18-year veteran of the temporary employment industry, is pictured in front of his "Wall of Fame."

Preferred Temporaries is headquartered in the red brick Sears Crescent Building adjacent to the Government Center plaza (left).

Viewlogic Systems, Inc.

AS TECHNOLOGIES LIKE CELLULAR TELEPHONES, PALM-top computers, multimedia, and satellite communications become commonplace, chances are good that Viewlogic Systems, Inc. helped make it possible. Located in the Boston suburb of Marlboro, Viewlogic is known as a leader in electronic design automation (EDA). Because of the complexity

of designing circuits with the millions of transistors found on today's microchips, electronic design engineers have had to turn to sophisticated software tools and high-speed computers for help. EDA software companies like

design times to develop each new generation of advanced products.

Studies show that design complexity is increasing tenfold every two years. It used to be an amazing feat to put 100,000 transistors in a microchip; now de-

damaged. Consequently, electromagnetic interference, design simulation, and test analysis are new EDA technologies with extremely high growth potential. Viewlogic is among the few companies that have mastered these.

Headquartered in the Boston suburb of Marlboro, Viewlogic is known as a leader in electronic design automation.

Viewlogic provide the specialized application software that electronic engineers need to design the next generation of complex products in smaller packages with higher performance and quality—all at a lower cost.

These factors are extremely important in the highly competitive world of electronic products where market leadership is often determined by who gets there first. Using Viewlogic products, designers of electronic products around the world are able to deal more quickly and easily with increasing complexity and shorter

signers using Viewlogic tools are routinely placing millions into a space smaller than a fingernail.

The scope of the task at hand is even more challenging: the chips get smaller, while the circuitry inside gets bigger. The miniature circuits are so close to each other that they can actually interfere with a neighboring circuit's function. Engineers need to confirm that their designs will work before building them. They must also provide a mechanism for testing the board after manufacture to ensure that it has been built correctly and has not been

A Unique, Open Strategy

Viewlogic has also distinguished itself in its unique approach to user needs. Most EDA companies virtually force their customers to use only the software that they manufacture. This outdated strategy is used to dominate a user's environment. With the challenges of the 1990s, users have rebelled and now insist on selecting their own "dream team" of tools to suit their unique design requirements. Viewlogic recognized this from the outset and devised an unprecedented strategy built on emerging industry standards. As a result, Viewlogic users can easily add tools from other vendors to devise their own unique environment. That freedom, coupled with being the only EDA vendor to offer its solutions on both UNIX workstations and Windows personal computers, has truly set Viewlogic apart.

The company's approach also has paid dividends. Customer preference for Viewlogic products has been increasing, and the company's software tools have become de facto standards for many parts of the design industry. This en-

dorsement prompted a public offering in 1991 on the NASDAQ system (VIEW). During the fiscal year ending in 1993, Viewlogic achieved sales of more than $97.9 million. In 1994 the firm continued its movement upward and was ranked 13th in *The Boston Globe*'s regional listing of the top 100 publicly held companies.

CARVING OUT A NEW NICHE

The company's Powerview,® Work-View® PLUS, and PRO Series™ design environments are even more popular than earlier View-

logic products. With its roster of world-famous customers, including Xerox, Siemens, Saab, Ford, and Toshiba, Viewlogic now stands among the true successes of Greater Boston. "Every electronics engineer in the world needs to be able to do things better, faster, and at lower cost," says Alain J. Hanover, Viewlogic's chairman, president, and CEO. "We have the tools that make it possible."

As if its product strength were not enough, the company has also set the pace in establishing the industry's most comprehensive distribution network. In addition to its second-to-none direct sales force, resellers, and distributors, Viewlogic uses telephone sales to provide users in every corner of the world access to its products and services.

CHOOSING BOSTON

Selecting the Boston area as a home for Viewlogic was easy, according to Hanover. "I had always dreamed of starting a com-

pany," he explains, "and my undergraduate studies at MIT and graduate school at Harvard gave me a chance to discover all this region has to offer." Hanover, who was born in France and grew up in New York, says he is also impressed with the region because of the talent pool. Although Viewlogic recruits outstanding people from all over the world, Hanover adds that the company's proximity to the area's well-known schools and its base of experienced, high-technology professionals is invaluable.

"We invest millions to make sure our employees have the state-of-the-art equipment and software tools that they need to do the job," says Hanover. "But it takes more than equipment to make a successful business. It also requires top-notch people and a clear vision. It's in these areas that we've really distinguished ourselves."

The Powerview® design environment is the company's flagship product line (left).

Alain J. Hanover (below), Viewlogic's chairman, president, and CEO, established the company in 1984.

Avalon Partners, Inc.

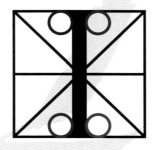

I T MAY SEEM LIKE A LOGICAL IDEA TO REPRESENT ONLY tenants in commercial real estate deals, but according to Avalon Partners founder William Goade, the concept was revolutionary when his tenant consulting and brokerage firm was established in 1985. ■ Traditionally, commercial real estate firms perform leasing services on behalf of the

Avalon has served as tenant representative for many firms, including Lotus Development Corp.

The firm's key employees include its five principals and senior associate. Seated, from left: William Krasnow, Maureen Richard, and Edward Fothergill. Standing, from left: Jack Burns, founder William Goade, and Robert Shulman.

landlord. This often creates a conflict of interest when a company tries to fill an office building for the landlord while locating office space for a tenant in the same market. Avalon was founded on the premise that a tenant gets better representation when its broker has no other allegiances. The company is unique in that its principals are all former corporate real estate executives. This experience has allowed Avalon to be used as an "outsource" by many companies to meet their real estate requirements.

The company does much of its work in the Greater Boston area, where it represented tenants in the largest lease transactions of the year in 1990, 1992, and 1994. However, Avalon has also completed projects outside of the Boston area totaling over 1.5 million square feet in more than 100 cities nationwide during the past five years.

SKILLED ASSISTANCE—START TO FINISH

A typical Avalon project begins by creating a detailed outline of a client's needs, compiling a survey describing current conditions in a desired market, and obtaining detailed information on properties for rent. A request-for-proposal document is then generated, addressing the specific needs of the client. Avalon evaluates the proposals and provides a financial and nonfinancial summary of each for the client's review.

After the tenant has chosen one or more sites, Avalon Partners negotiates the business transaction and writes a detailed letter documenting the terms and

conditions of the agreement. Unlike most firms, Avalon stays fully involved in the negotiation of the lease document and prepares a summary of the lease for its clients.

A good example of Avalon's work is a project it completed for an international computer software company. The firm needed 350,000 square feet of mixed-use space in a suburban campus setting with long-term growth potential and an option to purchase. Avalon helped the client consolidate its expiring leases, reviewed 90 potential sites, analyzed and summarized 20 proposals, and

negotiated business points with five finalists. Once the client chose the finalist, Avalon negotiated the lease agreement and then prepared a summary of the agreement. The client estimated its savings to be more than $30 million over 10 years.

Since 1985 Avalon Partners has expanded from three to 11 people in downtown Boston. This growth was spurred by the fact that the company specializes in multiple transactions of all sizes and represents 15 firms on a na-

tional or regional basis. Over the years, Avalon has served as adviser to Lotus Development Corporation, Sun Microsystems, PictureTel Corporation, Aetna Insurance, Liberty Mutual, Wang, Bell & Howell, and many others. The company was also a founding member of the Corporate Real Estate Services Alliance (CRESA), a nationwide group of affiliated tenant representation firms. Avalon helped create the entity to better serve its clients by aligning with like-minded firms of high integrity.

Goade expects the tenant representation business to develop

as more brokers expand their traditional business. However, he believes that Avalon's focus on tenant representation, combined with the corporate real estate background of its principals, will allow the firm to remain distinct and to continue to grow despite increased competition. "Tenant representation is the future of the business, and we understand it better than our competitors. The more educated the tenant is in the process, the more often we are selected," says Goade.

Wainwright Bank & Trust Company

WAINWRIGHT BANK & TRUST COMPANY IS A LEADER IN meeting local financial needs, offering a range of services including mortgages, business loans, commercial real estate loans, credit cards, and savings, checking, and money market accounts. Recently, Wainwright Bank expanded its retail presence with the purchase of a new headquarters building

in the Boston financial district. In addition, the bank has branches at Harvard Square and Kendall Square in Cambridge.

As the 14th-largest commercial bank in Massachusetts, Wainwright Bank also has the highest capital to deposit ratio (10 percent). But financial strength is only a part of the value Wainwright Bank offers to local residents. The other is a commitment to a social agenda that is unique in the banking industry. According to Robert Glassman, cofounder and chairman of the board, "We're a conventional bank doing unconventional things."

SOCIALLY RESPONSIBLE BANKING

Homelessness among AIDS sufferers is a problem in Boston, as it is in many American cities. Ill and often unemployed, AIDS patients frequently have no place to turn. When a group of local activists decided to address the problem recently by building low-income housing for people living with AIDS and their families, they turned to Wainwright Bank for financing.

"It is excruciatingly difficult to obtain construction loans from Boston's local banks," says Caleb C. Clapp, a developer who initiated the project. "Without the substantial involvement of Wainwright Bank, the project would not have been possible." The Sheila D. Daniels House in Roxbury, which houses 11 families coping with AIDS, opened in 1993.

In 1992 Wainwright Bank created the one-year Community CD, which provides consumers

the opportunity to safely channel their deposits into community development projects while earning a highly competitive rate of return. Community CD deposits helped finance the Sheila D. Daniels House, as well as other projects such as a new warehouse for the Greater Boston Food Bank, a women's facility at the Pine Street Inn homeless shelter, and a new wing of affordable single-room housing at the Cambridge YWCA.

The bank's internal commitment to diversity extends from the boardroom to the mail room and is outwardly demonstrated with the Community Card, a credit card that generates funding for organizations associated with the gay and lesbian community. One percent of the value of purchases made with the card is donated to groups such as the AIDS Action Committee of Massachusetts, Fenway Community Health Center, and other organizations providing legal advocacy, housing, and scholarships to the community.

While the company was formed in 1987 by Glassman and his partner, President John Plukas, as a European-style private bank offering a full range of conventional banking services, the organization is committed to the belief that some of the most responsible borrowers are those associated with community and philanthropic organizations.

"We found that the socially responsible constituency was also a financially responsible constituency," Glassman says. Involvement in community devel-

opment has become the bank's signature, underscoring its Banking on Values theme.

Stephen Lydenberg, a principal of Kinder, Lydenberg & Domini, Inc., which specializes in social investment research, says, "It is refreshing to find any cor-

poration, especially a bank, dedicated to doing business from an entirely new and socially progressive perspective. There are few enough such companies around. But it is especially gratifying to see that a bank with such a mission can grow and thrive."

With a combined control of 57 percent of Wainwright Bank's voting stock, Glassman and Plukas have been able to build a successful business around that mission—proving that it is possible to do well by doing good.

Members of Wainwright Bank's board of directors are committed to financial strength and socially responsible banking. From left: John Reed, Charles Desmond, Ranne Warner, President John Plukas, Chairman Robert Glassman, James Hyman, J. Frank Keohane, and Brenda Cole.

Office Environments of New England, Inc.

FOUNDED IN 1986 AT A TIME WHEN THE STATE AND national economies were entering a prolonged depressed cycle, Office Environments of New England (OE) has grown from a start-up company to become one of the largest office furniture dealerships in the country. Sales revenues in 1994 are expected to be in the $100 million range.

The company's owners include (from left) President Ed Marchetti, Executive Vice President-Chief Financial Officer Bill Nyhan, and Executive Vice President Walter Costello.

Committed to the quality of the products it offers, Office Environments is pleased to be associated with a broad selection of the industry's most respected manufacturers.

PHOTOS BY PETER LEWITT

INTERIOR DESIGN BY SUSAN GRECO, IBD

Although OE's founding group had over 100 years of combined office furniture dealership experience in the New England marketing area, they clearly understood that in order to survive and grow, Office Environments would have to be better than existing alternatives. Mediocrity, they believed, was not an option. Their focus was—and continues to be—on quality, experience, value, and service. To become bigger was never a corporate goal; rather, the founders believed growth should be the natural result of being better.

A quote from former ITT Chairman Harold Geneen is well known at Office Environments: "I think it is an immutable law in business that words are words, explanations are explanations, and promises are promises . . . but only performance is reality." This philosophy is deeply ingrained in OE's corporate culture and is evidenced in countless examples of the company's ability to get the job done professionally and on schedule—even in an industry laden with unpredictable manufacturing and scheduling surprises.

BUILDING LASTING RELATIONSHIPS

OE's owners—President Ed Marchetti, Executive Vice President Walter Costello, and Executive Vice President-Chief Financial Officer Bill Nyhan—are on-site and hands-on every day. They strongly believe that the company's ultimate success depends heavily on their ability to attract the best-quality talent at all levels and to provide employees with excellent training and a positive work environment. "Appreciated, enthusiastic employees become experienced, longer-term employees who are better able to professionally and effectively build long-term relationships with

architectural design professionals and OE's valued end user customers," says Marchetti. "Satisfied customers hold the key to our future."

Equally important at Office Environments is the quality of products offered by the company. OE is pleased to be associated with a broad selection of the industry's most respected manufacturers including Steelcase and its Design Partnership companies, Kimball, Gunlocke, and dozens of others. Steelcase is the industry's largest and most diverse manufacturer of high-quality furniture systems, filing, and seating solutions. "Current Steelcase research and development projects promise exciting breakthrough solutions to ergonomics, lighting, acoustical, and 'teaming' concepts for tomorrow's workplace—in the office or at home," says Costello.

A COMMITMENT TO CUSTOMER NEEDS

Office Environments is in a service business. "Our management strongly believes that we must offer additional service options and perform service in a superior manner for the company to be recognized by our clients as their dealer of choice," states Nyhan. To that end, OE offers a complete range of services including storage/warehousing in its own 150,000-square-foot warehouse, bar coding, inventory management, in-house delivery, installation and service capabilities, leasing, rental, total project management, and refurbished furniture options. In addition, the company's Office Extras

affiliate specializes in high-quality new or slightly used furniture bargains.

Ultimately, a company's clients decide if their suppliers are performing in a satisfactory manner, and if the supplier-client partnership is working at or beyond their expectations. Office Environments is proud to have long-term client relationships with many of the region's most respected companies such as Lotus, Thomson Financial Services, Fleet Bank, CSC-Index, Brown Brothers Harriman & Co., State Street Bank, John Hancock Mutual Life Insurance, Putnam Financial Services, and Goodwin, Procter & Hoar. Most utilize a broad range of OE's extensive service "menu" for their local and national facilities needs.

FOCUSED ON A BRIGHT FUTURE

While the road traveled thus far has been exciting and rewarding, OE's management remains focused on responding to clients' rapidly changing workplace needs in a creative, innovative manner. The company's recently expanded, 30,000-square-foot office/showroom facility at 280 Summer Street, with its breathtaking views of Boston Harbor, seems an appropriate setting for OE's management to discuss the bright future through the '90s and into the 21st century. "While tomorrow's concepts of office, workstations, and support equipment are likely to change, the importance of professional, value-added, positive relationships between suppliers and clients will only increase in significance," notes Marchetti.

Profitable every year since its inception, Office Environments is financially strong and eager—each day on each project—to earn the opportunity to continually serve its clients by performing in a superior manner.

The Registry, Inc.

WHEN DREW CONWAY FOUNDED THE REGISTRY IN 1986 to sell software consulting services, the company was a modest, three-person operation with a good idea. Eight years and a lot of hard work later, The Registry is one of the fastest-growing full-service information technology consulting firms in the United States. Based in Newton, it has become a multimillion-dollar, 20-branch firm that provides a full range of information technology consulting and professional services to clients nationwide.

EXCELLENCE IN INFORMATION TECHNOLOGY CONSULTING SERVICES

The Registry's rapid growth is attributable to the integrity of its business practices and innovative vision. Conway started the company because he believed that the increasing complexity of integrated computer systems would create a need for computer specialists beyond what most companies could typically keep on staff. He developed an extensive network of software consultants from across the country who provide their expertise to client companies on a per-project basis. Today, that network includes over 1,200 technical employees serving customers from coast to coast.

Before employment at The Registry, candidates are put through a rigorous hiring and selection process. "We are constantly working to identify the top technical professionals in the country to be a part of our team," Conway says. The screening process, which has received national recognition, includes testing for technical expertise as well as "softer" consulting skills. Conway emphasizes, "Although technical skills are necessary, the softer skills are a critical element in the consulting business."

The Registry has a focused sales strategy. "We identify specific clients in targeted industries and focus on under-standing their business," Conway says. "Only then can we add value and help them to meet their information technology objectives. Our ultimate goal is to cultivate long-term client partnerships."

The company has developed specific expertise in four areas of information technology: Networks and Communications; Database Development; Workgroup/Desktop Solutions; and Legacy Systems. The Registry's resource managers specialize in one of these technology areas, enabling them to stay abreast of changes in the field. By fully understanding their area of expertise, the resource managers can identify the right professionals for project teams more efficiently and effectively.

In order to better serve clients, the firm selectively enters

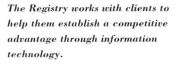

The Registry works with clients to help them establish a competitive advantage through information technology.

From its headquarters in Newton, Massachusetts, and a network of 20 branch offices, The Registry serves clients nationwide.

into "virtual corporation" strategic partnerships with companies whose areas of expertise complement its own. These strategic partners are established businesses that exhibit skills in both business and technical areas. The partnerships are designed to give The Registry depth in new markets as well as extend the breadth of services for existing clients.

The company maintains a highly trained business development staff of about 200 employees. The Registry is committed to continuous improvement and helps develop its team members by maintaining a full-time training department that supports all sales, recruiting, and administrative personnel with numerous educational programs and services. One example is "Registry University," which holds intensive training programs for employees four times per year. The classes are taught by guest speakers from within the company, as well as by outside experts.

Combining all these resources, The Registry works with its clients in helping them establish a competitive advantage through information technology. The company provides services by mobilizing a team with the right business, technical, and industry expertise to partner with its clients to meet the specific engagement needs.

BUSINESS SOLUTIONS
Over the years, The Registry has expanded to become a full-service information technology consulting firm, providing professional support services through business and information technology solutions consulting. The company provides numerous value-added services for both clients and technical staff, including engagement orientations, formal project reviews, productivity seminars, focus groups, competency modeling, and technology exchanges. In some cases, the firm designs entire information technology systems, implements the project, and manages the client's staff. "We provide a prescriptive approach to each individual engagement," Conway says.

And to make sure its efforts are on the right track, The Registry constantly surveys clients,

targeted markets, and employees.

Conway's approach seems to be working. In the last three years, The Registry was named by *Inc.* magazine as one of the 500 fastest-growing privately held companies in the United States. The firm also was featured in the 1993

ABC television series "Building America" for its excellence in customer service and its hiring and training methodology. In 1994 The Registry was selected as a finalist for *Sales & Marketing Management* magazine's Ninth Annual Best Sales Force Award, which recognizes the nation's top sales organizations. In addition, The Registry was named a semifinalist in the Best of America awards, sponsored by Dun & Bradstreet Information Services and the National Federation of Independent Business Foundation.

The Registry's growth is also reflected in its financial success. From a modest start in 1986, the company has evolved into a $100 million enterprise. In 1993 and 1994, revenue increased by more than 50 percent, nearly tripling revenue in fiscal year 1992. Currently, the firm has branch offices across the United States, servicing 42 states, with plans for international expansion in 1995.

Since Drew Conway founded The Registry in 1986, it has become one of the fastest-growing full-service information technology consulting firms in the United States.

Lynch Murphy Walsh & Partners

OSTON HAD ITS SHARE OF REAL ESTATE BROKERAGE firms when the five founders of Lynch Murphy Walsh & Partners started their brokerage business in 1987. They were convinced, however, that they could differentiate themselves from the competition by focusing on a niche of specialty services—commercial real estate brokerage, con-

sulting, research, and appraisal—and deliver them better than anyone else. "We felt we could be the best in those fields if we concentrated all our resources on them," says President Thomas A. Walsh.

Indeed, Lynch Murphy Walsh & Partners has pursued its strategy with great success. In just seven years, it has become the region's largest commercial brokerage firm, as measured by the number of square feet leased or sold. Between 1991 and 1993, the firm increased its annual number of completed transactions by 50 percent, from 270 to 400. And in 1992 and 1993, Lynch Murphy Walsh & Partners was included in a list of the country's top 100 commercial real estate firms compiled

by *Commercial Property News*, a national trade publication.

The company regularly does business in all of the New England states. For clients whose needs extend beyond the region, Lynch Murphy Walsh & Partners conducts assignments across the United States through its participation in a nationwide network of 70 independently owned commercial real estate firms, known as The Commercial Network.

Brokerage services, the largest part of the company's business, consist of representing landlords/sellers and tenants/buyers in lease or sale transactions. Lynch Murphy Walsh & Partners handles a wide range of property types, from manufactur-

ing to retail space to executive offices. The firm represents seven of the 10 largest U.S. insurance firms and all of the region's major commercial banks in completing real estate assignments in New England. Corporate representation balances the company's brokerage transactions.

The company's consulting services provide advice to a variety of clients on diverse real estate issues. A developer, for example, might hire the firm before construction begins to make its office park more appealing to tenants. Lynch Murphy Walsh & Partners frequently advises building owners on repositioning properties. This may involve rebuilding the lobby, putting on a new facade, or adding

Lynch Murphy Walsh & Partners has offered its expertise in brokerage and consulting services to clients throughout Greater Boston.

Clockwise from top left:
One Cranberry Hill is a first-class suburban office building sold on behalf of Prudential Real Estate Investors.

Located in the Boston suburb of Natick, Apple Hill is a 166,850-square-foot office project with a unique retail component.

The firm leases a variety of laboratory and biotechnology space.

Metropolitan Corporate Center, owned by MetLife, is a 3.5 million-square-foot, 1,000-acre, multiuse business park located in Marlborough.

tenant amenities like on-site day care centers, fitness rooms, or food service facilities. The company also gives guidance on the best way to structure a lease to attract tenants. Some situations call for traditional rental agreements, while others require leases with options to buy or other creative arrangements.

In the past, landlords, tenants, and investors only sought real estate advice when transactions occurred. But, increasingly, companies want commercial real estate consultation on an ongoing basis. "We are constantly monitoring the pulse of the market," states Walsh.

Much of the information Lynch Murphy Walsh & Partners uses to formulate its advice comes from its research. Beyond tracking activities in New England's commercial real estate market, the firm prides itself on delivering the information to clients in a way that is meaningful. "Clients have to make multimillion-dollar decisions about their real estate assets," Walsh says. "Rather than providing them with a snapshot of current conditions, we produce an interpretation based on trends and future market conditions that offers a moving picture of the state of commercial real estate."

In addition to its in-house database, Lynch Murphy Walsh & Partners draws on another valuable resource—the years of practical experience held by its 25 brokers. Each of the company's five principal officers has an average of 17 years in commercial real estate, and all are actively

involved in the business. This hands-on experience gives the company's leaders a better perspective since each project is overseen directly by one of the principals.

Appraisal—finding the value of a piece of property—is another specialty. Property appraisals are needed whenever a real estate transaction occurs, or for litigation or tax purposes. Lynch Murphy Walsh & Partners' affiliate, Valuation Associates, has appraised everything from office towers to golf courses. The appraisers look beyond the bricks and mortar when calculating property values. Issues such as demographics, economic trends, and population growth are con-

sidered when setting a value to a property.

Lynch Murphy Walsh & Partners has carved out a niche for itself in the crowded Boston-area commercial real estate market by focusing the significant expertise of its real estate professionals on creative solutions for its clients. Concludes Walsh, "Our formula for doing business is simple. First, we need to analyze and understand our clients' real estate and business goals. We then develop and aggressively execute a comprehensive plan while maintaining the high ethical standards for which we are known. In short, we combine the art of sales with the science of marketing to achieve results for our clients every day."

Sixty State Street, managed by Koll Management Services, totals 820,000 square feet of first-class office space in the heart of Boston's financial district (near left). Lynch Murphy Walsh & Partners handles leasing for the property.

The firm's principals are (standing, from far left) Gregory P. Lucas, Stephen J. Murphy, Stephen D. Lynch, (seated, from far left) Timothy R. Halloran, and Thomas A. Walsh.

Fallon Hines & O'Connor, Inc.

ALLON HINES & O'CONNOR, INC. IS A BOSTON-BASED commercial real estate brokerage, consulting, and advisory firm that pools the talents of 20 or so professionals with diverse and complementary real estate backgrounds. Since its inception in 1988, the firm has made its mark on Boston's real estate landscape by offering the highest standard of

service possible. Despite its relative youth, Fallon Hines & O'Connor's strength—its distinguishing characteristic—is found in its unofficial maxim: "Experience. The Difference." Indeed, it is the firm's clients who are the direct beneficiaries of an average of more than 12 years of experience for each of the firm's leasing and investment sales specialists.

Situated in Boston's financial district, 99 High Street (right) is a 32-story, 730,000-square-foot office tower owned by P&O Properties and Rose Associates.

Fallon Hines & O'Connor has had direct involvement in many of the Boston area's largest and most significant lease and sales transactions. The firm sold One Faneuil Hall Square, a 42,000-square-foot vertical retail store, to an offshore investor for $22.55 million (above).

The idea for the new firm was hatched by a group of seven people, three of whom were classmates at the College of the Holy Cross—Joseph P. Fallon, Brian T. Hines, and Charles S. O'Connor. The trio quickly added the talents of four additional principals— Michael T. Brown, Richard A. Graham, Kathleen T. O'Connor, and Robert M. DeLaney. More recently, Richard A. Fahey and Robert E. Griffin, Jr., joined the firm as principals. From headquarters offices in the city's financial district, the firm focuses on commercial/industrial leasing and investment sales in the four major Boston-area submarkets: downtown (including Back Bay), Cambridge, and the suburban markets within Boston's Interstate 495 and Route 128 beltways.

SUCCESS THROUGH PERFORMANCE

Fallon Hines & O'Connor has emerged as one of the fastest-growing real estate firms in the city and one of the most visible and respected in the Northeast. To ensure that its clients' best interests are served, the firm's brokers are compensated on a salary (plus performance bonus) basis, rather than a straight commission. "That way," Principal Robert DeLaney explains, "individuals are not independent players, but rather part of an identifiable and reliable team that works at the client's pace and direction."

Fallon Hines & O'Connor has built its reputation through performance; the firm's goal is not to be the largest firm in its industry, but the most focused, determined, creative, enthusiastic, and persistent. Nonetheless, the firm has grown steadily through several years in which local real estate conditions have been challenging. As a result, the Fallon Hines & O'Connor name has become synonymous with seasoned professionals who provide efficient, effective, and individualized attention to clients. The firm's hallmarks include team orientation, a fervent dedication to performance, and, most importantly, a belief in and emphasis upon relationships.

RELATIONSHIPS: THE KEY TO GROWTH

Since its formation, Fallon Hines & O'Connor has more than tripled in size and has provided advisory services to hundreds of institutional, corporate, and entrepreneurial clients. The firm's client list spans every major industry and reads like a "who's who" of top regional and national companies. Fallon Hines & O'Connor has represented firms such as Kenneth Leventhal & Company and BOT Financial in consulting/ accounting; Amgen, Biogen, Genzyme, PerSeptive Biosystems, and Boston Scientific in the biomedical area; Allmerica, Merrill Lynch, The Prudential, and United Asset Management in financial services; EMC Corporation, Molten Metal, and Sapient Computing in high technology; Blue Cross Blue Shield, Pilgrim Health Care, Delta Dental, and Tufts Associated Health Plans in the health care industry; ITT Hartford and UNUM in the insurance sector; Keane, Inc., Kronos, and Parametric Technology in software; and nonprofits such as Elderhostel and Oxfam America. The firm believes it is the intimate ties Fallon Hines & O'Connor enjoys with such clients that will prove crucial in coming years.

Assignments have included portfolio and single-asset dispositions, market studies, land and building opinions of value, appraisals, lease analysis and renegotiations, highest- and best-use studies, lease-versus-purchase analyses, and partnership agreement analyses. Serving these clients has involved leasing millions of square feet of office,

laboratory, and warehouse/distribution space. Accomplishing such a feat required not only an intimate knowledge of the area's diverse markets but also a sensitivity to and intimate understanding of the client's needs and business strategy. On the landlord/ owner side, Fallon Hines & O'Connor has represented P&O Properties, London & Leeds Development Corporation, Teachers Insurance & Annuity Association, Sumitomo Life, and the Massachusetts Institute of Technology, among many others.

The firm's knowledge of and direct involvement in the Boston area's largest and most significant lease and sale transactions

only adds to Fallon Hines & O'Connor's expertise. The firm has executed the sale of some of the most distinctive and visible investment properties in the metropolitan area, representing such firms as Aetna Realty Investors, Bank of Boston, Copley Real Estate Advisors, Homart, JMB Properties Company, Mellon Bank, MetLife Real Estate Investments, and Prentiss Properties. In 1993 the firm sold $175 million of office, retail, warehouse/distribution, flex, and multifamily properties.

REACHING OUT

Fallon Hines & O'Connor also works closely with brokerage organizations in other markets to

provide services to its clients— both for the sale of properties and to assist with setting up satellite offices or subsidiary operations. "Our approach is to take what we have learned about the business in our local markets and apply it through strategic alliances in other markets across the nation," DeLaney says. As a result, Fallon Hines & O'Connor has completed lease transactions from Seattle to Charlotte and from Chicago to San Jose. "Although we have not set our sights on being the biggest in our business, that does not mean we can't strive to be the best—the company that our clients keep coming back to," adds DeLaney.

London & Leeds' 830,000-square-foot Bay Colony Corporate Center is a three-building, world-class office park located in Waltham, Massachusetts.

As a Boston-based business, Fallon Hines & O'Connor has also made a commitment to support a number of local charities and community organizations. The firm has shown a particular interest in children and education through a business-to-school partnership with the Dearborn Middle School in Roxbury. Fallon Hines & O'Connor participates in a mentoring program through generous donations of time, resources, and funds. The firm also has provided seed money to establish a new private school on Thompson's Island in Boston Harbor.

High Street Capital Partners, Inc.

WE HAD SPENT OUR LIVES BUILDING A REPUTATION FOR integrity, honesty, and quality, and we didn't want to lose it," says Charles Raffi, Jr., of the Wilmington-based Raffi and Swanson, Inc., a 70-year-old specialty chemicals and coatings company. The partners were starting to think about retirement, and with no heirs in sight, they were looking for a buyer who would protect their life's work.

High Street Associates, Inc. met that need. High Street is a Boston-based acquisition and management company founded by a group of former Fortune 500 manufacturing executives, including Peter M. Jarowey and Walter F. Greeley, former Cabot Corporation executives. The company specializes in acquiring and nurturing small and mid-sized privately owned, family manufacturing businesses.

High Street's primary focus is growing businesses in the specialty chemicals and materials industries.

PHOTO BY PHILIPPE SION / THE IMAGE BANK

Typically, when a large company buys a smaller business, it recoups its investment by absorbing the enterprise and cutting overhead—often by laying off staff. High Street takes a different approach, treating healthy small businesses as resources that can be developed with the assistance of broader experience and a different perspective. "The High Street group is made up of builders who look at these companies as opportunities for growth," says Bernard F. Meyer, senior partner of High Street Capital Partners and a former Norton Company executive vice president.

When High Street purchased Raffi and Swanson in 1990, the firm had been run since the 1950s by Raffi and three other partners, all descendants of the company's founders. High Street worked to develop the business and, especially important for the owners, retained the 100-person workforce. Since then, sales have increased by over 30 percent. "We are very pleased with High Street," says Raffi. "They've added some new thinking to the company."

BUILDING SOUND FUTURES

High Street Capital Partners, Inc. was recently established as an outgrowth of High Street Associates. Jarowey and his partners set up the company to develop the value they saw in regionally focused, niche-oriented, private companies. Many of these businesses were successful and made money, but Jarowey thought they could benefit from the international experience and broadened perspective High Street offered. "Some companies are not positioned well to effectively exploit their excellent products and ideas," he says. "We help change a company's perspective from a regional focus to one that will allow it to compete on a broader scale, perhaps in national and international markets."

Huntington Laboratories, Inc., a supplier of germicidal and antimicrobial products for the infection control market, was in a situation similar to Raffi and Swanson's when High Street Associates purchased the Indiana company in 1990. The founder's heirs were not interested in running the company, and Huntington was looking for a buyer who would preserve its core values. High Street helped accelerate the company's product development, intensified its marketing effort, and introduced more detailed planning while leaving the staff intact. Since then, Huntington's business has increased by over 50 percent.

High Street's partners are skilled at turning a profit, but they emphasize that they are not financiers whose main function is to move money around.

"We are individuals with expertise in building businesses, selecting market niches, and serving them well, while manufacturing high-quality, low-cost products and supporting them with excellent technical service," says Charles Law McCabe, chairman of High Street Capital Partners. "We know what it is like to own and run a business. We're comfortable with entrepreneurs who want to preserve and grow what they've spent a lifetime building."

This commitment means that partnerships with High Street are win-win situations: High Street gains companies with proven track records and solid customer bases, while former owners rest assured that their companies, their employees, and their dreams will continue to prosper.

McFarland Associates, Inc.

cFARLAND ASSOCIATES MAY NOT BE THE LARGEST commercial real estate firm in town, but CEO Karyn McFarland sees that as a plus. "We're smaller by design," she says. "We give a higher level of service with more attention to detail." ■ The firm specializes in commercial and retail leasing, consulting, and investment brokerage,

representing both tenants and landlords. McFarland started the company in November of 1989 after nine years as a highly respected broker in Boston's downtown market. During its first year, the firm handled exclusive leasing assignments in excess of 1.6 million square feet. These

included 58,000 square feet of retail space at International Place and office space at the World Trade Center. In its first three years, McFarland Associates negotiated lease transactions worth more than $85 million.

The firm has established an excellent reputation for helping owners reposition office properties. For example, ORIX Real Estate Equities, Inc. owns a building at 185 Devonshire Street that in 1989 was only 50 percent full. McFarland Associates encouraged the ownership to place a concierge in the lobby—in order to set itself apart from the competition—and to improve all the common areas to reflect the same high level of finish as the lobby. The firm also increased brokers' fees and held

an elegant cocktail party on-site to reintroduce brokers to the renovated property. As a result, the building currently enjoys a 95 percent occupancy rate and is considered one of the finest rehabs in downtown Boston.

As the firm's reputation grew, so did the number of proj-

ects it was able to handle, which now total over 6.7 million square feet. "We tend to get the tougher assignments," McFarland remarks. "We're not afraid to tell an owner what needs to be done to reposition the building in order to get it leased; then we roll up our sleeves, and we do it."

McFarland Associates is also noted for its ability to offer many of the services of a much larger firm. One such service is a computerized database of the city's landlord and tenant activity. This type of technology helps McFarland Associates keep a pulse on space availabilities in the Boston and Cambridge markets, which represent an inventory of 46 million and 9.8 million square feet respectively. The firm also

tracks 7,000 tenants to accommodate the space and timing requirements of its clientele.

McFarland Associates recently formed a strategic alliance with Palladins, a highly respected real estate company in the northern suburb of Peabody. This alliance empowers McFarland Associates to fulfill the varied needs of its client base and remain on the cutting edge of commercial real estate services.

But it is the firm's intimate size and the resulting benefits that set it apart. McFarland Associates prides itself on its team approach, which includes sharing information internally to get the job done. "At some firms, brokers lock their drawers at night, but here we have a free flow of information," says McFarland. By utilizing its collective expertise and specializing in the local markets, the company can better serve its clients.

This smaller scale also allows for closer client contact with the firm's principals. "We're like a big company, only clients get more attention from key personnel," McFarland says. "Our success can be attributed to our ability to provide a broad range of services, combined with the attention to detail we offer in every aspect of the deal-making process."

Complementing its basic services in commercial and retail leasing, consulting, and investment brokerage, McFarland Associates offers a tenant newsletter, marketing materials, exclusive leasing services, and occupancy cost analysis.

Karyn McFarland (near left) started the company in November of 1989 after nine years as a highly respected broker in Boston's downtown market.

With the help of McFarland Associates, Boston's 185 Devonshire building (far left) currently enjoys a 95 percent occupancy rate and is considered one of the finest rehabs in downtown.

PHOTOS BY BILL HORSEMAN

THE UNITED STATES CREATES MORE THAN 13 BILLION tons of waste each year—solid, sludge, liquid, gas, toxic, and nontoxic. It is nasty stuff. But the traditional methods of burning or burying waste are more "out of sight, out of mind" than they are visionary. Both add tons of pollution to the environment annually. ■ Molten Metal Technology,

based in Waltham, Massachusetts, has developed a patented waste-disposal system that goes beyond visionary. In fact, it borders on the utopian. The system, called Catalytic Extraction Processing (CEP), recycles almost any waste into usable materials like hydrogen, ceramics, and metals without

making plastics and many chemicals. Another application is the breakdown of chlorinated solvents (like the ones used for dry cleaning), which creates a mix of gasses that can be used as fuel or made into more chlorinated solvents.

An even more dramatic use of CEP is the cleanup of

lems, to move away from burning and burying to recycling." CEP raises the possibility of wasteless industry, as well as the cleanup of existing waste materials. Not too long ago, those ideas would have been considered science fiction.

Molten Metal was started in 1989 in a converted warehouse in Cambridge. Christopher J. Nagel, Sc.D., then 31, and William M. Haney III, a 28-year-old Harvard graduate with two start-up companies under his belt, joined forces with Benjamin T. Downs and an initial $50,000 investment.

Since then, Molten Metal has grown into a $500 million enterprise that expects to continue to double its staff annually. Some things have not changed, however. Suits are still a rare sight, and a Ping-Pong table sits where a conference table would usually be.

The company operates a $25 million demonstration site in Fall River, Massachusetts, where prospective clients can peek at CEP by sending their industrial waste through the test system. Molten Metal has operating or planned partnerships with companies around the country, from Hoechst Celanese Corporation—one of the largest chemical companies in the United States—to Martin Marietta Energy Systems—the company charged with cleaning up the Oak Ridge weapons facility in Tennessee.

It may sound unbelievable, but that's all part of Molten Metal Technology's goal. "We're shooting to be too good to be true," Yates says. "If we sounded any other way, we wouldn't have set our sights high enough."

Molten Metal Technology's Recycling-Research and Development facility is located in Fall River, Massachusetts.

Catalytic Extraction Processing, the firm's patented waste-disposal system, recycles almost any waste into usable materials like hydrogen, ceramics, and metals without producing pollutants (right).

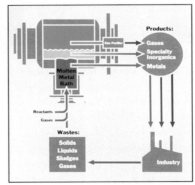

producing pollutants. It is done by immersing the waste in molten metal—in most cases, about 100 gallons of iron heated to 3,000 degrees Fahrenheit—which severs the chemical bonds and reduces the material to its basic atomic elements. By adding special reactants, the elements can be reconfigured into new commercial products.

REINVENTING INDUSTRY
Thanks to Molten Metal's vision, the plastic parts of an automobile can be shredded, dropped into the boiling metal, and transformed into carbon monoxide and hydrogen, both of which can be used for

existing weapons stockpiles. CEP can convert bombs—even those with nuclear components—into stabilized, isolated nuclear material and valuable metals. The process costs less than half as much as incineration and produces few or no by-products.

"We have a really special mission," says Ian Yates, vice president of sales and market development. "It is to change the way our world deals with its waste prob-

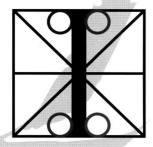

Sterling, A Division of Olsten Staffing Services

N THE 1980S, CORPORATE LEADERS FOCUSED ON MONEY as the prime motivator for all employees. Today, team cohesiveness, commitment to quality, and time for a life outside work are becoming important employee benefits. With the passing of the Family and Medical Leave Act of 1993, many employers have begun to rethink the structure of their organizations. This movement is just one factor contributing to today's booming temporary employment industry.

Sterling Office Services, a Boston-based employment firm with strong ties to the community, was founded in 1988 by professionals with many years of employment industry experience. Focused on serving both employers and employees, Sterling believes it is no longer sufficient merely to match individuals to job openings. With a diverse pool of over 10,000 assignment employees and full-time candidates, a skills match is a fairly straightforward task. Understanding preferences—such as which industries a person is most interested in, whether he or she is a team player or an individual achiever, and where a person is on his or her career path—is important when helping an individual find employment.

"The quality of Sterling's temporary employees and full-time candidates and the services they provide are fantastic," says client Donna Meserve, manager of human resources at John Hancock Property and Casualty. "Sterling took the time to really learn what we needed so they could go out and get me qualified individuals. They did their homework." John Hancock has been a client of Sterling since 1988.

HIGH-CALIBER INDIVIDUALS
All assignment employees and full-time candidates undergo rigorous screening. Interviews with prospective employees are in-depth; their business automation skills are evaluated, at least two references are checked, and all stated educational information is verified. "The goal is to ensure our employees can make an immediate contribution when they arrive at the client company," says Jennifer Hopkins, a Sterling area manager.

Once employees are accepted, Sterling provides them with customized training programs teaching skills required by the companies for which they may want to work. All skills evaluations are validated by the Educational Testing Service (ETS), ensuring they are unbiased and compatible with North American standards. "We are an equal opportunity employer, and we try to achieve diversity in every aspect of our organization," says Kathleen Quinn Votaw, a Sterling area manager.

A PARTNERSHIP WITH CLIENT COMPANIES
In 1993 Olsten Staffing Services, the nation's second-largest staffing services company, acquired Sterling. With support from this worldwide corporation, Sterling can now offer more extensive programs to assist client companies with human resources issues. Programs include Excellence Through Olsten People, the companywide quality initiative; Personnel Transfer Plan (PTP), which allows an organization to add contracted staff members without increasing permanent payroll costs; On-site Partnership Program, the option to have an Olsten personnel supervisor on a client site full-time to manage staffing needs; and the Precise® automated testing and evaluation system, which has set new stan-

dards for the staffing industry.

Sterling, A Division of Olsten understands that clients need more than office skills from an assignment employee; they require drive, enthusiasm, and resourcefulness. Providing companies in the Greater Boston area with these qualities and more is how Sterling, A Division of

Characterized by drive, enthusiasm, and resourcefulness, Sterling's assignment employees undergo rigorous screening and, once accepted, participate in customized training programs.
PHOTOS BY CHARLES ORRICO

Olsten has built a reputation and earned the respect of many employers. Says Rosemary Leach Matela, Sterling's controller, "We have a highly talented group of individuals who are extremely proud of what they do."

ANY OF TODAY'S MEDICAL ADVANCES ARE NOTHING SHORT of miraculous. Life spans are increasing, more and more people are surviving traumatic accidents, and patients with life-threatening illnesses are exceeding life expectancies. But as the medical community learns to prolong life, it must also consider the quality of that life.

Based in Woburn, AdvantageHEALTH Corporation has made quality of life its priority for more than 25 years. Advantage's reputation for quality care began in 1969 with the founding of the New England Rehabilitation Hospital, the state's first freestanding physical rehabilitation hospital and a nationally recognized leader in its field. Today, the company operates the largest integrated network of comprehensive medical rehabilitation facilities in the Northeast—facilities that assist individuals disabled by illnesses or accidents in recovering and maintaining their highest level of functioning. AdvantageHEALTH has established comprehensive multidisciplinary programs for the rehabilitation of physically disabled patients and has become a leader in such specialty programs as head trauma, cancer, chronic pain, young stroke, amputation, spinal cord injury, orthopedic problems, neurological disorders, and arthritis, among others.

INTEGRATION TO PROVIDE EFFICIENCY AND EXPERTISE

From its entrepreneurial Boston roots, AdvantageHEALTH has grown into a publicly traded industry leader that provides its comprehensive services from a broad and strong platform. The company has established a system for delivery of its services through an integrated network of freestanding rehabilitation hospitals, dedicated managed rehabilitation units within major acute care hospitals, and comprehensive and specialty outpatient facilities.

Advantage also delivers its services through its home health care division and senior living facility management.

Advantage's impressive performance has not come by chance. As health care issues have begun to play a larger role in the United States and its economy, AdvantageHEALTH has developed a model for comprehensive, fully integrated delivery systems to lead the health care wave of the future. It has implemented that model by carefully building a network of rehabilitation services over the past 25 years. The com-

When an aneurysm claimed her right leg, Joanne Scopa completed AdvantageHEALTH's specialized rehabilitation treatment program for amputees. Today, with the aid of a prosthetic device, she is able to get on with her active and independent lifestyle.

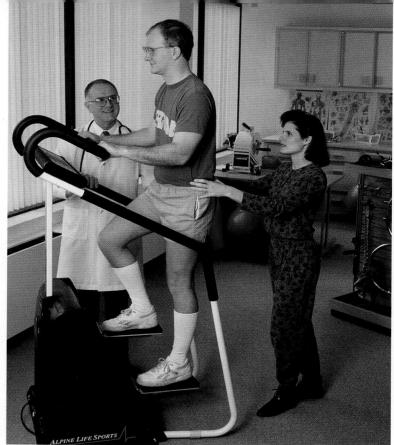

Simulation of real-life situations helps patients restore their capabilities to pursue the things that are personally important. Firefighter Scott Carpenter, injured on duty, incorporated into his AdvantageHEALTH treatment program movements that he performs on the job every day.

pany adopted a vision of integrated programs and delivery systems through an innovative strategy of affiliations, joint ventures, long-term management agreements, and partnerships with premier hospitals and health care delivery systems throughout New England and the Northeast.

As calls for reform in the health care industry are pushing providers toward integrated networks and greater consolidation, AdvantageHEALTH continues to advance, having already developed and implemented a successful model that demonstrates the integration of comprehensive rehabilitation services—delivered locally to patients in their communities through a regional network of inpatient rehabilitation facilities, outpatient facilities, and home care services. This integrated network of delivery can provide the highest level of care for the patient, while lowering the overall cost.

AdvantageHEALTH's network utilizes its freestanding rehabilitation hospitals as the hub of its services. The programs and protocols that are developed in these facilities can be rolled out and implemented through each delivery system. This hub-and-spoke model for service delivery is also the company's blueprint for

continued growth and expansion. The success of this model is evidenced by Advantage's history. In 1991, as a privately held company, AdvantageHEALTH had 31 sites of service. Within two short years of becoming a publicly traded company, Advantage's delivery system had grown to over 100 sites of service and now has developed a strong regional franchise. The company has developed premier provider affiliations with such nationally recognized providers as Geisinger Medical Center, Lahey Hitchcock Clinic, University of Massachusetts Medical Center, Maine Medical Center, Hartford Hospital, and Medical Center Hospital of Vermont. In addition, Advantage's facilities are affiliated with over 27 colleges and universities and offer a variety of residency programs. The company's facilities have also been distinguished with accreditation from the Joint Commission on Accreditation of Healthcare Organizations and the Commission on Accreditation of Rehabilitation Facilities.

In large part, Advantage credits the outstanding professional reputation of its clinicians for its ability to align itself with the region's most prestigious providers. The company has one of

the largest group practices of physiatrists—board-certified physicians specializing in physical medicine and rehabilitation. In addition, the company's ability to retain qualified therapists is largely enhanced by its continuum of care, which allows therapists to choose from inpatient, outpatient, and home care services. Says Chairman of the Board Raymond Dunn, "When people talk about the care they or a loved one received at our facilities, inevitably they do not mention the lobby, the rooms, or anything to do with the bricks and mortar. What they tell me about is our staff and how caring and giving they are. That unique quality is the seed that has allowed AdvantageHEALTH to grow and build upon a reputation that each of our employees enhances every day."

Thus having successfully executed its unique model for rehabilitation services, Advantage is in a pivotal position to grow through its regionally focused development strategy. Because there is broad recognition of the cost savings associated with rehabilitation, and because the company's business model corresponds to the expressed need for comprehensive, integrated service networks, AdvantageHEALTH is well positioned to efficiently and effectively serve the region's rehabilitation care needs.

Cambridge Technology Partners

C AMBRIDGE TECHNOLOGY PARTNERS HELPS A VARIETY OF successful companies around the world perform crucial aspects of their businesses even better. For Ingersoll-Rand Company—an international, $4 billion manufacturer of industrial machinery, construction equipment, and precision components—distribution is critical. To streamline the

order process and improve customer service, the company partnered with Cambridge Technology Partners to create the Global Business System, which links worldwide customers directly

it easier for customers to do business with Ingersoll-Rand.

That's business as usual for Cambridge Technology Partners. "We solve business problems through the use of information

else in the business." As the length of business cycles—the amount of time a new product can dominate the market before it is undercut by a competitor—decreases, companies cannot afford to ignore the competitive benefits information technology can provide.

KEEPING CLIENTS COMPETITIVE

In the past, the design, development, and installation of a typical information system could take from two to four years, with outside consultants using outdated techniques and old time and materials contracts. Systems were often built in a vacuum, relying on the expertise of the consultant and involving very little input from the users—those who often know best what is needed.

Cambridge Technology Partners has revolutionized the industry by delivering business-driven applications in six to nine months, partnering with clients to

Cambridge Technology Partners is headquartered along the Charles River in Cambridge (above left).

President and CEO James K. Sims (above right) worked with venture capital firm Safeguard Scientifics, Inc. to launch Cambridge Technology Partners.

to Ingersoll-Rand's supplying warehouses. The system provides one point of entry for all internal and external customers and allows distributors and affiliate companies to enter orders 24 hours a day. The new system reduces order entry and delivery cycle times, improves order accuracy, and makes

technology," says James K. Sims, president and CEO of Cambridge Technology Partners. "We help companies keep or establish a competitive edge in an increasingly compressed business environment by creating and implementing state-of-the-art information technology systems faster than anyone

build consensus and facilitate lasting change.

The firm's unique methodology and proven track record enable it to outpace its competitors. By agreeing to a fixed date of completion at a fixed price, Cambridge Technology Partners assumes the risk inherent in building these types of systems. The firm also shortens the design and development process by working closely with client companies to establish their needs and reach consensus on the right solution. Before the design phase of a project, clients often participate in a Rapid Solutions Workshop, an intensive, three-week process. In addition to speeding along the design process, the workshop generates in-depth specifications for the proposed system.

During the workshop, Cambridge Technology Partners and clients discuss business problems and technical solutions. At the end of three weeks, the Rapid

Solutions Workshop team delivers a prototype of the system so that clients can see the application before it is implemented.

By stressing client involvement in the early stages, the process allows problems to be spotted early, so that changes can be made with minimal disruption.

Working closely with clients also helps build consensus among client company staffers that the new information system is a valuable one. "Building consensus and involving users in the development process is just as important as establishing the right technical architecture environment," Sims says.

Clients are offered the opportunity to learn the technology and participate in the development phase, so they are knowledgeable and ready to go when the system is implemented. While Cambridge Technology Partners offers its clients full support services, the company prefers to train them well enough that they can solve problems and maintain and enhance the system on their own. This approach empowers clients by minimizing their dependency on an outside firm.

Cambridge Technology Partners recently joined with AT&T to create a new customer service system for its PersonaLink Services—a new network service for sending and receiving messages, accessing daily news and information services, and shopping electronically through the use of handheld devices called personal communicators. To continue to provide customers with its

trademark world-class service, AT&T selected Cambridge Technology Partners to help build a leading-edge customer service system. The system, which was developed in only one year, uses computer-integrated telephony to retrieve customer records and display them on the customer service representative's (CSR) computer screen before the CSR even picks up the phone. The system provides CSRs with direct access to customer, network, product, and service information.

A History of Rapid Growth

Cambridge Technology Partners' fast delivery of strategic, business-driven applications has made it one of the best-performing companies in the country. It became publicly traded in April 1993, and by the end of that year its stock value had more than tripled.

An important reason for Cambridge Technology Partners' impressive performance is the quality of the people who work there. They are committed, energetic, and knowledgeable in both the technical and business aspects of the field. While technical expertise is critical, the company also emphasizes "soft skills" such as the ability to build consensus and facilitate projects. "We always hire the smartest people we can find," Sims says.

By demonstrating to clients new and better ways to make information technology work for them, Cambridge Technology Partners continues to grow at an impressive rate—revenues in the first quarter of 1994 were up 84 percent over the previous year. The company has a proven track record of helping its clients increase productivity and efficiency, reduce costs, and gain a competitive advantage.

The company's executives and staff enjoy a rooftop barbecue (left).

Photographers

STEVEN ALEXANDER, a native of Waco, Texas, has lived in Boston since 1991. A freelance photographer since 1968, he specializes in location/destination, travel, and editorial photography. His clients include *Guest Informant*, *Travel Holiday*, *MacWorld*, *Reform Judaism*, *Home & Away*, *U.S. News & World Report*, *GE OnSite*, USAir, George Washington University, U.S. Department of State, *Discover America!*, *Washington: The Nation's Capital*, Mallard Press, and many others.

POLLY BROWN, a Bostonian since 1974, is an associate professor of documentary photography at the Art Institute of Boston. She has won a number of awards for her photography, including a National Endowment for the Arts Fellowship grant, and has been featured in one-person exhibitions all over the Northeast. Brown's photographic look at teenage mothers, *Children with Children*, was published in 1984, and her photography was also included in Northeastern University Press' *City Limits*, a photographic look at the people of Boston. Her photographic and editorial pieces have appeared in *New York Times Magazine*, *Self*, *Psychology Today*, *Mother Jones*, *Photo District News*, *PHOTO* (France), *Nieuwe Revu* (Netherlands), *Parade*, *National Geographic World*, *Americana*, *Signature*, *Travel Holiday*, *Nautical Quarterly*, *Boston Phoenix*, *Woodenboat*, and *Family Therapy Networker*.

NICHOLAS CARROLL, a citizen of Great Britain, is a visiting photographer in the Boston area.

WEBB CHAPPELL, originally from Bronxville, New York, has lived in Boston since 1982. He currently operates Webb Chappell Photography, where he specializes in people and location photography.

STUART COHEN grew up in Brighton, Massachusetts, and went on to attend Yale University. Now a freelance photographer living in Marblehead, he specializes in travel stock photography, and his photographs have been published worldwide, many of them in language textbooks.

DAVID COMB, a Boston-area native, attended the University of Wisconsin. He returned to Boston to open David Comb Photography, whose clients include Kendal Healthcare, Boston Scientific, New England Biolabs, Aetna Insurance, and Keystone Distributors. Comb enjoys shooting people on location and creating still lifes in his downtown studio.

JOHN CURTIS, a graduate of the London School of Photography, lived in England and South Africa before moving to Boston in 1981. He has won a number of national photography awards and recently completed a book, *Africa Style*.

JEFFERY DUNN, a graduate of Wesleyan University, operates Jeffery Dunn Studios in Cambridge. His assignments have taken him to many countries and his work has been published worldwide. Some of his clients include public television WGBH, Kodak, Blue Cross and Blue Shield, Fidelity Investments, Digital Equipment Corporation, and Simon and Schuster. Dunn has photographed Rodney Dangerfield, George Bush, Tina Turner, B.B. King, Ted Kennedy, Vincent Price, Peter Jennings, and Stevie Wonder. His most recent book, *Through Our Eyes*, was published by Little Brown.

MILLICENT HARVEY, a Boston native, attended the University of Arizona, Essex Photographic Institute, and the Art Institute of Boston. She operates Millicent Harvey Photography, where she specializes in environmental portraits. Her work has appeared in *Success*, *Business Week*, and *International Business*, and has been used by local and national corporations, including Fidelity Investments, Digital Equipment Corporation, Progress Software, and Deaconess Hospital.

BOB HUNG, originally from Newton, Massachusetts, has lived all of his life in the Boston area. A graduate of Boston University and Northeastern University, Hung is a freelance photographer specializing in seascapes and landscapes. His images of Cape Ann and Cape Cod have sold on postcards and in galleries, and have won several awards in Cape Ann Art Association shows. Hung's other favorite subjects include sports, antiques, music, and people.

LOU JONES attended Rensselaer Polytechnic Institute and the Massachusetts Institute of Technology. He now operates Lou Jones Photography, where he specializes in commercial photography. Jones has done work for Federal Express, Price Waterhouse, AT&T, KLM Airlines, Mobil, and others. He was also one of the founding members of the Advertising Photographers of America and is on the board of directors of the Photographic Resource Center in Boston. Other projects include coverage of the Olympics and conflicts in Central America, and a series of portraits of death row inmates.

BOB KRAMER, a Bostonian since 1982, has served as the staff photographer for Beth Israel Hospital and Northeastern Hospital, and as artist in residence at Bentley College in Waltham. Currently operating Bob Kramer Studio in Boston, Kramer provides clients with product, industrial, advertising, architecture, corporate, editorial, and public relations photography. His recent book, *Uncommon Footsteps*, was sponsored in part by Bentley College, Polaroid, the United Way of Greater Massachusetts, and a Cambridge Arts Lottery grant. The work is a collection of portraits of "special people"—people who are homeless, elderly, differently able, HIV positive, or otherwise challenged by everyday life and who show a special courage and tenacity. Kramer is currently at work on a second book, *Inner City Voices*.

JAMES LEMASS, a native of Dublin, Ireland, has lived in Boston since 1987. He has attended an art college in Ireland and is currently a freelance photographer, specializing in travel and people photography. Lemass' clients include the Boston Convention and Visitors Bureau, *Guest Informant*, and Cosmopulos Crowley Daly/CKG.

ADAM LEWIS is a panoramic photographer who enjoys photographing locations in the Boston area and abroad. A graduate of Tulane University, he has traveled the world and visits Japan regularly. Lewis now resides in West Newton, Massachusetts, and works with other family members in the Panorama International Company specializing in large group and scenic photography. His photography is also represented by the Pano-ramic Images photo library of Chicago.

STEVE LEWIS, a Bostonian since 1983, has a master's degree from the Rhode Island School of Design. A freelance photographer, he specializes in portraiture, and his work has been used nationwide, recently on the cover of the John Lee Hooker album *Mr. Lucky*. "By specializing in portraiture," Lewis says, "I have had the good fortune to photograph everyone from Henry Kissinger to a female Indian chief in Arizona."

STEVE LIPOFSKY, a lifelong resident of the Boston area, operates Lipofsky Photography. Specializing in sports photography, he is the official photographer for the Boston Celtics and has contributed to *Sports Illustrated*, *Sport*, *Esquire*, *Time*, and many other publications. Lipofsky lives in Nahant, Massachusetts.

ALEX MACLEAN, originally from Seattle, Washington, operates a photography studio, Landslides, in Boston. He has a bachelor's and a master's degree from Harvard and, since earning his pilot's license in 1975, has developed an expertise in aerial photography. He teaches aerial photography courses at the Massachusetts Institute of Technology, at the Boston Architectural Center, and in the continuing education program at Harvard University Graduate School of Design. He has had numerous exhibitions and publications, and his work can be found in the public and private collections of 3M Corporation, American Bell, Bank of America, Federal Express, GTE, Metropolitan Life, North Dakota Museum of Art, Steven Spielberg, Texaco, Texas Instruments, and many others.

HAL MILLER currently resides in Memphis, Tennessee, where he operates Miller Enterprises. He has studied at Northwestern University, New York University, University of Memphis, and Memphis College of Art. Miller specializes in cityscapes and landscapes, and his photography and paintings have won numerous awards. An avid traveler, Miller says, "I never leave home without my credit card, or my cameras."

RICHARD MITCHELL, a graduate of Pennsylvania State University, lives and works in New York City. He specializes in location portraiture, and his clients include *Boston Magazine*, *GQ*, *Self*, *Money*, *Inc.*, *Entrepreneur*, *Redbook*, *Adweek*, *New York Magazine*, Coach Leather, and Boston Publishing.

GREG NIKAS, originally from Ipswich, Massachusetts, now lives in Newburyport, an area he enjoys because of "its past and current association with the sea, its fabulous architecture, and its creative community of artists, designers, photographers, musicians, authors, and performing artists." Specializing in location and trade photography, Nikas has shot assignments in 30 states and 10 countries. He is currently working on a book about the Massachusetts coast.

PANORAMIC IMAGES is a Michigan Avenue, Chicago, stock photo library specializing in large-format panoramic views for advertising. Founded in 1987 by brothers Doug and Mark Segal, the firm represents the commercial artwork of 120 top panoramic photographers as well as the fine-art-for-advertising work of Mon-Trésor, a Japanese photo agency. Panoramic Images' clients include many major ad agencies, publishers, and graphic design firms in the United States and Europe, and their all-panoramic catalogs are distributed worldwide.

RICHARD PASLEY has been a Bostonian since 1980. His studio, Richard Pasley Photography, has provided photography for a wide range of international corporations, including AT&T (for whom Pasley spent a month in Argentina covering the installation of a nationwide cellular network system) and Polaroid (for whom he spent six weeks in Europe and North Africa shooting with the company's new Captiva camera). He has also completed more intimate projects, including fundraising efforts for the Little Sisters of the Poor and educational material for the National Park Service Visitor Information Services. Pasley's other clients include Gillette, Harvard Business School, Corning, Mellon Bank, New England Telephone, NYNEX, Omni Hotels, and Plimoth Plantation.

SUZANNE PLUNKETT is originally from Eden Prairie, Minnesota. After attending the University of Minnesota and Boston University, she joined the staff of the *Lowell Sun*, where she is a news photographer. Plunkett's photographs have appeared in *USA Today* and recently earned her a second-place prize in the National Press Photographers' Association regional clip contest. In 1994, she documented hospital conditions in Ukraine. Plunkett lives in Somerville and is an avid surfer.

SARAH PUTNAM, a Boston native, graduated from the University of Pennsylvania in 1974. Now working as a freelance photojournalist, she has photographed all over the world for a number of publications and corporate clients, including *Boston Magazine*, *Yankee*, *Parenting*, *New York Times Magazine*, *Time*, *Ms.*, *Forbes*, *Business Week*, *U.S. News & World Report*, *Fortune*, Polaroid, Fidelity

Investments, Brockton Hospital, Collaborative Technology, WGBH-TV, Harvard University, Boston University, Northeastern University, the Commonwealth of Massachusetts, and Grassroots International. She has also served in photography positions at the *Middlesex News*, the *New England Journal of Photography*, and *Sojourner*. Putnam lives in Cambridge.

RUSS SCHLEIPMAN, originally from Vermont, graduated from Dartmouth College in 1971. Operating Russ Schleipman, Inc., he specializes in location, advertising, and corporate photography, and his clients include Timberland, Reebok, Digital Equipment Corporation, and United Technologies. Schleipman's work has been published in numerous *Communication Arts* annuals and was among the winners of the Nikon Photo Contest International. A skier and a sailor, Schleipman enjoys traveling for work and pleasure.

JAMES SCHWABEL is a prolific contributor of large-format panoramic photography to the Panoramic Images photo agency in Chicago. Residing in the Hamburg, New York, area for most of his life, he began his career with a degree in accounting that eventually was converted into his now full-time position as location photographer. Schwabel specializes in panoramic scenics, landscapes, and travel photography. His work has been used by many major companies and advertising agencies on every continent. Schwabel recently bought a camper trailer and is continually traveling across America in search of the perfect photograph.

MARK SEGAL has pursued the perfection of the panoramic image since 1972, focusing on commercial and advertising usage. With his brother Doug, Segal operates three separate photography entities in Chicago, including Panoramic Images and its 250,000 stock pan photographs. Segal's clients include Air France, American Express, Sony, and Skidmore Owings & Merrill.

Index to Patrons

*T*HE OLD AND NEW CAN BE admired from the Cambridge side of the Charles River. Indeed, this is a city of contrasts, character, and grace—truly a special place.

PAGE 352, JAMES LEMASS PHOTO